D1274771

Anthropology & Education

The major objective of this series is to make the knowledge and perspective of anthropology available to educators and their students. It is hoped and believed, however, that it will also prove valuable to those in other professions and in the several disciplines that compose the behavioral sciences.

In recent years some educators have discovered that anthropology has much to offer the areas of professional training and educational theory and practice. In its cross-cultural comparisons of human behavior and in its inductive, empirical method of analysis is found a conceptual freshness that is intellectually liberating.

There are four major areas of anthropological theory that have direct relevance for education. These are the regularities of behavior and belief that we call culture; the transmission of culture and learning processes; the ways in which individuals group themselves for the accomplishment of communal purposes, from which comes organization theory; and the processes by which transformations occur in human behavior and groupings that can be explained by a theory of change. In addition, there are the subject-matter areas of child rearing; community and the relationships among institutions within it; the rites of passage; the cultural categories of social class, ethnic group, age, grading, and sex; and others. These several areas of theory and substance provide a rich source for this series. It is believed that the availability of such a storehouse of knowledge in the several volumes in the series will contribute immensely to the further improvement of our educational system.

SOLON T. KIMBALL, GENERAL EDITOR

Anthropology & Education

Series

THE WAY TO MODERN MAN
Fred T. Adams

PERSPECTIVES FROM ANTHROPOLOGY
Rachel Reese Sady

BECOMING A TEACHER
Elizabeth M. Eddy

THE CULTURE OF CHILDHOOD
Mary Ellen Goodman

LEARNING TO BE ROTUMAN
Alan Howard

FUNCTIONS OF LANGUAGE IN THE CLASSROOM
*Edited by Courtney B. Cazden,
Vera P. John, and Dell Hymes*

THE RITES OF PASSAGE IN A STUDENT CULTURE
Thomas A. Leemon

LIFE CYCLES IN ATCHALÁN
Alexander Moore

370.193
K 52

9.15

Culture
and the
Educative Process

AN ANTHROPOLOGICAL PERSPECTIVE

SOLON T. KIMBALL

Teachers College Press

Teachers College, Columbia University
New York and London

61586

Copyright © 1974 by Teachers College, Columbia University

Library of Congress Catalog Card Number: 73–21760

Cataloging in Publication Data:
Kimball, Solon Toothaker, comp.
  Culture and the educative process.

  (Anthropology and education)
  Includes bibliographical references.
  1. Educational anthropology—Addresses, essays,
lectures.   I.   Title.
LB45.K5   1974   301.5'6   73–21760
ISBN 0–8077–2422–X
ISBN 0–8077–2434–3 (pbk.)

Manufactured in the United States of America.

PREFACE

During the past two decades, a goodly portion of my intellectual endeavors has been devoted to a concern with the nature of learning. In a sense it all began in the fall of 1953 when I joined the faculty of Teachers College, Columbia University, as professor of Anthropology and Education. To this new assignment I brought the experience of community-studies research in New England, Ireland, Michigan, and Alabama; a decade of service with the federal government on the Navajo Reservation and with the War Relocation Authority; and academic appointments at Michigan State University and the University of Alabama.

My induction into the enterprise of education was assisted largely by colleagues and students during my thirteen years at Teachers College. One of the most stimulating intellectual experiences came from the course taught jointly with my colleague James McClellan, from which came our co-authored book *Education and the New America*. Other opportunities opened cross-cultural horizons. For a year I was a UNESCO specialist in education and community assigned to the Brazilian Center for Education Research in Rio de Janeiro. Subsequently I was research consultant to the Teachers for East Africa program and was in Uganda for several weeks. Later on I organized and was campus coordinator of the AID-Teachers College contract with the Ministry of Education in Peru.

As my knowledge of educational organization and practice in the United States and elsewhere expanded, so also did I begin to see more clearly the importance, indeed the necessity, of the anthropological method and perspective to the educational process. Ideas about various aspects of this contribution were developed in a number of papers. These dealt with such diverse topics as teacher training, administration, school organization, education and community, and learning theory. Although the range of topical diversity was great, the separate articles contained a consistency of intellectual perspective. Thus, when I set about the task of writing a book on the anthropology of education, I found that in these separate articles I had already written much of what I wanted to say. There was the problem of their sequential arrangement and of some editing. Although they had been written for other purposes and publications, I believe that their comprehensive treatment more than compensates for a minimum of repetition. Three of the chapters are new. In Chapter 14 I draw upon field research in Ireland and Brazil to demonstrate the value of community study and applied anthropology in developing educational programs. The focus on educational practice in Peru in Chapter 16 further illuminates the connections among world view, social patterns, and educational practice. The concluding chapter (Chapter 19) explores the importance of research results in anthropology to educational policy and program.

During the two-decade span of new experience and gestation of ideas, I was indeed fortunate to be associated with many individuals —colleagues, students, friends—who broadened my perspective and contributed to my growth. An attempt to acknowledge the nature of the contribution of each is, of course, impossible. Many provided the stimulation that comes from the exchange of ideas; others opened up new opportunities or were guides and collaborators in new ventures; some gave both friendly criticism and warm encouragement; and there are other ways in which their influence might be traced in some way or another in this book. The list of those who have added to my efforts is a full one. Those from my Columbia days include Conrad Arensberg, Mark Atwood, David Austin, Marian Rhodes Brown, Lyman Bryson, Ximena Bunster, Jacquetta Burnett, Freeman Butts, Harold Clark, Lawrence Cremin, Jo Danna, Wilton Dillon, Elizabeth Eddy, Jessica Feingold, Ralph Fields, Arthur I. Gates, Esther Lloyd-Jones, James McClellan, Margaret Mead, Rhoda Métraux, Frankie Beth Nelson, Yasuyuki Owada, Joan Roberts, Jerry Rosenfeld, Charles Wagley, Goodwin Watson, Sloan Wayland, and Esther Westervelt.

For each of the several countries about which I present data there were several individuals whose diverse contributions have assisted my account of the educational system of that country. In many instances my debt is both personal and professional. Those from Ireland include Dr. Henry Bugler, Mary (Batt) Callinan, Dr. John Counihan, Dermot Foley, Sean Gordon, Jane Harvey, Edward Kerin and his daughters Mary Ellen and Kathleen, Dr. Donough McNamara, and

Sean and Mary Quin. For Brazil I wish to mention Edwiges Florence, Robert Havighurst, Robert Moreira, Oracy Nogueira, Darcy Ribeiro, Dalila Sperb, and Anisio Teixeria. For Peru the list includes Oscar Gonzalez, Sydney Grant, Ruth Harwood (from whose research I quote extensively in Chapter 16), Carlos Salazar, and William Sayres.

Others of my colleagues who have contributed to my ideas or who have assisted in specific ways in the preparation of this manuscript include Kenneth Benne, Caroline Bird, Walter and Jean Boek, Bob Brown, William Caudill, Rosalie Cohen, Fred and Dorothy Eggan, A. T. Hansen, Everett Hughes, Ralph Kimbrough, Joseph Kitagawa, Alfred Kroeber, Hal Lewis, Alexander Moore, Richard Renner, David Riesman, John Singleton, and Lloyd Warner.

In preparing the materials for publication I have had the assistance of Barbara Coaxum, Lydia Deakin, Colette Tobin, Jean Jordan, and Louise Stearns. For their help I am truly grateful.

I also wish to express my appreciation to the Social Science Research Council. During the period that I held a Faculty Research Fellowship, I devoted some portion of my time to the problem of education and change. I also appreciate the fellowship provided subsequently by the Guggenheim Foundation, which gave me the opportunity to explore the relation between culture and learning. The products of these two periods of intense application are incorporated in this volume.

And finally, those of us who engage in professional writing and research know all too well the stresses we are likely to impose on our families as we bring some article or book to completion. Oftentimes we fail to acknowledge the forbearance, interest, and help that are so freely given. In consequence, as a token of a deeply felt gratitude to my family, I want to thank Hannah, Sally, Stan, and John, for their encouragement and help given over the years.

S. T. K.

CONTENTS

**Part IV
The Educational Challenge**

PART I   *An Anthropological Overview*

INTRODUCTION: ANTHROPOLOGY AND EDUCATION

Contemporary civilized man became the subject of anthropological scrutiny about a half century ago when the Lynds in Muncie, Indiana, and Warner in Newburyport, Massachusetts, began their respective researches. These have since become famous as the classic *Middletown* and *Yankee City* studies. Their pioneering efforts have both stimulated and influenced the social science disciplines in the study of communities and their institutions.

One of the important consequences of this new focus has been the expanding involvement of some anthropologists with the professions. Their contribution has ranged from basic behavioral research to instructional responsibilities as staff members of professional colleges. The path of collaboration, however, has not always been an easy one. For example, an unexpected discontinuity looms between the popular stereotype of the anthropologist as digger and classifier of old stones and bones and the first encounter with an anthropological researcher in the setting of a hospital or high school. Contrasting intellectual perspectives create other confusions. The research and analytic posture of the anthropologist contrasts sharply with the programmatic or diagnostic orientation of the professional. There are, however, some areas of mutual concern. These will be more meaningful if we summarize first the basic areas of study, method, and point of view of the anthropologist.

Anthropology is traditionally defined as the study of man. Theoretically, every aspect of human behavior or of the environmental condi-

Excerpted from "Anthropology and Education," *Educational Leadership,* Vol. 13, No. 8 (May 1956), pp. 480–483. Reprinted by permission of the Association for Supervision and Curriculum Development.

tions that affect the physical or cultural development of man is a proper subject of study. More explicitly, the central concern has been with man's exploitation of his environment through technology, his adjustment to other men through customs and social groupings, and his relationship to the supernatural. From the study of man's technical equipment, customs, activities, institutions, values, and symbols, the anthropologist records the culture of people. Cultural descriptions, however, are always within the context of a larger purpose. This is the search for generalizations that express the universalities of human behavior in time and space. In order to achieve this latter goal, the anthropologist works cross culturally and, through the comparative examination of cultures, seeks for the dynamics that explain the origin, diffusion, persistence, and change of social and cultural behavior. Inevitably, the anthropologist comes to appreciate the orderliness of the cultural universe as it is expressed in pattern and system.

The understandings drawn from various cultures oftentimes have direct applicability to formalized educational systems. For example, the informal or clique systems of grouping, prevalent among both students and teachers, meet basic needs that are provided for in no other way. These groups represent a powerful untapped social resource for advancing the goals of an educational enterprise. These natural groups are found in other institutional arrangements and have their parallels in simpler societies. As another example, the place and function of ritual in educational endeavor are seldom understood, a fact undoubtedly related to the overwhelming emphasis upon the individual in American education. Anthropology teaches us that critical periods in the life of the individual or group are eased through ceremonial observances, called *rites de passage,* and that values are reinforced and new learning accompanies such events. One may ask how do schools utilize, if they even recognize, these group building devices?

The productive use of cross-cultural materials must be within the framework of understanding basic aspects of human life. As an example, the family is an institutional arrangement present among all peoples. Its basic functions of regulating the sexual behavior of adults, providing protection for the immature, transmitting a large share of the cultural heritage to oncoming generations, and allocating tasks to old and young, male and female, for the welfare of the corporate whole, is a universal phenomenon. These are universal basic functions, although the details of family activities may vary enormously. Other cultural or social features provide comparable parallels. These may be seen in the division of labor between males and females; in agegraded systems sometimes accompanied by rituals that mark the transition from one status to another; in the relations between concepts of space and time and the rhythm of human activities; and in the connections between culture and personality.

The research methods utilized by anthropologists offer another tool for understanding problems of education. Up to the present, most educational research has been dominated by the tradition of experimental psychology. Anthropological method is quite different. The anthropologist uses the real-life setting as his laboratory. He seeks to avoid influencing the activities he records but rather to determine the characteristics of on-going systems as they operate within a set of conditions. Thus, he observes educative processes through the activities of individuals. He can then describe the characteristic patterns and offer certain conclusions about their functions. From such knowledge it is then possible to make predictions about the probable results of a given course of action.

The concern with the whole, in which each culture item is viewed in the context of its meaning and relation to the other parts, provides an essential perspective to an understanding of the educational process. The non-judgmental, comparative method of anthropology provides an intellectual device through which the educationist can escape from the superficial irrelevancies of the moment.

The inclusion of anthropological materials in classroom subject matter, particularly those describing the customs of primitive peoples, has made some headway in recent years. Such borrowings, however, can lead to negative results if they accentuate the ethnocentric tendency to establish the superiority of one's own way of life in contrast to the benighted peoples of other cultures. This result would contradict the very spirit of anthropological method, which avoids invidious comparisons but instead accords to most peoples respect for their ways. This does not mean that one needs to approve or attempt to adopt new behavior. On the contrary, the objective should be to derive a greater awareness of the meaning of one's own culture through the examination of others.

But there are other problems that fall within the interest and competence of the anthropologist. In this century America has been transformed from a pattern of multiple small towns and rural neighborhoods to a pattern of urban population concentrated in a few regional metropolitan cities and their adjunct suburbs. Accompanying this change have been modifications in the style of family life and in the relations and values within the family and between it and the other institutional arrangements within the community. These changes have their impact upon the educational enterprise.

The increase in organizational complexity is reflected in the ways by which we solve problems affecting education. For example, communities can no longer hold school boards directly accountable for their actions. These days, Big Brother, in the guise of federal and state courts and agencies, teacher unions, and professional associations, is now monitoring, regulating, and enforcing, with only incidental concern for community values, and sometimes with little apparent concern for the quality of education. School boards must either knuckle under to edicts imposed from without or face the consequences. The example illustrates how the use of external power affects the internal ordering. Under conditions of colonial administration, subjected peoples have experienced similar external supervision.

Other, more personal areas of life involving acceptable behavior for age and sex groups intrude themselves as problems with all the nagging uncertainties about the appropriate response to defined deviancies. Has the ability of the generations to communicate so deteriorated that they are now separated by a pathological void? The answer to such a question is related to the basic anthropological concern with transmission of culture. An answer may be found in determining the relative dominance of directional influence from either elders or peers. If youth no longer derives its images of maturity from the adult world, as those who espouse the emergence of a counter-culture claim, the shift represents a truly radical modification of the traditional educational process.

The areas mentioned thus far include only a few of the collaborative possibilities that fall within the broad spectrum of anthropological concern. They are suggestive rather than definitive. A much deeper understanding of the perspective and method of anthropology must be acquired, however, before the full measure of their relevance to formal education is understood. In the more detailed and systematic examination of various anthropological dimensions in the several chapters that follow, we hope to achieve that goal.

2. CULTURE, SOCIETY, AND EDUCATIONAL CONGRUENCY

Despite the great variety of their cultural forms, the communities of mankind have, throughout time, possessed in common the need to transmit their cultural heritage to each oncoming generation. It is thus that societies ensure their continuity and establish the conditions necessary for further cultural growth.

Although the methods, procedures, and organizations that are used to educate the young may vary greatly from one society or epoch to another, there is one aspect common to all: the young must pass through an extended stage of dependency during which physical maturity is reached and the skills and knowledge necessary for adulthood are acquired. It is during this period of dependency that basic learning occurs, but it should be noted that there is no causal link between dependency and learning. Furthermore, the period and nature of dependency vary according to the culture, as does the substance of the learning.

There are, of course, significant differences among various cultures in the methods used to instruct the young. Among some nonliterate peoples the process is, at times, so informal that untrained observers have reported that education of the young is lacking. Such comments reflect on the competency of the observers and not upon the effectiveness with which each new generation learns from, and is instructed by, its elders. The Western tradition, which links significant learning with formal classroom instruction, constitutes a much too narrow formula-

"Culture, Class, and Educational Congruency," in Stanley Elam and William P. McClure, Eds., *Educational Requirements for the 1970's: An Interdisciplinary Approach* (New York: Frederick A. Praeger, 1967), pp. 6–26. By permission of Phi Delta Kappa.

tion of what education encompasses. Only recently have we begun to recognize that success or failure in school learning is related to the pattern of learning acquired by the child in the cultural setting of his home.

The differences in methods of teaching and learning become particularly significant when examined in the context of the culture in which they appear. We are immediately struck by the correspondence between educational activities and those found in the familial, economic, political, and religious aspects of the society being studied. In traditional societies, the educational process reflects, and is in harmony with, the values, practices, and human groupings in other parts of the society. Such congruencies should not be surprising, but, since professional educators do not seem to have understood the importance of this observation, it is necessary to emphasize the point.

Examples of such lack of understanding abound. The history of the introduction of schools into colonial possessions by the British, French, and Dutch is one in which the practices that obtained in the mother countries were transferred almost unaltered, with no consideration given to native practices or needs.[1] In the schooling provided the American Indians, the Puerto Ricans, or the people of the Philippines, the policy of the U.S. Government was no different. The same insensitivity may currently be observed on the part of those education specialists who recommend the transfer of practices from their own to other countries without any regard for the prevailing traditions.

The principle of educational congruency applies with equal cogency to modern nations. Among these, change is accepted as normal, although its pace varies from one sector to another. Unless educational modernization is seen as deserving continuous attention, there is a great danger that innate conservative tendencies will prevail. Obviously, such a disjunctive condition would necessitate corrective measures.

The very fact of rapid change in the modern nation underscores our need to scrutinize the extent to which education is congruent with other aspects of the society. In the relatively stable traditional cultures, the very processes associated with the transmission of culture perpetuated the cultural heritage from one generation to the next under conditions of minimal change. The tempo of our times is vastly different. We accept change as a fact of life, and there are some who see current changes as revolutionary.[2]

[1] See, for example, John Wilson, *Education and Changing West African Culture* (New York: Teachers College Press, 1963).

[2] Robert Theobald, *Free Men and Free Markets* (New York: Clarkson N. Potter, 1963).

Under conditions of rapid change, we can no longer assume that the knowledge or practices that served us adequately in the past are sufficient for either the present or the future. Hence, we must rethink what we mean when we speak of education as the transmission of the cultural heritage. The sense in which we use this concept when we specify the Navaho Indians, the tribes of New Guinea, or even an early agrarian period in American history, is not applicable to the present. In such examples, the past and present are expected to be replicated in the future. Today, we cannot operate under such an assumption. Instead, we must consciously construct an educational system to serve a society that is in a state of continuous emergence.

If we had the opportunity to construct such an educational system, how should we go about it? As the first order of business, we must decide what segments of our cultural heritage should be included in the curriculum. This is necessary, not only because the cornucopia of knowledge from our intellectual and technical worlds is already overflowing and new knowledge is added daily, but also because differential utilities necessitate the setting of priorities. In recent decades, we have made such selective discriminations largely as a response to new demands rather than through rational assessment. Now we must build selective process into educational procedure.

Two additional problems confront us. We need first a new philosophy of curriculum practice and, second, a favorable environment for the teaching-learning process. This latter entails a reorganization of elementary and secondary school administration. The first of these two problems has already been examined in *Education and the New America.*[3] In that study, James McClellan and I argued that full participation in the modern world requires the acquisition of intellectual skills in the areas of mathematics and logic, aesthetics, experimentation, and the methodology of natural history. I shall not attempt to summarize our line of reasoning. I will repeat our belief that a modern educational system must emphasize the acquisition of cognitive skills of a different order from those traditionally stressed. We believe that our proposals represent a step in the direction of a new philosophy of pedagogy.

The need for reordering the administrative structure may be less obvious. Let us ask, however, if an urban school system that derives its structure and procedures from the pattern of a municipal bureau or from a factory system dating from the early part of the century, or from both, can provide the organizational framework within which the needed curricular changes can be realized. It seems probable that

[3] Solon T. Kimball and James E. McClellan, *Education and the New America* (New York: Random House, 1963).

any comparative study of organizational systems would readily establish that the structure and practices of urban school administrations
are more archaic than those of any other major institution. This in-
flexibility has been demonstrated by their reluctance or failure to
meet new conditions or to incorporate new programs. Until the learning function actually becomes the paramount goal, and until custodial,
housekeeping, and managerial functions are relegated to their proper
service roles, we can expect little change in the present situation. I
shall give further consideration to the current relevance of educational
philosophy and practice, curriculum, and administration later on.
These questions will then be examined within the context of the
congruency between the present corporate and scientifically oriented
society and human aspirations on the one hand, and the educational
process on the other.

THE ROOTS OF AMERICAN CULTURE

It is fashionable these days to derive the origins of American culture
from the Judaeo-Christian and Graeco-Roman traditions of the Mediterranean. Only in the most general sense should this postulate be
accepted. Although it is true that the Mediterranean influence spread
with the extension of the Roman Empire into Celtic and Germanic
Europe, it must be remembered that this cultural intrusion was
eventually assimilated and transformed. Our civilization shows evidences of Judaeo-Christian and Graeco-Roman influences from the
Mediterranean, but our cultural roots are based in the Anglo-Saxon
and Celtic traditions of northern Europe.

The more obvious aspect of this mixed inheritance is found in
our political system with its delicate balance of powers, its elected
legislature, its provision for judicial review and interpretation, and its
political and human ideals as expressed in the Declaration of Independence and the Bill of Rights. Human liberties are defended, new
perspectives asserted, and economic and social tensions adjudicated
through the ritual of law and the courts.

But a broad range of American values and organizational methods
have their origin in the religious tradition. The Protestant denomina-
tions encompassed the equalitarianism of the Baptists and New England
Congregationalists as well as the hierarchy of the Methodists and
Episcopalians and the strict, but human, posture of the Presbyterian
elders. Through all of them ran the theme of the need for man to shape
the world in the service of his and God's purposes. The individual
was the instrument through which this transformation was to be

achieved as each utilized his capabilities in work and sought the advance of the whole through the struggle for self-improvement.

These generalities of organization and thought are relatively easy to identify and give us a sense of similarity in cultural origin that closer scrutiny does not support. Our historians have called attention to the differences that distinguished Puritan, Quaker, or Cavalier, but only recently have we begun to assess these various groups as bearers of distinct cultural traditions. From this perspective, we now look for distinguishing features in settlement patterns, groupings, behavior, and values. This approach permits us to identify each group against a background of community and culture, to search for European origins, and to understand their transformations in the new environment.[4] These traditions became associated with geographical regions and provided the basis for sectional conflict. Only with the ascendance of urban industrialism, in the early part of the twentieth century, did we acquire a type of community that subordinated regional tensions to a more inclusive cultural and organizational framework. The evolving urban pattern, however, evoked its own distinctive set of tensions rooted in the cultural variations of race, ethnic identification, and social class.

My purpose now in examining briefly each of the cultural traditions is not only to further substantiate congruency but also to show the diversity in our origins. From Anglo-Saxon sections of England into the Northeast came peoples carrying the tradition of the agricultural village. They built their habitations around a central commons, or green, at one end of which they usually erected the meeting house that served the religious and civic functions of the commonalty. Only the addition of a miller, blacksmith, and other artisans broke the occupational uniformity of agrarian life. These village New Englanders were deeply committed to communal equalitarianism, preparation for which required a minimum level of literacy for all. As population increased and resources became fully claimed, the older settlement hived off its young into new colonies. These claimed unoccupied territory and perpetuated the pattern of life of the mothering group. The New England pattern of agrarian subsistence has long since been abandoned, but other of its qualities have been woven into the fabric of national life.

The plantation tradition of the tidewater, black belt, and delta areas of the South offers a vivid contrast in almost every particular.

---

[4] See Conrad M. Arensberg, "American Communities," *American Anthropologist,* LVII (1955); and Jackson Turner Main, *The Social Structure of Revolutionary America* (Princeton: Princeton University Press, 1965).

Production for a world market required large acreages and a plentiful supply of organized field labor. The need both for capital and for managerial skills contributed to development of a clearly defined upper class. The lower classes included those in servitude and the dispossessed or marginal whites. Extensive kinship linkages, the code of the gentleman, and governance by an elite gave the upper class a cohesive life style based on family, manners, and politics. The vital thrust of this tradition as a force in national affairs was shattered by the Civil War.

Three other traditions deserve brief mention. The hills and mountains of what we now call Appalachia attracted another breed of people. They were primarily of the Celtic tradition, which brought with it a sense of territory (but no love for the soil) and a subsistence pattern of agriculture based upon patch farming and unfenced pastures for grazing. Their strongest loyalty was to an extended kin group, and their code demanded direct physical retribution for personal offense. They were deeply egalitarian, even to the extent of rejecting schooling because it fostered inequalities among men. Since the middle of the nineteenth century, Appalachia has been outside the main stream of American development. Only recently has its plight become a matter of national concern.

The fourth and last of the principal agrarian traditions was the one I designate as "town and country." Here we encounter the farm homestead situated on its own tract of cultivated land. Each farm was occupied by a family whose ties to nearby and comparable families were contained within a web of reciprocal obligations. They called these activities "neighboring." Their early agricultural practices produced small surpluses, which they marketed in nearby towns and from which they received those goods and services that their homogeneous localities did not provide.

Townsmen and countrymen, although different from one another, created an economic and social symbiosis. It was this cultural tradition that was concentrated in the Piedmont of the southern states, in the Middle Colonies, and in upper New York State. From these areas came the settlers who poured into the great Mississippi heartland and, once there, built a society of Main Street towns and rural neighborhoods that gave the predominant cultural tone to American civilization until superseded by the forces of industrialism. Later, with the appearance of the new agricultural and transportation technology, this tradition rapidly evolved into the pattern of commercial production and soon lost the older social cohesiveness of the locality.

The urban and commercial tradition that flowed from London and other European cities represents the fifth major cultural stream.

Research by Bridenbaugh [5] has given us a clear picture of the organization and ways of life in the chief port cities—Boston, Newport, New York, Philadelphia, and Charles Town—at the time of the Revolution. All were significant as points of transshipment of goods to and from the hinterland. Three of them were also important centers of political power. Their cultural heterogeneity was expressed in institutional arrangements for commerce, government, and religion and in distinct social classes based on wealth and prestige. They were religious and educational centers where literature, the arts, and theater were cultivated. Merchants, bankers, and professional men could follow an upper-middle-class way of life, which allowed for refinement of taste and freed their wives from onerous domestic or home industry tasks. The environment favored intellectual stimulation, and some scientific societies were established even at this early time. It is significant that the cultural richness here was much greater than anything that provincial towns or agrarian countryside could provide.

EDUCATION AND COMMUNITY

It is when we examine the formal educational arrangements for each type of community that we can observe the broad congruency between education and the social and cultural aspects of a society. The communal egalitarianism of New England required a level of civic and religious participation possible only with a literate citizenry. Hence, both family and community were held responsible for educating the young. The contrast with the two-class system of the plantation South further illuminates the principle of congruency. There, formal education was primarily a privilege of the elite and was provided by tutors or private schools. Other groups were not excluded from access to formal learning, except under later restrictive laws that governed the treatment of slaves. But, where facilities existed, they were oftentimes the result of philanthropic (upper-class) benevolence. Moreover, there was neither a public nor a private responsibility that required literacy of field hands. In the context of such limits on early schooling, it is clear that it was no cultural anachronism that Virginia and North Carolina established the first free, public universities. Through educating their own children for the professions, especially law, a governing elite could assure the perpetuation of a political and social system; the risk of a lower class availing itself of the public universities was minimal.

[5] Carl Bridenbaugh, *Cities in the Wilderness: Urban Life in America, 1625–1742* (New York: G. P. Putnam, 1964).

The other cultural traditions of early America also exemplify the principle of congruency. The egalitarianism of the Appalachian uplands was rooted both in a system of family obligations, which prescribed the behavior of an extended kindred, and in a religion based on the belief in other-worldliness, which emphasized the spirit rather than the intellect. Such a cultural posture denied the relevance of formal education; in fact, the development of the intellect was correctly seen as creating inequalities among men and contributing nothing to spiritual insight, which came as a gift from God. Only through a countervailing thrust of vigorous individualism could the force of education gain a foothold. Those who were thus caught up faced both exclusion and isolation and were usually lost to another cultural tradition. Abraham Lincoln was born in this tradition and he carried many of its homespun mannerisms and egalitarian values into the Presidency.

The system of formal education in the "town and country" pattern yields yet another variant and further substantiation of congruency. Each rural neighborhood was served by its own school—the romanticized one-room school—presided over by a schoolmarm drawn from the same cultural milieu as her pupils. The school was basically an extension of the family, and the teacher's role was little different from that of an older sister or spinster aunt. The schools of the town reflected the greater heterogeneity of its environment. The town's elementary schools were an extension of the community, but the advanced schooling provided in the private academies, which were later replaced by public high schools, was for children drawn from the town's higher social classes and for ambitious and talented children from the countryside. Here, again, we observe the symbolic relationship of town and country in operation.

The relatively complex pattern of the urban schools mirrored the divisions based on social class, religion, and ethnic background. There were schools for rich and poor, for those of varying religious faiths, and for other groups. Entrance into many occupations, however, came only after one had served an apprenticeship in shop, office, or profession.

Some aspects of community and congruent educational practice may still be encountered in the educational situation today. But it would be misleading to assume that today's school system or its practices represents a direct evolutionary development from the past—although we cannot deny certain connections. Changes in the human environment have produced innovations and contributed to the loss of some aspects. The one-room school has almost disappeared. Private academies evolved into public high schools. Teacher-training institutions, technical institutes, land-grant colleges, and the graduate school have appeared and spread in response to new conditions. Moreover, innovation and elaboration accelerate as evidenced in the transformation of technical schools into universities, the spread of community colleges, the growth of the university complex into the multiversity, and in other ways. If the congruency between community form and educational organizational practice is valid, than what are the changes in American life that explain the facts?

THE NEW AMERICA

American civilization has moved on a course that takes us ever further from our agrarian past. The mill town appeared in the first half of the nineteenth century as the new industrial processes and the factory system spread from England. Then came the growth of the industrial cities associated with new industries and mass production. Now we are in the new age of science, and metropolis is the shape of the new human community. It possesses many features that distinguish it from the past.

The cultural outlines of this new America are readily discernible. Its physical manifestation is metropolis, where the spatial grouping reveals the social and cultural directions of an emerging civilization. The new monumental civic centers attest to the growth of public service and of a rising interest in the arts. In the great new office buildings, one finds the centers of control and planning for commercial and industrial enterprises whose operations may be purely local or may reach to the far corners of the earth. Within the central city, one may find clusterings of facilities and people that give expression to other functions, such as education or health. Moving outward, one encounters suburb, shopping center, and industrial park.

Among some of our older cities, such as New York, Philadelphia, or Chicago, a double transformation is occurring in the core or inner city. Immense wealth is being expended for the reconstruction of the central business and financial districts in an attempt to revitalize these areas. In contrast, the nearby residential areas have received tens of thousands of Negroes and Puerto Ricans dispossessed from areas once based on the older agrarian tradition, but now in the process of transformation to modern agriculture. In many respects, these people are the casualties of the transition. Metropolis becomes their refuge, but the skills they bring with them are inadequate for anything but menial employment; hence, they must either remain marginal in their participation in the new America or, even more debasing, become parasitic.

The attention we now give to programs of rehabilitation is a measure both of the problem and of our need to help the newcomers make adjustments.

The main thrust of American civilization, however, is elsewhere, and in order to understand its significance we need to examine the three truly distinguishing social groupings of the modern era, namely, corporate organization, nuclear family, and voluntary association. We must also keep in mind the sharp division between public and private activities and organizations because the separation between these sectors is accentuated in contrast with the past. Finally, we should understand that formal schooling is the channel that links the two and prepares the child for his participation in the public world.

The corporate form of organization provides the framework within which the majority of Americans now work. In structure and operation, it bears little resemblance to the town meeting of New England, the threshing ring of the rural neighborhood, the labor gang of the plantation, or the workshop of the city artisan. These were forms of human organization of another age. Furthermore, we must distinguish the corporate form from the classical bureaucracy described by Max Weber (although it may contain bureaucratic elements) and from the system of ranked positions found in a traditional army (although the principle of hierarchy may be present). The corporate form is able to assemble quantities of energy and diversities of skill for the purpose of solving specific problems. Its variety of internal distinctions should be viewed less as an arrangement to express status and more as the basis for achieving its multiple goals. The postwar American university typifies the emergent corporate structure more clearly than does either government or industry, although both are undergoing a massive reformation in this new direction. Unfortunately, the structure of the urban American public school system has shown little modification since the days, in the early part of this century, when it was set in the mold of municipal and industrial bureaucracy. An extensive restructuring is long overdue.

Within the private world of the individual, the significant group is the nuclear family.[6] It is the unit of reproduction and nurturance, and it provides a sanctuary of intimacy for all its members. From their relationships comes the psychic pattern that prepares and commits its young to participate in the public world.

The modern American family differs from other family types in

[6] For an exploration of this theme, see Solon T. Kimball, "Cultural Influences Shaping the Role of the Child," *The National Elementary School Principal, Those First School Years,* XL (1960), 18–32. (See Chapter 8 below.)

several respects. Neither parents nor young expect that the children, as adults, will necessarily remain associated with the household of their birth, the locale in which they came to maturity, or occupational choices of the preceding generation. The discontinuity is not significant, however, because the basic posture of poised mobility, in both the geographical and social sense, is firmly preserved. But mobility cannot be achieved through the family alone; it depends upon the learnings that the child receives from formal schooling.[7] If the school does not, or cannot, provide the young with necessary skills and knowledge, or if it provides these in inadequate measure, then the individual is excluded from full participation in our type of civilization.

We must also accept, however, that the failure may be attributed in part to the cultural milieu from which the child comes. Gans [8] has shown, for example, the restrictive impress of Italian families, which prevented their children from partaking, or wishing to partake, of the full possibilities of education as a device for advancement. The Italian parents clearly understood the threat to group cohesion that education posed and actively discouraged such educational ambitions as their children might show.

The principle we derive from this illustration has broad applicability. We can state it as follows: Those who hold a prior commitment to the cultural particularism of family, community, race, ethnic group, or social class are in greater or lesser measure barred from full participation in our society. To the extent that they impose these restrictions upon their children, the children are also disadvantaged. The magnitude of discrimination may not be quantitatively large or limited primarily to those who are descendants of a defunct agrarianism, but even the exclusion of a few represents a defect in our society. That the changes in American society have engaged the great majority of our people is a testimonial of strength. In fact, Americans have been the architects of their own transformation.

The last of the major types of formal social groupings that are characteristically American is the voluntary association. This is the technical term that encompasses the vast number of clubs, associations, organizations, societies, councils, fraternities, lodges, and other groups that surround every aspect of American life. There is no activity, category, or interest that lacks some organized kind of espousal. From

---

[7] A study that throws light on this subject is John R. Seely, R. Alexander Sim, and Elizabeth W. Loosley, *Crestwood Heights: A Study of the Culture of Suburban Life* (New York: Basic Books, 1956).

[8] Herbert J. Gans, *The Urban Villagers: Group and Class in the Life of Italian Americans* (Chicago: The Free Press of Glencoe, 1962).

stamp collecting to investing, from barbering to surgery, from young
to old, or rich to poor, Americans join with their similars to investigate,
protest, compare, or celebrate.

The American's capacity to create and utilize organization is a
trait that reaches to our very beginnings. In the now famous May-
flower Compact of 1620, the Pilgrims set down the rules that were to
govern their relationships. Two hundred years later, de Tocqueville
marveled at the ease with which Americans joined together to solve
their problems. He also observed that, once the particular issue had
been resolved, they would disband, but could reconstitute themselves
readily if the necessity arose. During the Civil War, most of the military companies that marched from the towns of the North, and many
from the South, were formed on the associational pattern. Today, in
our schools and colleges, students and professors alike are confronted
by a vast array of activities and interests calling for the coordinate
efforts of like-minded peers.

It is in and through these associations that the young learn the
social skills they later carry into adult roles. Only among the poor do
we find a deficiency in this organizational capacity, a fact that those
who are now attempting to organize representational councils among
them are discovering anew. And, if we look closely, we also discover
that the schools that serve the children of the slums are the most deficient in providing extracurricular programs. Educators might well
contemplate the significance of such a fact.

In these three forms of social groupings, then, we encounter the
significant structures of American society. The corporate form provides
the instrumentality through which much of the work of the world is
accomplished. The family nurtures the young, offers a haven from
stress, and perpetuates flexibility for adaptation by means of the posture of mobility. The voluntary association provides the interstitial
fibers that connect the parts into a vast interrelated whole. There is
more, however, that requires attention, and this analysis leads, next, to
the inner life.

THE PSYCHIC PATTERN

Earlier, I called attention to the psychic pattern that the child acquires
within the family, but which holds such great importance for his
participation in the public world. Our task now is to establish the
relevance of psychic patterns to the individual's behavior in the social
order. In examining the connections among psychic, cultural, and
social spheres, we come to understand both the extent to which there
is mutual reinforcement among them and the kind of tensions they

generate in the individual. For example, there is no aspect of human need or aspiration for which our society fails to offer the possibility of unlimited realization. We find one expression of this in the widely prevalent belief that money, although the root of all evil, can buy anything—that is, almost anything. Of course it cannot buy happiness, which must be pursued.

The more sophisticated know that there are many routes, other than the monetary one, by which to move toward goals. None escapes, however, making the payment that pursuit of the dream exacts, although the fairy tale fantasies of childhood would lead us to believe otherwise. The fact is, before an individual can hope to reach any of the promised rewards, he must prepare himself, and the magnitude of his effort is believed to be roughly commensurate with the magnitude of his achievement. Each forward step, however, engenders new efforts for reaching succeeding goals; thus, preparation becomes a never-ending requirement. Those whose original preparation was inadequate, or those who have withdrawn or been defeated, may be counted as the casualties. That they are not now involved does not invalidate the manner in which the system works. Their failure may be due to an inadequate internalization of the psychic base necessary for commitment. It is to that aspect that I now turn.

If the child-rearing practices of the middle-class American family are successful, the child learns that full achievement of adult status is accomplished outside the home. He also expects that, during a portion of his preparatory period (the years of advanced schooling), he may be absent from his family. The preparation for separation from family has been called "independence training." Although the physical displacement is obvious and necessary, the achievement of full independence is largely illusory. Quite apart from the difficulty of shedding deeply embedded habituation to parental direction, the individual has been bound by psychic ties that he can seldom, if ever, escape. These are particularly evident in the areas of anxiety, shame, and guilt.

The obvious expression of anxiety appears as prudence—the need to be careful. The child has been carefully schooled to avoid the dangers that threaten his own well-being and that of others; he has also been taught that, if "things" work, it is because of the care and attention bestowed upon them. Both humans and machines need checkups and tune-ups, and extraneous items must be removed. The consequence of such training is to develop a sense of the orderliness of time and space and of the placement and movement of objects in them. Orderlinesss becomes a *sine qua non* for accomplishment and finds no better expression than the insistence of teachers that, in the classroom, the orderly behavior of pupils is a necessary condition for learning. How else may we interpret the distress teachers show when they encounter children who have not been thus socialized?

The less obvious expression of anxiety manifests itself in a pervasive insecurity. Although we continually make demands upon the individual, as a child or adult, we have few ways of giving reassurance concerning successful performance. The individual remains uncertain of his own capabilities and of his performance in relation to these. He must continually seek assurances, and failure or rejection can be devastating. Whatever the response to his efforts, he has also learned that the resolution of his difficulties resides within himself and, hence, he must continue to struggle. For those who remain with the struggle, even the accolade of others furnishes a doubtful proof of success, since each achievement is a transitory phase toward the next step. Those who attempt to escape the tensions of struggle by withdrawing from the competitive situation experience relief only temporarily, since competition is primarily an internal state.

Giving up, however, is far more difficult than might be imagined since anxiety is coupled with shame and guilt. Through the formative years, each individual acquires an enormous and unpayable debt to his parents. He is in debt to them for the opportunities they have given him—for life itself. It is his duty, as a child, to utilize the benefits accorded him; as an adult, he validates the trust that has been placed in him. He does this by fulfilling his sense of their aspirations, an assignment that cannot be forgotten, even after his parents' death. It is an obligation he also transmits to his children and, hence, its perpetuation is transgenerational. The pangs of conscience that erupt following the violation of some moral rule are superficial pains compared to those that one suffers consequent upon the violation of obligations to oneself and to one's family. Thus, anxieties about one's capabilities and the wise use of opportunities are linked to a fear of shaming oneself and others and of the guilt that ensues if one is unable to meet one's moral obligations. Although the poor are not fully exempt from the anxiety-guilt-shame complex, the obligations toward their elders are met more directly in the care of aged parents, a practice once prevalent among the middle class.

Intimately associated with the pattern of anxiety, shame, and guilt is the need to act upon the world. Many foreigners have marveled at American vitality and have explained our behavior as youthful exuberance. We can hardly accept such an interpretation. As we grow into mature nationhood, there is no sign of a slackening of the energy with which we attack problems. In politics, in sports, in courtship, in business, in the invasion of outer space, even in the muted infighting of a university campus, we are playing orderly but violent games. Even those who proclaim their desire for peace use violent measures to attract attention to their cause. If this aggression erupts into uncontrolled violence, orderliness is destroyed, and feelings of anxiety and guilt are intensified. Therefore, the destructive aspects of aggressiveness must be contained, and this we do by turning our activities into games the rules of which must be strictly observed and their observation impartially enforced if we are to avoid chaos.

Thus far I have been describing and tracing the interconnections of the characteristic American social groupings and of the psychic qualities of those who are fully participant in our society. As the analysis proceeds, remarkable congruencies, which contribute to our great cohesion as a people, become evident. Our social framework contains and directs the lively tensions that arise among and within groups and, in most instances, channels aggressive energies into productive purposes. There still remains, however, one major area for exploration. It is essential that the aspects of world view that are distinctly American be made explicit. We need to know about these in order to understand ourselves as individuals and as social beings. Once this question has been explored, we will be ready for the final task—to seek the relevancies between the educational enterprise and contemporary society and, if necessary, to offer some advice.

WORLD VIEW—INTERDEPENDENCY AND SYSTEM

Each of the cultural traditions that rooted in American soil during the colonial period reflected somewhat different views about the nature of man, his relation to the world, and his destiny. Nevertheless, the similarities among them were probably greater than the differences. The Old World rigidity, encompassed in a pattern of thought that accepted absolutes, a fixity of the universe, and sharp polarities, was particularly evident in the religious tradition. But there was also a strong current of empirical pragmatism, which granted to the individual the capacity for intervention. In addition, the literary legacy left by the cultivated minds of this early period shows much more than a concern with theology and the supernatural; it also reveals a strong bias toward rational explanation and experimentation.

Periods of crisis provided fertile ground for the transformation of older views and the introduction of new ones. The rapid development of the North and West after the Civil War provided a favorable environment for the doctrine of progress that Herbert Spencer espoused in a series of popular lectures in Eastern cities. Until the advent of the Depression of the 1930's, Americans held no doubts about the superiority of their way of life, about a future filled with unending rewards. We are all aware of the great changes that followed in the wake of the two world wars and of the intervening trauma of boom and crash. Their detailing has no particular relevance at the moment. What I should like to do, however, is attempt to describe an emerging pattern of thought that flows out of these changes and constitutes the conceptual basis for a world view only now being formulated.

The cornerstone of this pattern is the concept of interdependence. Although most of us are accustomed to thinking in terms of identities and particulars, we are gradually learning that this atomistic point of view cannot give us a comprehension of the whole. We are only now beginning to understand that the sum of the parts does not constitute a whole. We likewise recognize that the whole is not an addition, but a process. In the nature of the relationships that lead to cooperation or strife between the nations of the world, in the connections between industrial processes and pollution, in the effect of human environment upon normal and pathological behavior, and in many other ways, we are beginning to understand *interdependencies*. We are beginning to view the events of the world as expressions of systems—what Darwin called the web of life.

This new view is of immense significance because it brings with it, and is built upon, correlative changes in other habits of conceptualization. For example, when we think in systemic terms, we study change rather than statics. Because we know that modification of a system's environment, or of its components and their relationships, will have repercussions on either environment or system, or both, we seek to discover what these changes are and the processes associated with them. Under such circumstances, we can no longer accept the fixity we have attributed to absolutes; we must accept variability as an aspect of the natural world. Variability must not be confused with either relativity or uncertainty. The latter term has been applied to certain problems connected with measuring the behavior of subatomic particles, and the former pertains to the perspective from which a phenomenon is viewed. In contrast, variability refers to the capacity for modification.

When we accept the viewpoint of variable interdependencies, we no longer concentrate upon determining the fixed qualities or essences of things. In fact, we can no longer assume that things stand as isolated particulars that can be examined in and of themselves. Instead, we must now seek for the relationships among things. We discover that, as these relationships change—such as those between digestive and neural processes, or those between the members of a family—the quality of the particulars also changes. In this approach, we see items as variables, and our search centers on the relationships between them, since from discoveries of regularities among them comes the power of prediction.

Inevitably, this method of thought brings changes in the kinds of questions we ask when we attempt to understand the nature of the world. Definition and identification become subordinate to the search for principles that explain *process.* This difference can be illustrated by comparing the collector, who seeks to classify and arrange the specimens he has gathered under some *a priori* scheme of classification, with the ecologist, who attempts to observe and explain the succession of plant or animal types under conditions of an unstable environment. The latter is concerned with process; he asks questions about the nature of change under certain conditions. The classical taxonomist is a collector and classifier, concerned exclusively with the nature of things. His approach can lead us no further than static formulations.

This new mode of thought necessitates imparting a new meaning to the concept of knowledge. The quiz-kid is knowledgeable in that he has a great store of facts ready for instant recall. An encyclopedia and an almanac are inert repositories of facts. No one can deny that facts may prove to be useful bits of information. They may also turn out to be utterly worthless. The point is that information acquires significance only when it becomes relevant to a problem. Under such circumstances, the important intellectual quality is the capacity to recognize and solve problems, and this is what the thrust of deliberate education ought to be about.

Those who contend that this is what the schools now do had better look again. In particular, they should look at examinations if they are to discover what knowledge is being sought. They will find that "acquaintance with facts," one of the definitions Webster gives for knowledge, is the basis upon which we judge student competence in most areas of study. This standard of judgment is of a piece with the pattern of thought that deals in particulars, absolutes, statics, and essences. It views learning as a causal sequence of the rewarded response to stimuli, a theory that requires of the learner no greater cerebral capacity than that of a dog learning tricks. This simplistic view of learning is far from adequate. Humans resemble other animals in their need for motor skills, but mankind, with its use of symbols and its capacity for abstract thought, possesses mental processes that are immensely more complex. Man is capable of making explicit those very processes that differentiate him from other forms of animal life. The cognitive skills he must have, before he can think in terms of systems, variability, relationships, and processes, are not inherent in the information he accumulates; they are a derivative of the capability to define and solve problems. Within this formulation, the concept of knowledge is extended to include the processes as well as the results of our cognitive activities.

EDUCATIONAL CONGRUENCIES

The problem with which we must now deal is that of deciding what kind of educational enterprise is needed; once again, the basic issue is congruency. On several occasions earlier, allusions were made to the existing situation in education. The evidence from these illustrations leads to the conclusion that the present situation is disorderly and disjunctive. It may well be that the legacy inherited from our past, during which education was primarily a conservator rather than an innovator, explains this condition. Certainly, the long insulation of the schools and of professional educators from the main streams of development in technology, thought, and organization would seem an equally plausible reason. Whatever the explanation, the fact remains that those who run our schools do not evidence an awareness of the crucial position and role they now hold, and schools are woefully deficient in meeting the educational needs of society.

This is not the place to offer specific prescriptions for the modernization of the educational system. I assert now, however, that it cannot be accomplished by reshuffling the bits and pieces of a curriculum, adding a little of this or subtracting a little of that. The transformation that is required is much more fundamental. It means bringing the organizational structure of the schools into accord with those corporate forms that now serve other functions so well. It means modifying the curriculum so as to emphasize the teaching of basic disciplines of thought and to put subject matter particularism in a subordinate position. And it means testing for problem-solving cognitive skills: for the ability to demonstrate an understanding of the variabilities and interdependencies of systems. Finally, it means building into our teaching practices the self-testing and self-correcting measures that are essential for the functioning of any viable system. These goals imply a very different philosophy of pedagogical practice and learning from that now prevalent.

3. THE RELEVANCE OF ANTHROPOLOGY

Any appraisal of the relation between anthropology and education should first specify the areas of common concern. From the anthropological perspective, the most inclusive concept is the transmission of culture, which encompasses not only what is taught and learned, but also the organization, pattern, and processes of education in their social and cultural settings.[1] Professional educators usually would agree that the transmission of culture also is their major concern, but they would then insist that, as practitioners, their orientation is primarily programmatic. They would say that their job is to know what to do and how to do it, although some might add that they could use assistance in developing new understanding of their problems and in learning how changes in current practices could produce improved results.

The sharpest differentiation between educator and anthropologist is likely to appear in the perspective, definition, and solution of educational problems. Teachers, school administrators, and other educational specialists are primarily trained for and engaged in activities subsumed under instruction. In contrast, the anthropologist, proceeding from the perspective of his discipline, seeks to describe the social system and cultural behavior within the educational institution and to

---

"Education," in Otto von Mering and Leonard Kasdan, Eds., *Anthropology and the Behavioral and Health Sciences* (Pittsburgh: University of Pittsburgh Press, 1970), pp. 112–122. © 1970, University of Pittsburgh Press. Used by permission.
[1] Solon T. Kimball, "The Transmission of Cultures." In *The Body of Knowledge Unique to the Profession of Education* (Washington, D.C.: Pi Lambda Theta, 1966). (See Chapter 12 below.)

place it in the context of the community. By ordering this accumulated knowledge, the anthropologist may suggest modifications in organization or procedures that will increase the effectiveness of the educational system. When he works with educators, he functions primarily as a consultant and refrains from direct intervention in the responsibility of those trained to operate the system, the professional educators. Anthropologists who have worked in applied anthropology are aware of the connection between preliminary, traditional field research on a problem, and the preparation of innovative proposals based upon the findings of this research. They also are aware that they must resist becoming practitioners because this responsibility belongs to those whose training, experience, and aptitudes have prepared them for this role.

I should draw attention to another fundamental distinction between educators and anthropologists, since they may view such specific problems as those of school dropouts, under-achievement, or discipline from quite different perspectives. The cross-cultural and holistic perspective of the anthropologist permits him to interpret the data from specific research in a wider context than can the educator, who usually is concerned with one specific situation. Furthermore, some aspects of behavior that educators may ignore, treat casually, or even be unaware of, such as informal groupings or induction of new personnel or students, may strike the anthropologist as of major significance. In particular, the anthropologist's perspective gives him a strategic view of the relationships among schools, the educative process, and the community. His knowledge of cultural continuity and comparative analysis also should prove advantageous in understanding cultural change.

These differences in outlook and procedure need to be examined in the context of purposes and their associated values, although it is difficult for me to phrase or specify them, except in the most general terms. Let us assume that American anthropologists and educators are equally committed to the principles of democracy. Although no attempt will be made to enumerate these principles in any detail nor to assess the congruency between ideal and practice, for illustrative purposes I shall mention representative government, cultural pluralism, equality of opportunity, and protection of individual dignity. The immediate problem is of another kind: to examine the extent to which democratic tenets influence the American anthropologist, first, in his analyses of the school system operation either as implicit or explicit assumptions, and, second, in the solutions he recommends for an educational problem. Can we, as anthropologists, claim some deeper and more universal insights about human nature, culture, and social groupings than those implicit in the democratic creed and, if so, do these contribute to a dilemma by contradicting the validity of some goals that we readily accept?

Presumably, few educators need to be confronted with the doubts that I suggest face anthropologists. Although thoughtful educators are distressed by the gap between ideal and practice, the pressure of daily responsibility leads many to do their job without a sufficient understanding or questioning of the system and makes them largely insensitive to its inconsistencies. For example, the once prevalent belief that the United States was free of social class was supported by contrasting the United States to Europe, where a hereditary aristocracy barred the advance of the capable and ambitious. It was believed that in the land of the free any man could rise to great heights, as had Lincoln, Edison, and Ford. When the community studies of the early 1930's began to provide evidence for the existence of social class distinctions in the United States, some labeled both studies and researchers as un-American. Later, Warner, Havighurst, and Loeb, in *Who Shall Be Educated,* showed how children of different social levels were differentially treated in tne schools.[2] Subsequent studies in Chicago by students of Everett Hughes and in Detroit by Patricia Sexton confirmed the disadvantages that children of the working class faced through unequal distribution of educational resources and personnel.[3]

The assumption that equitable distribution of resources ensures equal educational opportunities or results is, of course, fallacious. Class biases appear in subtle and unconscious ways, even among those who profess ardent support of democratic equality. In Spindler's research, the teacher so stereotyped class behavior that he was unaware of the differences between his rating of students and their actual performances.[4] Jules Henry has shown the subtle and automatic rewards and punishments that teachers mete out to those students who conform to, or violate, their class-oriented sense of proper behavior.[5] Ruth Landes reported that Mexican-American students in California rejected certain aspects of schooling that threatened their cultural identity.[6] Thus, boys who took part in athletic programs were accused by their peers of becoming "Anglicized," and cultural values of

---

[2] W. Lloyd Warner, Robert Havighurst, and Martin Loeb, *Who Shall Be Educated* (New York: Harper and Brothers, 1944).

[3] Patricia C. Sexton, *Education and Income* (New York: Viking, 1961).

[4] George Spindler, *The Transmission of American Culture* (Cambridge, Mass.: Harvard University Press, 1959).

[5] Jules Henry, "Attitude Organization in Elementary School Classrooms." In George D. Spindler, Ed., *Education and Culture* (New York: Holt, Rinehart & Winston, 1963).

[6] Ruth Landes, *Culture in American Education* (New York: John Wiley and Sons, 1965).

Mexican girls were violated by what they considered the immodest exposure they suffered when they were required to shower in open stalls
in physical education classes. Landes further reported that when these
ethnic-based behaviors were understood by the teachers and efforts
were openly made to accommodate to them, much of the unwittingly
created tension disappeared. Perhaps stress generated by violations of
class identity might also disappear given the same treatment, although
traditionally subcultural variations expressed in social class have not
been accorded the same dignity and respect sometimes given autonomous cultures.

In other words, the American acceptance of cultural pluralism and
the anthropological value of respecting cultural autonomy are fairly
well in accord. But the problem gets sticky when we view social class
as a subcultural variant while adhering to a relatively uniform educational approach expressing only middle-class values. In the extension of
middle-class values in education, we witness an attempt to bring children of the lower class into the orbit of middle-class behavior. Many
attempts are made to justify this procedure, but this might also be con-
strued as an example of social class, or cultural imperialism. The recent
spot announcements on television that urge continued education, pre-
dicting a dismal future for the unheeding, are obviously intended to
reach working-class youth and, regardless of the validity of the exhortation, those who respond to the message serve middle-class values.[7]

It is generally accepted that the schools that serve the slums of
the big cities are relatively unsuccessful in their educational efforts
when judged by, and compared with, middle-class standards.[8] One
problem that plagues educators in slum sections is the inability to keep
older children enrolled in school. There are several ways in which this
high dropout rate may be interpreted. The school program may be so
inept and the school environment so punishing that they may contribute
to the high attrition rate. Perhaps those who withdraw or are rejected
represent the intellectually marginal. Perhaps they withdraw because
they equate a given age with adulthood and see school as only for children. Or perhaps all three ideas possess some validity as explanations
of the situation, although educators are less likely to look to the social
and cultural setting for explanations than to purely pedagogical ones.

From time to time some educators have had the temerity to suggest
special curricula for the so-called culturally disadvantaged, but such
propositions are repugnant in a democracy unless they carry a magical

---

[7] A strict application of this interpretation would view schooling for middle-
class children as a form of age-status imperialism.

[8] Whether educational programs are any more or any less effective than
other social betterment efforts in these areas is a moot point.

label such as "enrichment." Even these labels can be political dynamite. Nevertheless, differential schooling already is in effect. The "track" system is justified on the basis of vocational interests and aptitudes, whereas in reality it divides students on the basis of class background. A further separation appears with the special treatment accorded the mentally retarded and the emotionally disturbed, most of whom are recruited from the poorer classes, as exemplified in the "600" schools in New York City.

This brief excursion into aspects of social class and education is primarily intended to show some of the complications facing both educators and anthropologists in a society where practices and ideals are not, and cannot be, in accord, and where the complexities of a culturally diverse society create conflicting values.

If the problems confronting educators seem difficult, those facing anthropologists who attempt to analyze the educational system and to work with educators seem even greater. For example, should the degree of objectivity maintained when observing initiation ceremonies among Australian aborigines be any different from that maintained when observing a school monitor system, where students selected for their size use force to punish other students who have violated school rules? Is not the principle of cultural congruency demonstrated by the discovery that physical prowess is the basis for a pattern of dominance and submission among the same students outside the school? What should be the basis for intervention in either case? As anthropologists, we have not been overly sympathetic with missionary or governmental suppression of native custom. Is it possible that we have a double set of values when confronted by behavior we label offensive in our own culture? Instead of protesting the danger of going native, should we not recognize that we are already one with the natives when we make judgmental evaluations based on their values? If our perspective and method are to be useful to American education, we must learn to keep our analysis free of culture bias to the same degree demanded in our work elsewhere. Otherwise we had better steer clear of advocating educational reform, since its practitioners are far more competent than we are in their spheres.

Perhaps the distinctive role and contribution of the anthropologist in the field of education can be further clarified if we examine some specific area of research. Consideration of the informal group system of a high school student body can well serve this purpose. These groups are not areas of great concern to either school administrator or teacher, and I know of no books on school organization or curriculum, except those written by sociologists, that even mention the subject. From such evidence I think we are justified in concluding that educators do not consider informal grouping among students, or its absence, to be of any great relevance to the educative process. Some years ago, student peer group choices were explored when sociometrics made quite a splash; the interest continued for only a brief period, however. Like so many other innovations, the mechanics of determining student preference and rejection were adopted to serve the needs of teachers and administrators, but the flesh and blood of theory and the therapeutic goals of the method were never assimilated. Actually, small group theory in anthropology is genetically unrelated to sociometrics, although the techniques of the latter have some utility.

Three major reasons manifest the importance of informal or small group studies. First, we know that in many societies much of what a child learns is acquired from his peer group. Where education is institutionalized under the control of adults, the official knowledge of textbook and lecture must contend with the unofficial and possibly contradictory lore children teach each other. Furthermore, knowledge and experience always are assimilated through a perceptual screen that includes the criteria for discrimination and evaluation.

The relationship between the student's informal system and that of the community and of the institutional structure of the school provides the second reason for the importance of small group studies. Hollingshead's study in Elmtown, for example, shows that the high school clique system reproduces the parental status and value systems.[9] There are many intriguing problems in this area, such as the relationship between student and teacher cliques and the evaluations each group makes of the other; it is obvious that we need several studies to provide us with comparative data. Research on the school has not yet established the correspondences between formal and informal systems, but the results of studies in hospitals, factories, and prisons have demonstrated such relationships.

A final reason for the importance of small group studies is covered by such rubrics as morale, organizational health, job satisfaction, and productivity. Other ways of describing these phenomena include participation and involvement, organization and communication, or executive function. Here again we must turn to industrial research to provide us with the clues to what we might expect to find. Mayo's report on the consequences of changed conditions in the textile plant upon worker behavior seems particularly relevant.[10] In this plant, it will be remembered, the general malaise that afflicted all workers gradu-

[9] A. B. Hollingshead, *Elmtown's Youth* (New York: John Wiley & Sons, 1949).

[10] Elton Mayo, *The Human Problems of an Industrial Organization* (New York: Macmillan, 1933).

ally disappeared as they were brought into a meaningful relationship to their environment. Arensberg's analysis of numerous such studies supports the same conclusion.[11] A vitally important area of study is the extent and the ways in which student peer groups mediate a meaningful and participant relationship between students and the school environment.

The student system is much more than informal grouping as Gordon,[12] Coleman,[13] and Burnett [14] have told us in their major studies of high schools. It also includes the extracurricular programs organized around student government, athletic, literary, dramatic, musical, and club activities. Events associated with these activities are highly visible and involve varying degrees of faculty assistance and control and parental participation. Extracurricular activities provide a meeting ground between school and community that is not provided in any other fashion. In addition to being viewed as an extension of the academic program, these activities represent the varied social and cultural interests of the community and, as such, serve as a training ground for them. This, however, is not the perspective emphasized by educators. Although they are well aware of this phase of school life, with some misgivings I may add, they are more concerned with program and supervision than they are with the social cultural implications. This narrow emphasis of the educator provides the anthropologist with the opportunity, even the responsibility, to bring the systematic approach of social science analysis to this aspect of the educational system. Here the anthropologist can exercise his competency in describing the relationship between social structure and culture pattern in an institutional and community setting.

Thus, the student system is a social science problem with relevance for education, whereas its programmatic aspects remain the responsibility of professional educators. With this distinction, we can avoid distorting our results through culture bias. For example, the discovery that lower-class children opt for adult values and behavior at earlier ages than do middle-class children is a consequential scientific finding for educators who are programmatically concerned about dropouts. As applied anthropologists, however, we also have the right to evaluate or

[11] Conrad M. Arensberg, "Behavior and Organization: Industrial Studies." In John H. Rohrer, *et al.*, Eds., *Social Psychology at the Crossroads* (New York: Harper and Row, 1951).

[12] Wayne Gordon, *The Social System of the High School* (New York: The Free Press, 1957).

[13] James S. Coleman, *The Adolescent Society: The Social Life of the Teenager and its Impact on Education* (Glencoe: The Free Press, 1961).

[14] Jacquetta H. Burnett, *A Participant Observation Study of a Sociocultural Subsystem of the Students in a Small Rural High School.* Unpublished doctoral dissertation, Columbia University, 1964.

recommend procedures designed to change the situation in one or another direction. The ethics involved in offering such advisements have already been clearly stated by the Society for Applied Anthropology and need not be elaborated here.[15]

In order to broaden the scope of this inquiry, I will designate divisions for grouping specific problems of education, and discuss relevant anthropological theory for each of them.

There are six major areas that are broadly inclusive of the enterprise of education. These are (1) training of school personnel, (2) organization and management of schools, (3) the specification of curriculum and preparation of materials, (4) pedagogical practices, (5) the relations between school and community, and (6) philosophy of education. In no sense should these categories be considered mutually exclusive units for study. Obviously, the activities of a teacher and students in a classroom have relevance for all these, but for research purposes these items, singly or in combination, must be viewed as primarily topical. Although this does not invalidate them as appropriate research subjects, we should try to find some alternative or complementary arrangement, some frame of reference, that provides a more insightful conceptualization and serves the goals of social science as well as those of education. To do so we must turn to anthropology.

Anthropology utilizes an inductive, empirical, natural history method through which it seeks to describe the structure, pattern, and process of human behavior. It shares with other sciences the ordering of data as systems that reflect the qualities and relationships of individual items in their activities. From anthropological operations and from the results of analysis, we theorize about the connections between patterns of behavior and the forms of human grouping in stable or changing environments. We have developed theoretical formulations for many aspects of behavior. The problem here is to decide which of these areas of theory are most appropriate to educational research.

Earlier I suggested that the transmission of culture, inclusive of developing cognitive capacities and technical skills, should be the primary objective of an educational system. But the strict application of such a view would neglect the implicit, and often intended, socialization and growth of affective, evaluative capabilities, to say nothing of the purely physiological aspects. Obviously, all of these must be considered in framing research. Other ingredients in the teaching-learning process include the institutional setting, the traditional practices of school and classroom, and the relationships with other institutions in a specific community environment. Together, these items suggest four

[15] Society for Applied Anthropology, "Statement on Ethics of the Society for Applied Anthropology," *Human Organization*, XXII (1963–1964).

areas of applicable theory: learning theory, culture theory, theory of organization, and theory of change.

Learning theory, thus far, has not been a major concern of anthropologists. Wallace has been interested in this problem and has called attention to the contrast between stimulus-cue-response and cognitive learning.[16] In an earlier period, Mead, Hallowell, Linton, Kardiner, and others produced useful and exciting studies of child-rearing practices that helped us understand how personality is formed in a cultural environment. Their theory, however, borrowed mainly from psychoanalysis, gave much greater emphasis to psychomotor and affective learning and behavior than to cognitive or intellectual learning. Among both anthropologists and psychologists, the implicit acceptance of the stimulus-response paradigm and of the conditioned reflex as basic neurological processes may help to explain the neglect of the distinctly human, symbolic aspects of behavior, and the processes of their acquisition. If the study of culture transmission is to be truly comprehensive, it also must be concerned with the cognitive, symbolic structure, the cultural behavior, and the social groupings within which learning occurs.

The realization of such an objective requires that we broaden our area of inquiry considerably beyond the traditional description of child-rearing practices and specification of personality formation. We must look for the congruencies between culture pattern, social grouping, and the logics of mythology and language and their relationships to the cognitive screen through which experience is received and organized.

Once this objective has been realized, we are in a better position to seek solutions to some perplexing problems, such as defining the relationships among psychomotor, affective, and cognitive learning. What consequences will ensue in the results we obtain if we shift from treating directed learning as stages in development to focusing on transition or, alternatively, to viewing learning as pattern embellishment and expansion? Can we establish cultural levels of cognitive complexity and relate these to culture and community? It seems to me that learning theory based on solutions to these problems is directly applicable to curriculum materials and pedagogy, as well as to teacher training and the philosophy of education. Actually, the inductive, natural-history approach contains a powerful learning tool and implicit learning theory.

Culture theory, in contrast, has general applicability for all aspects of education. In particular, those understandings of continuity and persistence and of pattern and congruency will be useful in tracing the

16 Anthony Wallace, "Culture and Cognition," *Science*, CXXXV (1962), 351–357.

origin and development of custom and in explaining their function. Education has much to learn from specific research utilizing the time and space formulations of Hall [17] and the studies of body socialization and movement by Birdwhistell.[18] In international and cross-cultural education, many of the difficulties accompanying attempts to transfer educational systems from one culture to another without taking into account the distinctive culture patterns of the recipient culture could be alleviated or eliminated if these anthropological concepts were available.

Theory of organization has particular relevance for the training of administrators, for school organization and management, and for relations between school and community. Studies in industry can contribute both method and theory to this area of interest, which is shared with some sociologists and social psychologists. The contributions of many individuals in these several fields are worthy of close study, specifically Arensberg, Richardson, Whyte, Hughes, Becker, Rossi, Sanders, and Sayles. Atwood has already demonstrated the utility of interaction theory in school organization.[19] One significant question, of course, is the extent to which custodial or supervisory practice facilitates or impedes the learning process. When we examine the dimensions of school and community relations, we encounter a much broader and less clearly defined area, but the technique of event analysis should help to place schools in the institutional setting of the community.

Theory to deal with problems of educational innovation and change comes from anthropology's long-standing interest in culture growth and spread, and from its more recent concern with the forms of human groupings and their dynamics, as well as with the relationship between culture and community. Anthropology's natural-history approach leads us to the processes of transformation, either those affecting the individual as they may be observed in rites of passage, or those of group and community as seen in stress or in the stabilizing rites of intensification. From this perspective, we seek to understand the process of group formation, modification, or dissolution, as well as what happens with individual induction or expulsion. The notable accomplishments of applied anthropology in the theory and procedure of innovation and change should give us confidence that the principles and procedures

[17] Edward T. Hall, *The Silent Language* (Greenwich: Premier Books, 1961).

[18] Roy L. Birdwhistell, *Kinesics and Context: Essays on Body Motion Communication* (Philadelphia: University of Pennsylvania Press, 1970).

[19] Mark Atwood, "Small-Scale Administrative Change: Resistance to the Introduction of a High School Guidance Program." In Matthew B. Miles, Ed., *Innovation in Education* (New York: Teachers College Press, 1964).

we have already tested also are applicable to educational problems and processes.

These, then, are the areas of anthropological research competence and theoretical concern that seem to have special relevance for education. The insistence upon framing problems in social science terms does not negate the importance of problems as they are seen and described by educators. It is our task, however, to translate these into research problems where our theory and techniques can apply. Also, the perspective and inductive methodology characteristic of our discipline can make additional and unanticipated contributions.

4. ANTHROPOLOGY AND TEACHER TRAINING

There is a widely prevalent belief that excellence in our educational system is directly linked with teacher preparation. It would be difficult to establish that there was no connection between teacher training and later performance and yet there are so many factors that influence teacher "productivity," quite apart from the murky area of its measurement, that it is indeed curious that the critics and reformers of education have taken this narrow area as their main ground of contention. Their almost exclusive focus on the relationship between performance and training ignores the social and cultural settings within which both processes occur, including the community of which institutionalized education is a component. Such limitations are clearly evident in the writings of Arthur Bestor, Jacques Barzun, and Admiral Rickover. As illustrative of this orientation, I shall summarize the Carnegie-sponsored study directed by the noted educator, Dr. James Conant.

In *The Education of American Teachers*,[1] Dr. Conant surveys the existing situation and offers a series of proposals to reduce the confusion and deficiency. He believes the considerable flux in certification requirements proves, among other things, that there is uncertainty about them even among those with superior wisdom. The situation would be improved, he contends, if the certification were primarily a responsibility of the institutions that train teachers. Each institution would develop the curriculum that would ensure competence in subject

---

"Anthropology and Teacher Training," in D. B. Gowin and Cynthia Richardson, Eds., *Five Fields and Teacher Training*, Project One, Cornell University (Ithaca: Cornell University, 1965), pp. 1–11.

[1] James B. Conant, *The Education of American Teachers* (New York: McGraw-Hill, 1963).

matter, teaching methods, and such related areas as psychology, and would provide extended periods of supervised apprenticeship.

The biases of Dr. Conant are easily identifiable. He is repelled by a system that establishes standards but then negates them by the numerous loopholes that allow evasions. He rejects the senseless and elaborate bureaucratic control that attempts to specify too narrowly who is competent. He is fearful of the oligarchic power, narrow vision, and self-perpetuating tendencies of the educational establishment, and he emphasizes autonomy and responsibility. He believes skill is perfected under the direction of a master, in the tradition of the graduate school and the guild.

His tightly prescribed curriculum attempts to reach solutions through modification of existing practices. There is only the slightest evidence that he understands that the educative process is something more than subject matter competence and teaching skills. He directs major attention to courses and classroom experience as bases for certification, and ignores the larger issue of the function of formal education in our society.

There is nothing startlingly new in the curriculum proposed by Conant. Only when he calls for direct accountability and certification by the training institutions does he depart from accepted practice. This latter proposal is one that the more philosophically minded educators might let their fantasies run with on a balmy afternoon, but the politically hard-headed would predictably shun both poke and pig.

On what basis then might we make decisions about a teacher training curriculum? Even the age-old basics of subject-matter competence and pedagogical skill appear simplistic when we begin to look at the dimensions of the problem. The mere possession of these two qualities will in itself neither assure their application in the classroom nor, if used, guarantee that students will learn. For example, custodial management seems to be the primary skill asked of inner-city teachers in some classrooms. What we mean to say is that the successful discharge of the teaching function depends upon a lively grappling with the realities of students, school, and community, and never in this world can any formula of so many hours of this or that prepare for the encounter—state certification requirements to the contrary.

Let us return to the question we posed above but phrase it more broadly by asking what are the essentials common in all professional training? These include intellectual skills—a logic of cognitive organization; personal skills—a way of thinking about and responding to experience; the acquisition of knowledge; and technical skills—the use and communication of knowledge. When we begin to flesh out this listing with the insights and practices anthropology can offer, it is then that the prescription for the training of educators becomes novel—even radical.

Reference to Dr. Conant has been necessary to set the framework within which we may discuss the contribution of anthropology to teacher training. The main issue is the relationship between American society and the form and function of the educational enterprise. This is a problem to which my colleague, James McClellan, and I turned our attention in *Education and the New America.*[2] We showed that Main Street and rural education were adaptable only in part to industrial cities that emerged early in this century. These cities required radical transformations of the educative process and organization, largely because of the social upheaval—a sharp separation between the public and private aspects of life.

It is not the distinction between public and private that is so novel, but rather the tenuous, even conflicting, relationship between the two. Where the connections between institutions once made a community, there have now been interposed supra-community institutions requiring loyalty apart from any responsibility to the individual or his family. In the shattering of the traditional community, man's private world has become disconnected from his public one.

The private world is family and friend. Its locale is home, but not always neighborhood. Activities uniting parents and children are labeled "nuclear," and in these personal relationships, which extend to friends and relatives, the individual expresses the emotional needs of love and suffering and dependence. But only in part does the emotion of family events distinguish it from behavior in the public world. It is also a separation based upon organization and function.

In contrast, "public" America comprises great superstructures in business, government, education, health, even religion, and their interconnected associations. To these organizations belong the responsibility for the goods and services needed by a large, diverse, and highly specialized society. Civilization requires high technical, professional, and organizational skills, which are consciously sought through education; they cannot be supplied, as in agrarian America, through instruction provided within the family. Furthermore, it is no longer possible for a man to count himself prepared in his self-chosen career through completion of a single course of study. In order to keep abreast, it is often necessary to return to formal study. Teachers are not exempt from this necessity, although current certification procedures ignore the reality.

[2] Solon T. Kimball and James E. McClellan, *Education and the New America* (New York: Random House, 1962).

In this counterpoised system of public and private worlds, formal education becomes the process of preparation for participation in the public world. Moreover, the measure of a man's success depends to a considerable degree on his social achievement. Recent concern over dropouts and over the inadequacy of slum schooling recognizes the consequences for those who cannot, or do not, assimiliate the skills that education provides. Their handicap almost certainly relegates them to an inferior social level.

A further aspect of our civilization is of utmost importance to any rational system of education. Unlike the simpler forms of community life exemplified in the New England town, the plantation, or the Main Street towns, it is all but impossible to experience directly a whole metropolitan community, because of its massiveness, complexity, and its specialization of activity. Within large organizations, most individuals are limited to their own special activity and to that of the levels above and below them. The situation of residence is somewhat different. Participation in local affairs is limited to a few things that were once concerns of autonomous communities.

Direct participation in everything is impossible, but if we are to have a viable society, there must be some device by which a vicarious or at least symbolic comprehension of the society can be achieved. It is our belief that this can be won only through understanding the functions of family and superstructures, the tensions between them, their relation to the individual and his self-fulfillment, the course of life itself, and the symbols that express and give meaning. Obviously, only through deliberate education can this understanding be acquired.

What then is the relevance of these social realities for the training of teachers? Mr. McClellan and I addressed ourselves to this problem in an indirect manner only. We asked what kind of academic experience adolescents should have, and, by inference, what training teachers must have to provide this experience. We rejected any solution merely listing academic disciplines, since by nature they restrict interest and attention. We proposed, instead, that the curriculum be organized around four disciplines of thought and action inherent in the social order that together encompass human experience not as inclusive categories of knowledge but as tools by which comprehension is gained.[3] The disciplines we proposed are: (1) logic and mathematics, (2) experimentation, (3) aesthetic form, and (4) natural history. It is in the last area that the major contribution of anthropology to teacher training is to be found.

The natural-history method is not widely known and its central

[3] *Ibid.*, pp. 297–304.

position in the methodology of anthropology is not understood.[4] This situation may be attributed in part to the unbelievably successful utilization by the physical sciences of the logico-deductive approach after they had incorporated the tools of mathematics and statistics. Unravelling the secrets of the universe and their relevance for technology combined to eclipse the theoretical significance of the great scientific insights achieved by Charles Darwin through inductive analysis. The world's attention was directed to his proposals about the origin of species and man's genetic connection with other forms of life, and not to the theoretical and intellectual procedures that brought him to that understanding. Only now, slowly and grudgingly, is there a developing awareness of the far more important methodological contribution of Darwin.[5]

What has yet to be fully understood is that the Western intellectual tradition includes two complementary but distinct approaches to the study of the universe. The logico-deductive method of physical science creates hypotheses from mathematical and abstract models, and verification is sought through research and experimentation. The empirical, inductive approach of natural history builds from the data of organic and social behavior the principles of structure and variability. Hypotheses come from the observation of events and are substantiated or modified through further observation.

Anthropologists' concern with all aspects of man's behavior explains the several traditions from which anthropology has borrowed its point of view and techniques. From history, literature, and the arts has come a humanistic approach, which helps to counter a coldly objective view of humanity. Anthropology shares with sociology a common interest in group life and has been influenced by the latter's approach to community and society. From biology comes the empirical, inductive method of observation and analysis, and a common concern with man's evolution and physiology. This eclectic propensity may be observed in other areas as well.

The important fact, however, is not that anthropology has borrowed from many fields but that influences have been successfully adapted to the central purpose of anthropology, the study of man. This purpose has always been linked to empirical, inductive research— the natural-history method. The emphasis upon method is not intended to exclude the value of anthropology's content, but to incorporate it

---

[4] The public associates natural history with museums and bird watching or specimen collecting. The physical scientist thinks of the early and primitive stages in the development of a scientific discipline when he uses the term.

[5] Solon T. Kimball, "Darwin and the Future of America," *The Educational Forum*, XXV (November 1960), 59–72. (See Chapter 6 below.)

alone into teacher training would be to miss the vital essence of the discipline. Its richness is its perspective and ways of thought, which help reshape our apprehension and interpretation of the world. Perhaps the use of an example would help to clarify the matter.

Everyone would agree that the prospective teacher should know something about the operation of a school. Just what that something is, and just how the knowledge should be gained, are moot points. The anthropologist would argue that a simple description of the roles of administrators, teachers, and pupils, no matter how skillful, is inadequate. At best, it portrays a static picture of responsibilities; at worst, a schematic, idealized version of what ought to be. The idea advanced by Cubberley in his text on school administration is an example of the latter.[6]

An anthropologist would treat these writings as data, not necessarily as any representation of reality. For him, understanding school organization comes from slow and painstaking field research. Often, the specific questions and observations develop from the immediate situation, a procedure vastly different from the use of a set schedule or questionnaire. In contrast to the recognized lack of specific knowledge in given areas is the established body of concepts and procedures with which a research is initiated. These represent the scientific heritage from previous studies and assumptions about the nature of human groupings. The idea of social system is central among these.

The anthropologist seeks relationships between individuals as they participate in events. These provide the data from which he builds his abstractions of structure, function, and process. Thus the emphasis is not upon things but upon processes. Since the significant data are not quantitative, or only incidentally so, enumerations are only byproducts, and since sample characteristics are irrelevant, the statistical measures used so widely in psychology and sociology are applied infrequently.

Another objective is to identify the connections between subsystems and the whole system. The goal is to discover how a system maintains itself by internal dynamics and its changing relations with larger systems. A simple cause-and-effect formula is inapplicable. The relations within and between systems are multidimensional and must be so handled.

Although this explanation is only a partial statement of the natural-history method, let us test its applicability by looking at a high school from this perspective.

The major social categories in a school coincide in part with the

[6] Ellwood P. Cubberley, *Public School Administration* (Boston: Houghton Mifflin, 1916).

well-known divisions of administrators, teachers, students, and grade levels among students. This is only an initial step whose results must be verified, but our method can classify and provide a basis for further analysis. When we being to examine the variety of events in which different people interact, and begin to chart this behavior in relation to time and space, we are faced with a situation of great complexity. But by classifying events, we see that the school contains three major subsystems: the administrative, the academic, and the student. Although these correspond with the previously identified social categories, we also encounter some that do not, such as those involving ·members of the community. When parents or others join school activities, their effect must be accounted for.

The problem is crucial because it involves the criteria for devising categories and is central to all questions of taxonomy. When the Greeks hit upon the common-sense designation of basic elements into earth, fire, water, and air, they prescribed a framework that persisted for centuries and hindered rather than aided advances in scientific understanding. But when the physicists decided upon atomic weight as the basis for classification of the elements, they went a step beyond the experience that is immediately available to the ordinary man. There is a quite different classificatory principle at work, however, in a taxonomic system based upon utilizing the attributes of any class of entities, as in the construction of the table of atomic weights, and the establishment of subsystems based upon events. In the latter instance, the criteria are derived from actual happenings in time and space; in the former, they are based upon the qualities of a thing.

Although these brief remarks are hardly more than a hasty excursion into the problems of classification, they do emphasize another aspect in which the method of natural history differs from that of the physical sciences. In the former, the systematics of classification are derived from within the system; in the latter, they depend upon some defined attribute of entities.

We are still very far, however, from completing an examination of all the possible ramifications. It will be remembered that each subsystem should be viewed as a part of another subsystem. Part of our problem is to see how some types of relationships contribute to stability, others to stress. Behind our search is the assumption that tension is inherent in any situation involving several systems. We also begin to note the rhythm of interaction expressed in periods of social time. For example, the class period is a significant unit of time in the academic subsystem and the football season in the student subsystem. One research goal is to discover the rhythmic regularities of activities and their interconnections. When completed, an initial step will have been taken toward the prediction of significant variations in system relations.

With this kind of systematic analysis of behavior, we have gone far in eliminating the witless involvement of the innocent who adhere to the customary because it is comfortable and safe, who test the new by trial and error, and who judge consequences in terms of affective standards. We are on the way to a cognitive apperception of systems, and that, after all, is what much of formal schooling ought to be about. This type of analysis also offers possibilities for understanding practical problems. A principal who has been trained to think in these terms can predict when his action will produce an eruption among teachers or students, and vice versa.[7]

We can deepen our understanding by examining the student sub-system. In other than a few metropolitan high schools, programs of extra-curricular activities are prevalent. Educators express uneasiness about the emphasis on such activities, especially sports, and purists would eliminate all activities that do not contribute to intellectual development. Most educators would agree, I believe, that to the extent that these activities develop aesthetic, vocational, and physical talents, the programs are desirable. They contribute to school morale, and, on occasion, they provide a beneficial link with the community.

There are several aspects of these programs, however, that are given little heed, partly because school officials have never been trained to be sensitive to them, and partly because they do not see that they are relevant to official school goals. For example, to assess the relative contribution of classroom learning and extra-curricular activities to adult participation in community life would be an intriguing problem. A child must somehow learn those techniques and values that allow him to participate in his community. Except for vocational skills, formal study contributes very little. Indeed, where else can an individual learn and practice social skills if not in extra-curricular activities? Within their semi-autonomous activities, students learn to nominate and elect, they plan programs and events, buy and sell, account for receipts and expenditures, direct and are directed. From these activities emerge their judgment and morals.[8] These are essential skills in the world of community and corporation, and although their acquisition does not promise success any more than intellectual per-

    [7] Mark Atwood, "Small-scale Administrative Change: Resistance to the Introduction of a High School Guidance Program." In Matthew B. Miles, Ed., *Innovation in Education* (New York: Teachers College Press, 1964), pp. 49–77.

    [8] Jacquetta Hill Burnett, *A Participant Observation Study of a Sociocultural Sub-System of the Students in a Small Rural High School.* Unpublished doctoral dissertation, Columbia University, 1964.

formance in the classroom does, they favor the opportunity for development.

The easy assent of the educator to this line of reasoning is not enough because it provides no proof of understanding the intellectual processes by which it is won. Such findings must be evaluated in the context of other cultures. It is here that the anthropologist possesses the advantage of a comparative view of human behavior. He knows from the study of child training in other societies that children are prepared for adult roles by both formal and informal means. He also knows that much of this learning comes from one's peers, that its acquisition is self-generated, and it is often autonomous and without direct rewards from the adult world.[9] Furthermore, he knows that most of the essential knowledge is won by the child without direct adult intervention. It is mostly in the realm of the esoteric, the secret knowledge contained within ritual and cosmology, that the child must be taught, sometimes forcibly, and thus fully initiated into adult responsibilities. In part, the adolescent is teaching himself a great deal about adult behavior through extra-curricular programs.

There is still another unsupervised aspect of the student subsystem whose outline may be only barely visible to those not trained to see it. I refer to the pattern of friendships and cliques, "the informal system," whose study has been popular during the past two decades. Hollingshead's book *Elmtown's Youth*[10] was one of the first to provide us with a systematic description of these groupings, although other social scientists had observed them. Until recently, educators gave scant attention to them except as they impinged upon the operation of the formal system. In the clique, students resembled others who directed organizations. Some viewed them with suspicion as being undemocratic and possibly subversive. The truth is that the dynamics of the small group remain the dark continent of human behavior.[11] Nevertheless we have begun the exploration, and much more knowledge is available than is being profitably incorporated in teacher education.

The initial step in the important study and analysis of small groups is research into interactions of types of events. These, however, must be viewed within the context of other subsystems. We must examine relationships in cliques, the hierarchy of values, prestige rankings, participation in extra-curricular activities, and academic per-

[9] Dorothy Lee, "Autonomous Motivation." In F. C. Gruber, Ed., *Anthropology and Education* (Philadelphia: University of Pennsylvania Press, 1961), pp. 103–121.

[10] A. B. Hollingshead, *Elmtown's Youth* (New York: John Wiley & Sons, 1949).

[11] George C. Homans, *The Human Group* (New York: Harcourt, Brace, 1950).

formance. Empirical observation has already established some connections, but the full measure of these has, as yet, not been worked out. Those educators concerned with dropouts might learn a great deal about their problem if they considered student participation as one of their variables. For example, we know that students of a lower social class are more likely to exhibit adult behavior in their out-of-school activities and shun the formal student subsystem. The same principle applies when we examine the relationship between the student and the academic subsystem. In past attempts to account for academic performance and achievement, educators have relied almost entirely upon the relationships between the quality of teaching and teaching materials and the intelligence and motivation of the student. Our insistence that the school must be understood in its totality should indicate just how inadequate and wrong the interpretations may be when they are based upon such limited variables. They ignore the relevance of environment or social skills in the learning process, and do not recognize social skills as an important consequence of the school system. Although impatient with this intellectual myopia, we cannot expect too much change until another point of view, supported by research findings, is injected into teacher education.

It should be clear by now that anthropology's contribution to teacher training is much broader and more fundamental than its subject matter. The natural-history method, as exemplified above, imposes its own logic on the interpretation of behavior, and requires a recasting of the processes of thought. It provides a model for classroom instruction through which students are actively engaged in discovery on their own.[12] In an educational environment that used this method, the goals of formal education would extend beyond the acquisition of knowledge and skills, and would incorporate the utilization of the cognitive processes through which all the great minds have extended our comprehension of the universe. These are the processes available to anyone for the interpretation of experience. Their acquisition is essential for our society.

Implicit in the method of anthropology, and explicit in the organization and presentation of data on human behavior, is a point of view relevant to the training of teachers that is integral to the method already elaborated upon. We have touched upon this indirectly and now must do so directly. The perspective sees cultural variability as a function of the social context. In this view, absolute standards may

[12] Solon T. Kimball, "An Anthropological View of Social System and Learning." In Esther Lloyd-Jones and Esther M. Westervelt, Eds., *Behavioral Science and Guidance: Proposals and Perspectives* (New York: Teachers College Press, 1963), pp. 11–30. (See Chapter 9 below.)

be recognized in any particular society, but custom, when projected on a world screen, must be seen relatively, as Ruth Benedict in her *Patterns of Culture* has so ably argued.[13] But relativity is only one aspect of this complex, and the danger of linking this concept with amorality is lessened by the anthropologist's concern with the universals of human behavior. Like other forms of life, man reproduces himself, brings his young to maturity, provides for his basic needs, and protects himself from his enemies. Man is distinguished from other animals, however, by the learned behavior his young must acquire, and in the use of symbols for the transmission of culture. The relationships among physiological, cultural, and social processes, then, form the data from which we abstract what is universal.

Within anthropology, this is achieved by cross-cultural studies and the comparative method. Familiarity with the customary behavior of numerous cultures gives the anthropologist a resource not traditionally available to other social scientists. If, for example, he wishes to test some idea about the relation between learning and rites of initiation, he examines the practices of several societies.[14] Comparative analysis protects against unwarranted generalizations, and, when joined with empirical, inductive reasoning, it generates new connections between culture and society. These, then, are elements that give anthropology a distinct approach. It treats human data relatively and universally and it examines them without moral judgment.[15]

If the scientific heart of anthropology is the natural-history method, the spirit of that method is preserved in the sense of the web of life. Materials are not gathered as accumulations of information, but as comprehensions of mankind. This is why there is great danger of distortion in any educational program that enumerates a list of desirable courses, but loses the essence of their use. Humans, cultures, and societies must be seen whole.

We turn again to the central problem of the contribution of anthropology to training for teaching. This time, however, our focus is on perspective, not method. Although all education should act as a liberalizing influence, what carries the student outside his own culture should prove particularly effective. This is what anthropology attempts to do, although the shedding of one's ethnocentric bias may prove traumatic. As our cultural shell begins to fall away, whole new perspectives come into view. What we thought absolute is seen against a

[13] Ruth Benedict, *Patterns of Culture* (Boston: Houghton Mifflin, 1934).

[14] John D. Herzog, "Deliberate Instruction and Household Structure: a Cross-Cultural View," *Harvard Educational Review*, XXXII (1963), 301–342.

[15] George Spindler, "The Character Structure of Anthropology." In George Spindler, Ed., *Education and Culture* (New York: Holt, Rinehart and Winston, 1963), pp. 5–14.

background of time and place and is accepted in the cultural whole.

The fortunate student begins to grasp the upward sweep of civilizations and accords dignity to the accomplishments of man. If the perspective is fully assimilated, it can be carried to the classroom, where children of diverse backgrounds are not judged by middle-class norms, but on their own terms. The teacher can then help those who are hindered from learning because of the cultural gap that together they must bridge.[16]

A full discussion of the uses of anthropology in the teacher training processes would necessarily include phases not here developed. For example, only passing reference has been made to the contribution anthropology makes to understanding the learning process: how different cultures teach the child that learning is an act in itself, and how there are both subtle and gross differences in the preparation for learning.[17] From this we would move to consideration of the relation between culture and personality, between world view and cognitive process. In the study of the individual from birth to death, the student would be introduced to those ceremonies, universal in practice, that mark the transition from one stage of life to another.[18] These rites of passage have their counterpart in our graduation exercises and in the ritual marking of other events. Inevitably, we would examine the variety of human groupings and the cultural behavior associated with each. In this effort, problems of the relation between community and culture, and of variations in educational processes associated with different forms of community, would appear.[19] Nor could we ignore the relevance of those other great divisions of anthropology that focus upon man's biological characteristics, his linguistic behavior, and his attempts to understand and direct the processes of change.

If education is to prepare the young to participate in the new American society, it must undergo a great transformation. The schools of the future must emphasize cognitive and social skills and cross-cultural perspective. The preparation of teachers for such an endeavor cannot be achieved through the juggling of existing courses. The goal is attained only after a thorough change in the intellectual approach to the acquisition and use of knowledge.

[16] Ruth Landes, "Culture and Education." In George F. Kneller, Ed., *Foundations of Education* (New York: John Wiley & Sons, 1963), pp. 320–352.
[17] Margaret Mead and Martha Wolfenstein, *Childhood in Contemporary Culture* (Chicago: University of Chicago Press, 1955).
[18] Arnold van Gennep, *The Rites of Passage* (Chicago: University of Chicago Press, 1960).
[19] Beatrice Whiting, Ed., *Six Cultures: Studies of Child Rearing* (New York: John Wiley & Sons, 1963).

5. TEACHING ANTHROPOLOGY IN PROFESSIONAL EDUCATION

During the past few years there has been a gradually increasing awareness of the contribution anthropology can make to graduate professional education. Its evidence may be seen in the inclusion of data derived from anthropological sources in texts and materials used in graduate instruction. Equally substantial proof is found in the dozen or more anthropologists who hold full or part-time appointments in graduate schools of medicine, public health, nursing, social work, education, or theology. Anthropological influence has also been significant in a few graduate schools of business.

Although the total number now engaged in graduate professional teaching is small at present, we may expect that the relative significance of anthropology in such programs will show a continued and possibly accelerated expansion. Not only will these schools seek to add anthropologists to their staffs, but also relevant anthropological materials will continue to find their way into teaching materials.

The grafting of an academic discipline onto professional root stock creates some special problems. It should be remembered that professional activity is primarily the practice of skills in the performance of service to others. Training is for the purpose of perfecting the arts of practice. Training also includes imparting ethics, theory, and, in some instances, the findings of science. It is in the area of theory and scientific results that some academic disciplines have contributed to professional training. In medicine, for example, the biological sciences

"Teaching Anthropology in Professional Education," in David K. Mandelbaum, Gabriel W. Lasker, and Ethel M. Albert, Eds., *Teaching Anthropology*, Memoir No. 94, American Anthropological Association (Washington, D.C.: American Anthropological Association, 1963), pp. 493–502.

constitute a firm basis of the medical arts. Psychology and, to a lesser extent, the other social sciences have provided foundations to educational practices. Social work has drawn upon several fields. Thus, the pattern of the relation of anthropology to professional training has already been established by precedent.

The anthropologist will be expected to transmit those aspects of his discipline that are relevant to the problems of training and practice in a profession. He can do this through teaching, research, and publication, and through such personal influence as time and place permit. Although these several activities can hardly be separated, our primary focus is that of the teaching of anthropology, and it is to that phase of the problem which I now turn.

Most of my comments will be based upon my own experience as professor of anthropology and education, 1953–1966, at Teachers College, Columbia University. I am aware that the conditions and needs will vary from those of my colleagues in professional education elsewhere. Nevertheless, I suspect that there are sufficient similarities in the expectations of the institutions in question, in the degree of student sophistication or its absence in the subject, in the problems of choosing, adapting, and interpreting anthropological data, and in the relations with teaching colleagues who are primarily professional in their outlook, that the problems we have met are much alike although our solutions may have been different.

It is not my intention, however, to examine all of the aspects of teaching anthropology in a professional school. Instead, I wish to concentrate upon the contribution anthropology can make to methods of teaching and to the area of general education or, if one prefers, liberal arts education. (In this sense, I refer to the nontechnical presentation of subject matter that has as its goal increasing knowledge, widening perspectives, and, hopefully, contributing to the capacity to interpret intelligently events in the world.) These were major objectives in my one-semester course entitled "Anthropology and Education," which each year enrolled about 400 students. My other courses were more technically or professionally oriented and will not be discussed.

The sequence in which the several aspects of the teaching of anthropology in graduate professional education may be examined appears to me to have a certain logic. For example, the conditions of teaching in a graduate professional school are bound to affect organization, objectives, and content of a course. In addition, the background and future expectations of students will have their effects. These are limiting conditions that have a direct influence on the other aspects and should be described first. Objectives, basic concepts, and content constitute an additional three factors that are related, not alone to each other, but also to the conditions of teaching. Finally, the mechanics of course organization, including teaching techniques, form another and related segment. It is proposed that each of these be considered in turn.

LIMITING CONDITIONS

Those who teach foundation subjects—psychology, history, philosophy, and the social sciences—know that the student in a professional program can devote to them only a limited number of hours outside his special field. Anthropology is one of several such courses from which the student may choose. Under these conditions, one assumes that few of those who enroll in anthropology will do further work in this field. Thus, a course in anthropology is not intended to serve as a preliminary to advanced work, or for the purpose of recruiting students. Freed of these objectives, there is greater latitude for inclusion and exclusion of materials to approximate the tradition of liberal education, although choice is always made in the context of relevance to educational problems.

Academic background, professional aspirations, and intellectual characteristics are factors to be considered in course organization and content. A tabulation of students in the anthropology course at Teachers College for the academic year 1959–1960 revealed that four-fifths received their bachelor's degrees from a liberal arts college or university. The remaining fifth were graduates of teachers colleges. Distribution of students based upon area in which undergraduate degree was received gives the following percentages: arts and humanities, 30%; social sciences, including psychology, 23%; nursing, 20%; education, 15%; science, 10%; other, 2%. The overwhelming proportion of students from liberal arts colleges and universities, with a preponderance of degrees in the arts and sciences, should provide a student group possessing a broad academic base for professional training. It is my impression, however, that they have not received the kind of integrated cultural perspective that educators seek in liberal arts training.

Further analysis of student characteristics, based upon degree sought and field of professional study, revealed considerable diversity in professional goals. Nearly two-thirds were candidates for the M.A. degree, most of them being in the first year of graduate study. Of the remainder, slightly more than one-fourth were candidates for doctoral degrees; the others were seeking special certificates or were unclassified. The heterogeneity of academic background, level of graduate training, and professional goals does little more than hint at the qualitative characteristics of students. Although these are far more difficult to assess, a statement of impressions based upon several years' experience should serve, at least, as the point of departure for further study.

The questions asked, the point of view presented in papers, and written replies to a solicited request for reactions to the course reveal an almost universal and deeply imbedded system of middle-class values. It is not surprising to find the students are committed to equality, democracy, and the superiority of Western and, in particular, American culture. They have been heavily impregnated with a psychological and atomistic view of the world. For them the significant item of interest in the human world is the individual, and the understanding of oneself and others is a primary goal of learning and experience. They have weakly developed capacities for thinking systemically or scientifically. In fact, scientific learning is equated with the acquisition of knowledge; method or philosophy is hardly appreciated. Few of them have had training in research methods, nor do they show evidence of possessing systematic criteria for evaluative criticism. It is my belief that these students are fairly representative of others who have completed an undergraduate education. They reflect the failure of a piecemeal and specialized course program to develop intellectual depth. The deficiency is not so much in knowledge or skills as it is in an absence of a conceptual system and associated intellectual tools for interpreting the events of the world. On the other hand, these students were a pleasure to teach. They are intelligent, cooperative, and receptive; and happily, only rarely did I encounter one who is the captive of dogma.

An assessment of general and specific expectations may also be risky, but some observations that apply to a majority should be offered. There are two main aspects of professional training, the development of skills and the inculcation of moral and ethical standards governing professional practice. It is legitimate to ask the extent to which method and subject matter of anthropology could do either. The objectivity anthropology requires in cross-cultural analysis, or in the examination of customs and social groupings, also requires that the learner eliminate his ethnocentric biases. Anthropological relativism or determinism could conceivably weaken moral perspectives. Moreover, no direct connection between method, theory, or subject matter and pedagogical skills is easily discernible. It is my belief, however, that it is precisely in the areas of professional morality and of teaching skills that anthropology has much to offer, and that its presentation within a humanistic and general education tradition will produce the best results. One measure of achievement would be to examine the objectives sought, concepts utilized, and content included. It is to these aspects that we now turn.

OBJECTIVES, CONCEPTS, CONTENT

A concern with educational problems has been expressed by American anthropologists from time to time over the past several decades. Interest in the processes of cultural transmission alone should have proved a sufficiently strong bond with educators to have produced some fruitful cross-stimulation. Until recently, unfortunately, the results of the occasional contacts have been meager, at least in comparison with the influence of psychology. One difficulty has been the problem of deciding what aspects of anthropology have relevance for education and their subsequent adaptation and even translation for use by educators. This difficulty is in process of being overcome.

A significant forward step was the Stanford conference in 1954 on anthropology and education organized by George Spindler.[1] His "overview" of the conceptual and historical relations between anthropology and education included an enumeration of fields and interests in anthropology that possess relevance for education. The major areas as I have abstracted them follow:

1. As a basis of *general education*—"an introduction to a new perspective on human life." Relativity and universality.
2. Biological base of behavior—race, evolution, growth patterns, maturational sequences, sexual differences, and glandular processes.
3. Personality in culture.
4. Cultural dynamics—the processes of growth, change, stability.
5. Growth and adaptation of the child—socialization. Transmission of skills, knowledge, attitudes, and values.
6. Cross-cultural education—comparative study of educational processes.
7. Social structure—class, group alignments, prestige ranking, status and role, social control.

The point of view represented and the topics included are those that can and must be presented in graduate course work for educators. There are, however, some areas of theory and method that, I believe, also deserve major consideration. These are:

1. Methods of systemic analysis—community, institutions, autonomous groups, personality.

[1] George D. Spindler, "Anthropology and Education: an Overview." In George D. Spindler, Ed., *Anthropology and Education* (Stanford: Stanford University Press, 1955).

2. Event analysis—regularities of human behavior in time-space context.
3. The method of natural history—inductive empiricism based upon methods of classification and interdependencies of components.
4. Commitment and perception—cultural and individual aspects.

These additional aspects are necessary ingredients if students are to have the basis for understanding the distinctive world view from which anthropologists operate. Findings may have ends in themselves but they cannot serve the larger objective alone. We must also transmit an understanding of the theory and processes that we utilize in our analyses. Only then will the larger conceptual framework, which examines the individual in his physical, psychical, social, and cultural contexts, become meaningful; cultures will be seen as wholes, and the relation among individual, group, and culture made explicit.

The crucial test in determining the validity of any method used in the organization and presentation of data is, of course, whether it achieves the objectives and produces desired results. My immediate objective was to demonstrate the use of anthropological data and theory for purposes of general education. A related goal was to demonstrate the relevance of anthropology to problems of contemporary civilization.

For students seeking professional careers in education, an understanding of the cultural context within which American educational institutions and processes developed is particularly appropriate. This goal can be met in part by the application of anthropological method to the analysis of Colonial and Post-Colonial periods in American history. The presentation includes description of settlement patterns, their European cultural antecedents, environmental, technological, social, and cultural characteristics and variations. Particular attention is directed to educational institutions and practices and to their interconnections with other aspects of social and cultural systems. For most, the cultural interpretation of history represents a new approach, as does the kind of specificity that delineates regional differences and their meaning. The historical perspective that emphasizes the interconnection between cultural aspects is, however, related to other distinctly defined anthropological purposes. Of major theoretical significance is the concept of *system* developed alongside an examination of *culture as a whole*. There is demonstration and insistence upon treating cultural items in *context*. *Continuity* of culture is exemplified in reference to European antecedents. *Diversity* and *variation* may be observed in the *comparative* analyses of regional agrarian patterns. Some aspects of *cultural dynamics* are derived from an examination of changes that flow from adaptation to new environmental and social conditions.

It is also possible to show how understanding American culture in its original and developmental stages has relevance for contemporary problems. If an appreciation of the value of history is one of the by-products, this in itself is a worthy contribution.

Another topic used to explicate other aspects of anthropological method is that of the study of European pre-history. Further justification for the inclusion of this subject can be found in the assumption that a liberally educated person should know something about the cultural origins of civilization. But the method of presentation serves several other purposes beyond those of merely presenting facts. Once again, the vehicle chosen is utilized to carry a particular theoretical burden; in this instance, the method of natural science with emphasis upon man and culture in time and space. Data from the Paleolithic and Neolithic are utilized to show how they can be organized in categories based upon similarities and differences. The method of organization demonstrates the operation and utility of principles of taxonomy. Interrelationships between technology and environment, and between both of these and characteristics of population, are described. Through the use of these categories and others, there is presented the cultural *macro-system* and the interdependencies of its components. The processes of *inference* through comparison are utilized. The emphasis upon systemic analysis shows how the methods of inductive, empirical science may be used to organize data about the universe and, at the same time, how it provides a method for eliciting their meaning through functional interrelationships.

The objective of this latter analysis is to provide conceptual tools that permit a logically consistent understanding of man and culture in time and space, to see the relation between different levels of cultural development, and to comprehend the processes of change. These intellectual tools make possible comparisons with methodological systems of other disciplines as well as with the world-embracing schemes developed by particular individuals. For example, the scientifically based approach of anthropology may be contrasted with and used to interpret methods and results of such diverse theorists as those represented by Marx, Freud, Spengler, Sorokin, or Toynbee. The applicability of the methods of an empirical, inductive science to the interpretation of cultural evolution and world history is certainly a significant contribution to general education.

METHODS OF TEACHING

In professional education, where considerable emphasis, properly and by tradition, is placed upon moral and ethical standards of practice, it is of utmost importance that the practitioner view the world in an empirical, inductive manner. Otherwise, there is the danger that rigid adherence to learned precepts will hamper the individual in his response to the variety of changing conditions he must meet. Thus, there is an unusual opportunity for the anthropologist in his teaching methods to exemplify the very system of thought he represents. He can provide a model, not alone for interpreting professional experience, but for all subject matter areas that provide general education to the student.

Few individuals possess the capacity to view themselves and the world around them either objectively or as parts of interrelated systems. Their formal education has prepared them to seek explanations of events within an already formulated system of thought and perception. Intellectually, they have been isolated from new insights through adherence to established formulas, dogma, or other rigid systems of beliefs. In considerable measure, the kind of teaching they experience contributes to this condition. The emphasis upon fact and the equation of detail with knowledge have perverted their capacity to be receptive to the concepts of a world organized in systems. The deductive process limits, if it does not determine, how new experience is to be categorized and understood. Unfortunately, most teaching in general education and the liberal arts as it is now practiced is cast in this mold.

An earlier statement asserted that one of the major contributions of anthropology to pedagogy could be the transference of its scientific methods to the art of teaching. This means, specifically, the presentation of empirical data inductively for the purpose of deriving general explanatory statements about the universe, or some part of it. Under such a procedure, the facts are seen to be justified, not in themselves, but as they constitute the essential detail for grasping the nature of a system. Systems, in turn, are not to be treated as conclusions or results, but as expressive of the internal dynamics that govern stability and change. Comprehension of the processes of human beings as physical and psychic entities, and of the cultures and societies they create and transmit, remains the ultimate goal.

Before we examine the problem further, it is best to remind ourselves that anthropology utilizes the natural science approach.[2] In this tradition, it is inductive and empirical in its operation. Its practitioners proceed from a series of assumptions and a body of theory that believes regularities in behavior can be made explicit through system analysis. Furthermore, it is not necessary to formulate hypotheses before initiating research, as is the custom with other social sciences. Anthropological

[2] Solon T. Kimball, "The Method of Natural History and Education Research." In George D. Spindler, Ed., *Education and Anthropology* (Stanford: Stanford University Press, 1955). Solon T. Kimball, "Darwin and the Future of Education," *The Educational Forum*, XXV (1960), 59–72. (See Chapter 6 below.)

research may be justified on the grounds of gathering more data, examining a problem, or for purely exploratory purposes. This activity, however, is never random. It is always formulated, at least by implication, within a framework of larger problems to which the discoveries may add new insights.

The question we now pose is the extent to which the anthropologist can transfer to the clasroom his procedures of gathering data in the field; the process by which he sorts, combines, and interprets his facts; and his theories of behavior and grouping. If the transfer were successful, classroom presentation would simulate data collection and analysis. The student would move toward results and conclusions utilizing the same intellectual operations as the instructor.

We should keep in mind that we are concerned with two interrelated but separate problems. The simulation in data presentation of anthropological operations is one; the other is the transmission of the skill of presenting subject matter inductively. Once again I must let my own experience serve as the basis for evaluation. Most, but not all, of the topics are presented within the inductive framework. Age and sex analysis seems to be presented more easily through deductive method. It is assumed that it is unnecessary to establish the validity of the categories. But with personality, small group, and social class analysis, it is possible to use an almost pure form of inductive logic. In small group analysis, greater emphasis is given to the method of organizing facts than to the substantive results. In this latter instance, it is the intention to demonstrate a technique of teaching.

Systematic examination of the results of this approach has not been attempted. But significant changes in point of view or professional practice should not be expected from such a brief encounter. If there is to be serious testing of the effects of inductive teaching, an experimental and research program should be established with these objectives in mind.

CONCLUSION

Its utilization of natural science method and its concern with humanistic aspects of behavior give anthropology a particularly wide scope in comparison with other disciplines. There is no broader coverage than its focus upon man and his works. Its concern with cultural relativity and pan-humanism and its method of cross-cultural analysis contribute to acquiring a wider perspective of the human condition. In subject matter, approach, and point of view, anthropology seems unusually suited to meeting the needs of a general and humanistic ingredient in graduate professional education.

Its contribution to the technical aspects of professional practice can also be considered. The utilization of inductive analysis in teaching techniques is of immense significance in a culture where the explosion of knowledge mandates that principles of organizing new information and experience exceed in importance the stacking of facts upon each other. Other applicabilities rest in such areas as personality, small group, social structure, and cultural dynamics. But let us always remember that the greatest impact occurs from an intellectual transformation that our theory and analytical processes initiate but that is not innate in our subject matter.

6. THE NATURAL-HISTORY METHOD AND EDUCATION

The celebration in 1959 of the centennial of Darwin's *Origin of Species* has been, primarily, the triumphal affirmation of a great man's contribution to our understanding of the origin and evolution of life. One aspect of his career, however, has been almost completely neglected. Practically no attention has been given to the applicability of Darwin's methods to educational theory and practice.

This serious deficiency needs to be remedied since the method of natural history, which Darwin utilized in evolving his theories, provides both philosophy and techniques of immense significance to the enterprise of education. Current pedagogical thinking will be enriched by such an addition. In part, the exploration of aspects of Darwin's intellectual development and his use of natural history method will meet this need.

It is necessary to understand something about the historical antecedents and consequences of the theory of evolution if we are also to understand the relation of Darwin to education. Our problem is neither that of describing nor assessing the impact of his theories upon the subject matter and interpretation of biology as it was then and later taught. We know that acceptance came slowly; that over the years new knowledge and theories have modified and extended understanding of the original formulations; and that there has been popular distortion of some of his basic ideas.[1]

"Darwin and the Future of Education," *The Educational Forum* (November 1960), pp. 59–72. Used by permission of Kappa Delta Pi, an Honor Society in Education, owners of the copyright.

[1] For example, the concept of the "struggle for existence" became connected with Spencer's phrase "survival of the fittest," which in popular understanding was

The bitter struggle around the validity of the concept of evolution, however, has tended to obscure other aspects of Darwin's contribution. These deficiencies and omissions are gradually being overcome as perspective and scholarship permit a more balanced evaluation. It may well be that in the future we will honor Darwin less for his discovery of variation and natural selection as the key to explaining the evolutionary process than we will for the principle inherent in such a conceptualization, that of inevitable and continuous change.

We know that for more than a century preceding Darwin, natural scientists, those who were delving into the mysteries of what today we call the earth and biological sciences—geology, paleontology, zoology, botany—were gradually breaking the shackles of a static time concept inherited from medieval scholasticism. Bit by bit the evidence was accumulating that would permit some synthesizer to break through the intellectual barriers that held men's imagination caught in the rigid theological dogmatism of the times. Darwin himself credits the influence of a number of men in the development of evolutionary concepts.

The period was right not only for the appearance of a theory of man's genetic relation to other forms of life, but also for a theory of change that would break the prevalent time-bound "Fall and Redemption" concept of the cosmos, which then prevailed. For example, in 1858, Darwin received a manuscript from A. R. Wallace, who was working in Malaya, with the request for an evaluation of a theory identical with the one he had formulated. Even earlier approximations were alluded to by Darwin in the "Historical Sketch" published with the third edition of *Origin of Species*. And as Huxley, the great supporter of Darwin, exclaimed after reading the theory, "How extremely stupid not to have thought of that!" In fact, Herbert Spencer had published a theory of social evolution four years before the appearance of *Origin of Species*.

Although since his day there have been great refinements and extensions in the methods he employed, the basic principles and procedures are as useful today as was his application of them during his famous scientific expedition in the *Beagle* in the years 1831–1836. Darwin does not systematically record for us, however, the procedures he used that led to his intellectual discoveries and scientific conclusions. Bits and pieces appear here and there in his *Voyage of the Beagle,* in his brief autobiography, and in his letters, and are implicit in his major works. On rare occasions he pulls aside the veil to permit us to see how he perceived and organized his experiences and how

---

interpreted as "dog eat dog," or the strong will prevail over the weak. Darwin's less competitive concept was that, in the process of "mutual interaction," the best adapted would survive.

eventually he transformed the facts of his observation into support of his hypotheses. His reasoning process has been characterized as one that combined both inductive and deductive logic. But Darwin expressed openly his suspicions of deduction. He always insisted upon careful and precise observation, and from the ordering of the facts he constructed interpretations and theories against which he tested new observations and facts.

It is unfortunate, perhaps, that Darwin never attempted a systematic analysis of the methods that guided him in his work. Historically, these were part of a scientific tradition elaborated by Sir Francis Bacon with his emphasis upon inductive logic and further elaborated in the eighteenth century and later by Linnaeus, Cuvier, Lyell, and other natural scientists. But self-conscious examination of conceptual processes and activities represents a later and more sophisticated phase in the history of science—the operationalism of Bridgman or the symbolic logics of Carnap.

Darwin and other scientists of the nineteenth century had quite other goals. They had a job to do and they were interested in getting at it. They were striving to elucidate the principles that would contribute to a rational understanding of the world in which they lived. Their progress was impeded by forces residing both within and without their ranks. Beliefs based upon prevailing theological dogma provided a hostile environment for ideas that challenged time-held verities. Older scientific explanations themselves gave ground slowly before the new evidence and hypotheses. And always there was so much more that had to be discovered, tested, and meaningfully related to the existing corpus of knowledge.

The qualities demanded of those who maintained their intellectual integrity and perseverance in the face of the criticism and difficulties were of a high order. But through faithful adherence to the principles of science, not alone as a method of observing nature, but also as a pervading and powerful ordering of one's life, it was possible to persevere against the many obstacles. Darwin gave expression to this when he said:

From my early youth I have had the strongest desire to understand or explain whatever I observed—that is, to group all facts under some general laws. . . . As far as I can judge, I am not apt to follow blindly the lead of other men. I have steadily endeavoured to keep my mind free so as to give up any hypothesis, however much beloved (and I cannot resist forming one on every subject) as soon as facts are shown to be opposed to it. Indeed, I have had no choice but to act in this manner, for with the exception of the Coral Reefs, I cannot remember a single first-formed hypothesis which has not after a time to be given up or greatly modified. This has naturally led me to distrust greatly deductive reasoning in the mixed sciences. On the other hand, I am not very skeptical—a frame of mind which I believe to be injurious to the progress of science.[2]

Darwin possessed an open mind, inquiring and receptive, but not devoid of ideas about the world around him. But his beliefs were never cast in the rigid mold of doctrine or dogma, for these would have prevented him from interpreting new experience except in already predetermined ways. This willingness to scrutinize each new bit of evidence in terms of already established conclusions demanded a toughness of mind that might not have persisted alone. But Darwin also possessed a dedication that carried him through great difficulties. As he stated it, "my love of natural science has been steady and ardent." [3]

Acceptance of the philosophy of natural science requires a commitment to the principle of the inevitability of change. The on-going processes of a dynamic equilibrium continuously reshape, usually slowly but under critical conditions perhaps at an accelerated pace, the nature and relationships of organic life. The mentality that operates from a static conception of the universe has closed itself to the perception of these changes or understanding of their processes. It can thus be understood that there must be a correspondence between the mental processes that perceive and interpret the external world, and the events that are experienced. Darwin possessed that mentality and held to that view. In fact, his niche in the history of science is secure because his search for the key that would explain the mechanism of change in organic life led him to postulate variation and natural selection as the mechanisms that accounted for the changes the facts presented. In retrospect, no person with an adherence to the absolutes of static time and the dogma of special creation could have broken through the enclosing membrane of existing traditional thought.

Commitment to natural history included more than an open mind and a love of the subject. Theoretically, the open mind could also be vacuous. The individual might receive new experiences in infinite number, but lacking the intellectual discipline with which to understand them or to organize them in terms of categories and principles, there is no new learning, no insights, no understanding of the meaning of the experiences of the changes of which they are manifest.

Observation is central to the method of natural history. Time and again Darwin refers to the necessity for minute, painstaking, and careful observance. This is a skill that is acquired through training. But

[2] *The Life and Letters of Charles Darwin*, edited by his son, Francis Darwin (New York, 1896), Vol. I, p. 83.
[3] *Ibid.*

observation in itself is not enough. One must know what it is he is looking for and he must have a conceptual scheme into which he can fit his experiences. When the new fact does not fit, then there is the need to re-examine and to change if necessary the assumptions, hypotheses, and conclusions already held.

Early in Darwin's career, this basic understanding was dramatically brought to his attention. In the summer of 1831, Darwin was concluding his studies at Cambridge. Professor Adam Sedgwick, a noted geologist, invited him on a field trip to North Wales and had come to Darwin's home preliminary to departure. Darwin told him of a conversation with a laborer who had found a large tropical (Volute) shell in a near-by gravel pit. Sedgwick said it must have been thrown there by someone ". . . but then added, if really embedded there it would be the greatest misfortune to geology, as it would overthrow all that we know about the superficial deposits of the Midland counties." [4] Darwin then recounts his surprise at Sedgwick's lack of delight in the supposed discovery and concludes, ". . . Nothing before had ever made me thoroughly realize, though I had read various scientific books, that science consists in grouping facts so that general laws or conclusions may be drawn from them." [5]

Through such anecdotes we learn much of the process of Darwin's education. We can see that experience and mental formation went hand in hand. There was no separation between the accumulation of knowledge and its utilization in apprehending the meaning of life. And we can also begin to comprehend the correspondence within natural history as a scientific method, as an educational procedure, and as a philosophical system. Its value for Darwin, its potentiality for education are contained within this harmonious unity. One of the lessons had been learned—facts to be understood must be grouped "so that general laws or conclusions may be drawn from them."

But there were additional learnings that Darwin was to acquire before he would be prepared for his own great discovery. The basis for another one was laid during the same summer. Darwin and Sedgwick had gone to Wales, where the student was learning the techniques of geologic stratigraphy. It was much later, however, that Darwin realized that both of them had failed to comprehend one aspect of the geologic record because neither had been trained to perceive evidence that was so sharply etched on the rocks around them. Darwin's words illuminate the point.

. . . On this tour I had a striking instance of how easy it is to overlook phenomena, however conspicuous, before they have been observed by any

4 *Ibid.*, p. 48.
5 *Ibid.*

one. We spent many hours in Cwm Idwal, examining all the rocks with extreme care, as Sedgwick was anxious to find fossils in them; but neither of us saw a trace of the wonderful glacial phenomena all around us; we did not notice the plainly scored rocks, the perched boulders, the lateral and terminal moraines. Yet these phenomena are so conspicuous that, as I declared in a paper published many years afterward in the "Philosophical Magazine" (1842), a house burnt down by fire did not tell its story more plainly than did this valley. If it had still been filled by a glacier, the phenomena would have been less distinct than they are now.[6]

The crucible of experience made the lesson clear to Darwin and we can benefit from the same insight. One cannot see, or, if seeing, will not comprehend if the principles for assimilating the meaning of facts have not been previously learned. Even when the principles have been ingested intellectually, they will be greatly strengthened by direct confrontation with a specific problem. It may be useful if we examine this point further for purposes of clarity and emphasis.

Some years ago I was crossing some craggy limestone hills in western Ireland in the company of a countryman. At one point he stopped and pointed out some impressions in the exposed limestone surface. The resemblance of the indentations on the rock were nearly identical to the imprint a horseshoe-shod pony might leave if traveling over a soft mud flat. The hoof prints did not have the regularity one would expect if these had been left by a pony, but my companion related to me a perfectly plausible account of their origin. For him these signs were evidence of the passage of a supernatural horseman whose magical power was sufficient to leave their impress on the hardest rock. That they should be interpreted as the fossil imprint from a period when the land was covered by the sea was beyond his grasp. He possessed, nevertheless, a magico-religious system of thinking that permitted him to explain natural phenomena within that context.

Darwin and the natural scientists had to contend against the power of such traditional supernaturally rooted explanations of natural phenomena. The arguments were lengthy and involved but the essential conflict was between the validity of supernatural and natural explanations. The dispute is no longer of great import in western intellectual circles. The scientific approach has triumphed in its insistence upon the interpretation of facts within the frame of rational empiricism. Although the significance of glacier engraved striations on the valley boulders was not comprehended by Darwin or his mentor, their eventual explanation was to be found within a system of thinking that sought meaning within natural events.

[6] *Ibid.*, pp. 48–49.

The history of Western thought is filled with examples of the inadequacy of observation alone unless its use is coupled with explicating principles. For example, the principles governing the inheritance of characteristics did not really begin to be understood until after Mendel's experiments. The linguist can elucidate the structure and dynamics of any language, although those who are its traditional users may be completely unaware that such exist. High school students operate daily in a complicated cultural and social system of which probably only a few could describe even a part of what they continuously experience. In all these instances, meaningful understanding comes only after the capacity for directed observation has been achieved. This understanding was a part of the education of Darwin that helped him on the path toward his great discoveries.

Within a few months after receiving his degree from Cambridge and his field trip with Professor Sedgwick, Darwin had accepted the position of naturalist and embarked on an extended scientific expedition. Darwin's education was profoundly advanced by his voyage on the *Beagle*. Darwin himself believed this to be the case and expressed himself as follows: ". . . I have always felt that I owed to the voyage the first real training or education of my mind; I was led to attend closely to several branches of natural history, and thus my powers of observation were improved, though they were always fairly developed." [7]

Through inference and an occasional comment, we are able to establish the manner in which this experience contributed to his education. Neither in the text nor in his available comments about the voyage does he make explicit the gradual development of his insights. Nevertheless, for those who look, the record is nearly as clear as are the striations on glacier deposited boulders. And if we are not able to pinpoint exact time and place for fruitful synthesis of ideas, we are able to observe the continuous accretion of the experiences that were later to be given maturity in his theory of natural selection.

"THE VOYAGE OF THE BEAGLE"

During the years 1831 to 1836, Darwin sailed as a naturalist abroad the British government ship, *H.M.S. Beagle*. Without this experience it seems improbable that he would have been able to achieve his later contributions. He himself recognized its importance when he wrote, "The voyage of the Beagle has been by far the most important event in my life, and has determined my whole career; . . ." [8] The results

[7] *Ibid.*, pp. 51–52.
[8] *Ibid.*, p. 51.

substantiate the statement, but his account in *The Voyage of the Beagle* is much more a naturalist's narrative than it is a specific contribution to understanding his development or the principles he was to enunciate later. Nevertheless, occasional gems of insight, inquiry, and reflection illuminate his thought processes.

Early in the expedition's travels, the *Beagle* touched the coast of Brazil at Bahia, where Darwin was enchanted with the beauty of the tropical vegetation. Keen observer of the present, his comment also shows that his mind was probing the past for cues to understanding the here and now. He observed the granitic formation that characterizes much of the Brazilian coast and that geologists believed to have been heated under pressure. The exposed solid rock formations led him, as he said, to some curious reflections. ". . . Was this effect produced beneath the depths of a profound ocean? or did a covering of strata formerly extend over it, which has since been removed? Can we believe that any power, acting for a time short of infinity, could have denuded the granite over so many thousand square leagues?" [9]

Much later, when the *Beagle* was on its homeward course and had stopped at the island of Ascension, where Darwin commented on the relation between climate and geology, he revealed again his concern with the problem of time and change when he asked, ". . . Where on the face of the earth can we find a spot, on which close investigation will not discover signs of that endless cycle of change, to which this earth has been, is, and will be subjected?" [10] In these, as in other instances, one may observe in the questions Darwin posed the operation of the dialectic of science. New facts are catalogued, tested against existing conceptions, and modifications made where the evidence demanded.

The experience of the first several months as the *Beagle* traveled southward along the east coast of South America, passed through the Straits of Magellan, and finally reached the Galápagos Islands off the coast of Ecuador had a powerful accumulative influence. He saw first-hand the contrasts in fauna and flora between coast and interior, or climatic zones of tropic, sub-tropic grasslands, forest, or mountain. He discovered extinct fossil types in areas where existing fauna showed clear genetic relationships. Although the new facts may have posed more problems than they answered, the basic questions were coming into ever sharper focus, namely: those of time and space, of distribution and sequence, and of change and persistence. Most important of all, he was beginning to pose his questions in terms of the relationships within and between organic life and the conditions of the environ-

[9] Charles Darwin, *The Voyage of the Beagle* (New York, 1909), p. 22.
[10] *Ibid.*, pp. 497–498.

ment. He was emerging from the mold of the descriptive taxonomic naturalist to one who was seeking answers through understanding the dynamics of change by examining the relationships of things as they were and are. This was the new dimension, this search for process and the mechanism through which change operates. But it was when he encountered the dramatic forms of life to be found on the Galápagos Islands that the intellectual seeds waiting for germination began to grow.

Of his experience in the Galápagos, Darwin writes, "The natural history of these islands is eminently curious and well deserves attention. Most of the organic productions are aboriginal creations, found nowhere else; there is even a difference between the inhabitants of the different islands; yet all show a marked relationship with those of America, though separated from that continent by an open space of ocean, between 500 and 600 miles in width." He professes astonishment at the great number of aboriginal beings within such a confined range and concludes, "Hence, both in time and space, we seem to be brought somewhat near to that great fact—that mystery of mysteries—the first appearance of new beings on this earth." [11]

From such comments, we can see the cumulative effects of comparative experience upon Darwin as he moved toward profounder insights. The preparatory years of learning to observe and classify, the absorption of the principles of scientific generalization, the several months of first-hand exploration along the coast and in the interior of South America had provided, in their entirety, a breadth of experience that would permit him to solve some of the perplexing problems with which he was confronted by organic life on the Galápagos. Probably, it is indeed fortunate that he encountered these islands only after months of previous observation rather than initially, otherwise he might not have been struck with both the striking differences and yet admitted similarities between organic life within the islands and that of the nearby continent.

The Cape Verde Islands, possessing variants of African life forms and visited early in the cruise of the *Beagle*, never excited the same wonderment. We must assume that Darwin was not then ready to pose those questions on the "mystery of mysteries" of the origin of life. In fact, it would not be until 1838, two years after his return, that he read Malthus's essay on population, which was to stimulate him to make his first formulation of the origin of species. For us, the important consideration is not the developmental sequence of new insights or the accumulative effect of new generalizations, but the use of a conceptual

[11] *Ibid.*, pp. 381–383.

method that permitted the organization of new experience into meaningful relationships and, if necessary, the revision of existing generalizations.

The practitioners of natural history meet this requirement through the use of comparative analysis. The process is not one of merely listing and describing the differences that exist between forms of organic life within a given locality, or between areas. An enumeration or inventory provides us with nothing more than just that. The result may represent a commendable addition to knowledge, but there are other questions that must be answered if the dynamics of change are to be comprehended. In particular, the difficult problem of "mutual interaction" must be met. In essence, this was what confronted Darwin if he were to make sense out of the strange forms of life he encountered on the Galápagos Islands.

Committed as he was to seeking explanations within a theory of natural causation rather than one of supernatural creation, he must still search for an hypothesis that could contain the divergences he observed. At this point, his comparative method stood him in good stead and prevented, at least, erroneous conclusion. He did not become trapped into following a unilineal deterministic position by attributing the distinctive organic types to environmental conditions. He commented upon the great similarity in geology and climate of the Cape Verde and Galápagos Islands, but noted that, although the great majority of plants and animals in the latter islands are aboriginal productions with an association different in kind and number from that on the continent, they nevertheless show affinities with America. For him the significant question was ". . . why were they created on American types of organization?" [12]

In later years, Huxley stated the problem succinctly when he said, ". . . That which we were looking for, and could not find, was a hypothesis respecting the origin of known organic forms, which assumed the operation of no causes but such as could be proved to be actually at work. We wanted, not to pin our faith to that or any other speculation, but to get hold of clear and definite conceptions which could be brought face to face with facts and have their validity tested. . . ." [13]

THE METHOD OF NATURAL HISTORY

It is not our major purpose to trace the evolutionary process in Darwin's thinking that eventually brought him to the epochal discoveries

[12] *Ibid.*, p. 398.
[13] *The Life and Letters of Charles Darwin*, pp. 550–551.

of the relation among variation, natural selection, and organic change. We are obligated to many others who have set themselves this task. Nor are we primarily interested in the subsequent substantiation, refinement, or modification of the theory of evolution. Our focus has been upon how the utilization of a particular method of thinking, that of natural history, aided Darwin in formulating a theory of the origin of species that was in accord with the facts as they could be observed. To accomplish this, it was necessary for him to break through traditional and static modes of thought that were imbedded in religious dogma ànd prevailing scientific doctrine.

Our problem is how best to summarize the contribution of this method to Darwin's education. What is there distinctive about the method of natural history that gives it a unique advantage in organizing knowledge and experience? A complete exposition of this approach would require a treatment far beyond the scope of my purpose. But its basic outline can be readily grasped and, in fact, has already been outlined in preceding paragraphs.

The method of natural history requires two quite different but related operations. There is a need to establish an orderly system for classifying, in categories, the items of the universe. As an example, the simplest of such divisions is that drawn between animate and inanimate. Within the realm of organic life, we differentiate between plants and animals. And within each of these broad headings we make many further distinctions. This aspect of natural science is called taxonomy. The systematic work of Linnaeus in the eighteenth century advanced and gave great impetus to the collection and naming of species. Identification, however useful, does not answer basic questions of process, function, or origin, and, in particular, the nature of the relationships that obtain between organisms and the conditions of the environment. These questions required principles that explained change.

The natural historian studies the origin, growth, persistence, and decline of individuals and of species. But he is also interested in much more because only as other questions are answered is he able to understand his basic problems. Secrets of the laws of change are also contained within the sequence and distribution of organic forms. In the one instance he is probing for the succession of life forms, in the other for their distribution in space. Even with this knowledge much remains to be understood. He must determine what relations exist between the prevailing conditions, such as those of climate and soil, and the appearance, persistence, modification, or disappearance of plants and animals. Furthermore, what are the internal mechanics of the organic processes, the factors of mutation and inheritance of characteristics? From this condensed and oversimplified statement, it can be readily grasped that the problems are not simple, and nature does not readily give up her secrets. But the natural historian is provided with a set of working tools that, applied with patience and persistence, permit slow penetration into the mysteries of nature.

Among these is the insistence upon prolonged, careful, and repeated observation of natural phenomena. When possible, these data are tested through experimentation. The mountain of detailed knowledge that accumulates from such activity, however, is relatively useless until another operation is performed. This requires the formulation of generalizations that explicate the relationships observation establishes. And there is the further necessity to test these through further observation and, if possible, to establish even broader generalizations that include wider classes of data.

Through the application of these devices, Darwin was able to verify the fact of variation and the struggle for existence. He observed that competition was greatest between species that were closely related and that "the same spot will support more life if occupied by very diverse forms." From the need to explain such generalizations as these came the formulation of his theory of natural selection and the law of life and the universe itself—evolution and change.

We have now reached the point where we must return to the question we posed earlier, that of the relation between the method of natural history and education, and of the importance of Darwin to us in understanding this relationship. As a first step we shall examine Darwin's reaction to his own formal schooling.

DARWIN'S EDUCATION

The formal education to which Darwin was subjected evoked little interest or enthusiasm from him and such references as appear in his brief autobiography were mainly critical. For seven years (between 1818 and 1825) he attended the famous Shrewsbury School under Dr. Samuel Butler. Of this period he wrote,

Nothing could have been worse for the development of my mind than Dr. Butler's school, as it was strictly classical, nothing else being taught, except a little ancient geography and history. The school as a means of education to me was simply a blank. . . . Much attention was paid to learning by heart the lessons of the previous day; this I could effect with great facility, learning forty or fifty lines of Virgil or Homer, whilst I was in morning chapel; but this exercise was utterly useless, for every verse was forgotten in forty-eight hours.[14]

[14] *Ibid.*, pp. 29–30.

There were, however, some extra-school activities that Darwin found profitable. He recalled these as follows: "Looking back as well as I can at my character during my school life, the only qualities which at this period promised well for the future, were, that I had strong and diversified tastes, much zeal for whatever interested me, and a keen pleasure in understanding any complex subject or thing. I was taught Euclid by a private tutor and I distinctly remember the intense satisfaction which the clear geometrical proofs gave me. . . ." [15] But his real pleasure and much of his learning came from other activities. These included an avid interest in shooting, the collection of insects and minerals, and serving as an assistant to his brother in a home-made chemistry laboratory. About this he stated, "This was the best part of my education at school, for it showed me practically the meaning of experimental science." [16] But he also commented that the head master publicly rebuked him "for thus wasting my time on such useless subjects. . . ."

Darwin's experiences at Edinburgh University, where he was sent by his father in 1825 to study medicine, were little more rewarding than those at Shrewsbury. By his own admission he never exerted himself because of a belief that his father would leave him sufficient property for his future needs. This fact may have contributed to his characterization of the lectures as deadly dull. But in his second year he became acquainted with several young men who had an interest in natural science. These were members of a society that gathered regularly and read papers. Darwin presented two. He also attended meetings of scientific and professional societies and heard scientific papers and discussion. But his lack of interest in medicine led his father to propose he become a clergyman and thus in 1828 he entered Cambridge, from which he received his degree in 1831.

Darwin's reactions to formal education at Cambridge duplicated almost exactly those at Edinburgh and Shrewsbury. He spoke of his time as being wasted with the exception of study for his degree examinations. Once again, however, the activities outside the classroom were to prove of great interest and importance. He voluntarily attended the lectures of Professor Henslow on botany and accompanied him on field trips. From this association there grew a friendship that led to his meeting students and professors who were interested in natural science. During the latter half of his time at Cambridge, he and Henslow took long walks almost every day and Darwin admired his broad knowledge of the natural sciences, his conclusions based upon minute observations, and his excellent judgment and well-balanced mind. It was

[15] *Ibid.*, p. 30.
[16] *Ibid.*, p. 32.

through Henslow that he was persuaded to take up the study of geology under Professor Sedgwick and finally it was upon his recommendation that Darwin accepted the fateful opportunity to join the voyage of the *Beagle* as naturalist. Darwin was now poised for the beginning of the Great Adventure in education, a journey from which, once started, he never turned back, the life-long ceaseless quest for those principles that would make understandable the ever-changing natural universe.

The circumstances and influences that set him upon this course were many. If we accept his own evaluation, the classical and formal education contributed little and might even be considered a detriment. The significant factors, as he recorded them, were really few. Basically, there was an almost obsessive interest in nature evidenced in his love of hunting and of collecting. In themselves these were not enough and he could easily have become a country squire or parson typical of the period. Fortunately, in his school days he caught a glimpse of the methods of experimentation through his brother's interest in chemistry. Then came the gradual acquisition of understanding the need for systematic and detailed studies while at Edinburgh University when he joined with students and scientists in learning and discussing the facts of natural history. Finally, there were the long conversations with Professor Henslow, discussions with other men of science at Cambridge, and the field trips for purposes of systematic observation. Through all of these experiences the seeds of commitment were sown and sprouted and grew. The boy became man, and the man utilized and expanded a method of observing, synthesizing, and generalizing about the world that made of Darwin's life a perpetual voyage of discovery of the wonders of the world.

What are the implications for our system of education of Darwin's life and his contribution? This is the significant question. We might enumerate his personal qualities as those that should be emulated, but these are possessed by many and in themselves do not lead to any necessarily profound understanding or contribution. We might join with him in his rejection of classical education as not providing an adequate training for the mind, but modern education has long since abandoned the once complete emphasis upon this type of pedagogy. We might point to the epoch-making theory about evolution and its consequences in literally redirecting the course of man's thinking about himself and nature. Singly, or taken as a whole, these aspects of Darwin's life have had great effect. But it is my belief that the full impact of Darwin's contribution to education has yet to be realized. It is to be found in the application of the method of natural history to the method and theory of education. It will come when we can transfer to the classroom and to the study of subject matter the concepts and accompanying techniques through which the dialect of science comprehends the world.

In earlier sections of this article, considerable care was taken to demonstrate the processes of learning as Darwin himself experienced them. This progressive accumulation of the evidence item by item is, in one sense, a faithful if greatly telescoped and limited recapitulation of what Darwin himself experienced. As such it resembles the natural history of the development of ideas and understanding. The summation that followed this reconstruction set forth the central ideas involved in the method, and represented valid generalizations upon the adduced facts. Let us now move one step further and make explicit how this method can be utilized to modernize our educational system, and why it is so important for us that we do just this.

NATURAL HISTORY AND EDUCATION

Behind the controversies that have erupted over the enterprise of education may be found manifold causes. Future appraisal will undoubtedly separate the bogus from the legitimate complaints. But in the meantime the American public is being bombarded by a barrage of accusations, denials, and countercharges that have created and contribute to confusion. It is not difficult to detect a widespread uneasiness that all is not as it should be.

Through the clamor of contending voices, however, there is one insistent note about which there seems no disagreement and to which we should pay heed. It is stated by educators and non-educators, by progressivists and traditionalists, by those who favor more or less of liberal arts or of science; in fact, it is the recurring theme to which each doctrine, each view, has attached itself. Simply stated, it is that education must prepare the individual to live in a world of perpetual change; that whatever else we may be certain of in an uncertain world, it is that the future will be different, perhaps vastly different, from the present. Only in its grossest form do we even pretend to predict this world to come, but we know it will come and that it will be different.

The implications of such a belief can be staggering. It means among other things that all of us must be poised to adapt to the changes as they occur. No longer can we have the security that knowledge and skills once acquired can be expected to serve a lifetime. Both may become obsolete at any time. In effect, we must be prepared to learn anew and then to relearn again. The much discussed displacement through technologic advance includes all other fields of endeavor as well. The practitioners of the sciences, arts, professions, and of management also find themselves in situations little different from those of unskilled or skilled workers. We must all learn to expect that the demands of life require the process of continuous learning as the conditions of the world in which we live are modified.

It is for this reason that the theory and method of natural history are of such vital significance. As it was given expression a century ago, and as it has evolved since, it has not only demonstrated that continuous change is a law of life, but has given us theory and techniques for its comprehension. There is the insistence upon the orderliness of the universe, a concept it shares with the other sciences. There is recognition that the physical, organic, and cultural worlds constitute systems, and within each of them there is a great variety of subsystems, all of which contain their own internal logics and dynamics. Its approach fosters humility in the face of the unsolved mysteries, and creates and perpetuates a sense of wonder at the intricately balanced but dynamic ways of nature.

There is no subject matter, no aspect of life to which the method of natural history is not applicable. As a method of instruction it is as readily applicable to pre-school children as it is to the most advanced kind of intellectual operation. Its emphasis is not upon the acquisition of knowledge alone, for it is already recognized that we are about to be engulfed in a sea of facts. In contrast, its emphasis is upon the utilization of principles through which facts and experiences may be organized and made meaningful. Equally important, this approach is in accord with what we know about the physical, psychic, and social development of the individual. Its utilization will, therefore, do no violence to the natural tendencies of the individual, but will strengthen his development.

What, we should ask, are the expectations that this method will be adopted by educators? There is really no answer to this question. Inertia and tradition rest heavily upon any who attempt innovation. But the crisis of reforming our educational system to conform to the realities of an ever-changing world provides a powerful incentive to seek some solution. Scattered evidences of the use of the method, particularly in the area of the teaching of science and arts, are already apparent. Its use is almost certain to spread. But if and when the full potentialities of natural history are utilized in our educational approach, the world will owe an even greater debt to Charles Darwin, and to those who preceded and followed him in giving us a method of understanding change, than is now apparent.

PART II   *Culture*
and Learning

7. INTRODUCTION: THE CULTURAL CONDITIONS OF LEARNING

The transmission of the cultural heritage and its acquisition through learning constitute one of the central concerns of anthropology. The problem is stated in such a way that its two dimensions of teaching and learning are examined separately and together. The simplest formulation of the question we ask in our attempt to derive knowledge about a single society or to work out the cross-cultural variations is, who teaches (or learns) what, to (or from) whom, when, where, and how, under what conditions, and with what consequences. The bare bones statement of the problem must be amplified if we are to understand what the anthropologist does, what he looks for, and how he organizes and interprets his data.

An essential characteristic of the anthropological method is the examination of all aspects of a people's way of life. Historically, this emphasis upon the whole arose from the fact that the tribal groups studied were relatively limited in population and homogeneous in cultural attributes and possessed few and simple social arrangements. These circumstances led to some consequences of immense conceptual importance. Among them was the realization that human behavior, of whatever type, could be understood only within the context of its relation to other aspects of the same society and that cultural and social behavior must be viewed as interdependent systems operating within a given set of conditions. Specifically, the number and variety of social groups, the kinds of activities characteristic of each, the nature

"An Anthropological View of Learning," *The National Elementary Principal*, Vol. XL, No. 7 (May 1961), pp. 23–27. By permission of the National Education Association.

of the values and symbols, even the manifestations of personality, were considered to be expressions of and related to the whole.

This understanding that a particular subject must be examined in terms of its components and the relationships between them is not unique to anthropology nor unappreciated in other professions. In education, for example, an increased awareness has developed of the relation between architectural form and the teaching function. Innovations in the teaching process have been hampered by the rigidity of the traditional school building with its box-like classrooms. The new architectural forms are giving emphasis to flexibility in the arrangement and utilization of space. This is an instance in which we incorporate our values into the physical environment we construct for our activities. It is also an example of the constrictions that older forms, whether they be material items of walls and chairs or cultural practices such as recitation or tests, may impose upon attempts to bring change. However desirable some of these modifications may prove to be, or however reasonable and justified a new or old practice may appear, the lesson that anthropology teaches is that unanticipated and unsought-for consequences may be the product of the best intentions. This conclusion should also prove no surprise to those people who have been willing to accept the reality of their own observations.

The realities of the learning process, then, must be viewed in the context of the total social arrangements and cultural practices that constitute education and the environment within which it operates.

About forty years ago, some of us began the study of what we termed modern communities. From these studies came descriptions of social class, ethnic, and racial groups, value systems and symbolic behavior, and, eventually, a specialized interest in some of the institutional arrangements such as health, education, and industry. Some of these findings, particularly those by Lloyd Warner on social class and of Allison Davis on the cultural bias of intelligence testing, have had their effect in educational circles. Other findings, such as those related to organizational dynamics, method, and philosophy of teaching, the function of age and status differences, and the function of induction ceremonies, have hardly penetrated educational literature or practice. Those aspects to which I wish to direct particular attention include the relation between our image of the child and teaching, cultural differentiation and learning, and the relation between the organizational environment of the school and the child's response to the teaching process.

CHANGING IMAGE OF THE CHILD

Our image of the basic nature of the intellectual and emotional aspects of the child, the structure of his mind, and the appropriate processes by which we can transmit successfully the skills, knowledge, and point of view that we believe are of greatest value to him as he moves toward adulthood, is in a constant state of flux and modification. If you pause to reflect upon this state of affairs for a moment, you must be struck with the incongruity of a situation in which we have to admit ultimately that we don't know what we are doing. If we did, we would not find it necessary, as we do continuously, to cast aside one approach and substitute another. Permit me to illustrate the point.

In the colonial period in New England, the child was viewed as basically an uncivilized creature, if not wicked and full of potential evil. The responsibility of the parents, minister, and schoolmaster was to use authority, supernatural and secular, in the necessary training that would discipline his contrary and perverse characteristics and make him a civilized and orderly member of church and community. Some aspects of this continue to exist, although the rationale no longer includes reference to religious dogma of sin, evil, and the devil.

Much later, when small town and rural life represented the dominant cultural pattern after the Civil War, child nature ceased to be viewed as containing an element of evil that needed to be extirpated through disciplined training. Instead, children were equated with the barnyard animals, and the responsibility of the owner and parent was to provide the care and protection that would eventually permit them to grow to maturity. There was an innate wildness that had to be controlled and, just as animals had to be broken to the harness, the saddle, or the milking shed, children were to be transformed to take their place in the adult world, a responsibility shared by family, church, and school. Tom Sawyer and his kind eventually had to be corralled and taught those essentials, which included reading, writing, and arithmetic. The process was often as painful to the subjects as to the adults charged with the task. What was taught and learned had little relevance to child life, but it did have necessity in the adult world and failure to learn could only lead to the "worthless" and "uncivilized" behavior associated with Huck Finn's father.

A few other examples will illustrate how frequently we change our rationale. You will recall the analogy once made between the mind and muscles. The teacher was responsible for exercising and stretching the mind's fibers, and it didn't really matter too much what was taught as long as there was mental "exercise." This notion was effectively dispelled by Thorndike, who reduced learning to the organization of stimuli by and in the neural system.

During the twentieth century, several images of the child have held currency at one time or another. We have changed from treating children with emotional aloofness to a posture that really we are all pals together, except that the lesser pal needs lots of love and security, which the bigger pals must give. We have become aware of developmental stages, which Erickson codified and linked with psychic crises as the child progressed from one to another. We are still in the phase in which each child should be viewed as a separate individual and the educational process should be geared to help him develop those unique potentialities that are his own. We are at flood tide in thinking that the child possesses unexpressed "creativities" that education can release. We are entering the phase when "intuitive intraception" will be education's slogan and goal. We are beginning to modify the concept that the child is an "empty vessel" that the process of education fills to one in which not knowledge, but the understanding of structural relationships and the capacity to organize new experiences in terms of preexisting intellectual and emotional canons of evaluation and interpretation, will be stressed. The teaching goal will be stated as one that helps the child to develop the processes of comprehending changes, whether these be inside or external to his skin.

The excuse for this excursion into various views about the nature of the child is to give emphasis to the point that the image the adult, parent, teacher, or administrator holds of the child influences in very considerable measure the "what" and the "how" of the teaching process. In turn, what the child receives and what he does with it affect his development and his later behavior as an adult. For this reason, we have the right to be concerned about what happens in the classroom. Fortunately, however, human beings have a tremendous resiliency, and while the adult world is in process of deciding what it ought to do, children somehow grow up to be pretty effective adults, on the whole. Nevertheless, the image of the child as learner and the associated teaching rationale represent one aspect of the realities of learning.

CULTURAL DIFFERENTIATION

Consideration of the image of the child and of his learning processes and the relevance of these to the educational process leads to my second major topic, that of cultural differentiation.

One of the major objectives of anthropology is determination of cultural variability. It is not difficult to convey the kind of differences that distinguish such tribal groups as the Hopi and Navajo. We now generally recognize that Orientals are not all alike and impossible to tell from one another, but that Japanese, Chinese, and Koreans represent distinct cultural traditions, although their geographical propinquity may have facilitated cultural borrowing from each other. It may be less easy to accept that there are deep and relevant differences between the people of Britain or France, or among Americans after the process of Americanization has had its opportunity to work. The field research of anthropologists, however, has established the validity for speaking of subcultural variants within the United States and elsewhere. Such a conclusion is supported by the results of community studies, which have described the subcultural groups we label social class. These studies have now been made in all sections of the nation. In all of them, social class emerges as a central aspect of the system of values and behavior. In addition, comparative examination of these researches establishes regional differences—that is, middle-class behavior in the South is not the same as in New England or the Middle West.

Other studies have been made on a number of America's ethnic and minority groups. These show the range of deviancy within a given city and across the nation. It seems unnecessary to belabor the point further. For those who wish to read or who will trust their own observations or both, there is evidence of group difference.

The relevance of this kind of knowledge has been made available to educators in several publications. Warner, Havighurst, Allison Davis, and Hollingshead are names we all associate with contributions in this area. The full implications of such research seem not to be appreciated, however. It is not proposed that students be grouped according to their subcultural background. Any such conscious separation would immediately be subject to the most vociferous criticism as un-American and undemocratic. These groupings are evident, however, in our cities, where peoples of different economic levels or ethnic backgrounds cluster in compact spatial areas. And although the educational problems of these areas may be different, we do not modify our programs for them in the same way that we do for different levels of tested intellectual ability. Perhaps we should not; but no matter how deep we bury our heads in the educational sands, the fact of the situation will not disappear. Furthermore, the failure to take cultural variation into account makes of some of the educational ideals and practices a farce and subverts the functions of education.

Let me illustrate the point by what may appear to be an extreme example. Let us assume that a teacher trained in Oklahoma takes a position on the Navajo reservation. There she attempts to put into practice the precepts of meeting the individual needs of her pupils, needs of which she hasn't the slightest idea nor the kind of training by which to determine them. Her best attempts would be to project from her own experience, which may or may not have any relevance to the ways of life, the personality system, or the methods of evaluation of her pupils.

What she actually attempts to do is convert her students to her way of life and thinking, and the evidence indicates that this is usually not very successful. What our teacher has not learned or is unable to apply is that new learnings always take place within the perceptive system of the individual being taught. Children from subcultural groupings other than those of the teacher face a difficult problem in adjusting, if they do, to the demands of the teacher and she, in turn, to their ways of behaving and thinking. The consequence is often a stalemate in which the teacher is frustrated and generalizes her experience through invidious stereotypes, and the students withdraw or become disengaged from the objectives of the educational system.

This is a serious problem in our big cities, where the children of the disadvantaged are not being effectively reached by educational processes. The failure is of a group, not of individuals, and arises because we do not adapt our educational procedures to the needs of groups whose perceptive systems do not permit them to learn, or who do not value learning in the same way as do children from middle-class homes. The failure is ours, not theirs. Thus, cultural differences constitute another of the realities of learning.

SCHOOL ORGANIZATION AND CLIMATE

Finally, I wish to address myself to the organizational structure and climate of the school. Organizationally, we have moved toward a sharper definition of the administrative role of the principal and super-intendent and, in consequence, a separation of the supervisory function from the teaching one. Additionally, we have recognized an increasing number of problem areas that we believe should be the responsibility of those specially trained for the task. As a result, the staff function and its personnel have expanded enormously. We employ specialists in testing and measurement, in handling psychological problems, in guidance, in curriculum, in health, in subject matter, and in many other fields. The number and variety of such specialists is a function of the size and wealth of the school district and of the success of the administrator in convincing his board of the need for such persons.

We rationalize these additions on the grounds that such persons are a necessary part of a progressive school program, that the ordinary classroom teacher is not qualified to handle special problems, and that other responsibilities make it impossible for the administrator to do so. The separation of these functions from the classroom teacher and their assignment to specific staff personnel has increased the complexity of administrative problems. What distinction is made in the advisory, supervisory, and teaching functions? What modifications have occurred in the relation between teacher and principal or pupil and teacher by the addition of specialists? What have been the consequences in pupil performance, quality of program, and relations with parents?

These are only some of the questions that have been asked. But the one in which we are most interested is the effect of these new innovations upon performance, and indirectly upon spontaneity and flexibility in personality. I do not have the answer for what is happening in the school situation, but I can relate what studies in industry show to be the effect of increasing the quantity of the downward flow of initiation when no compensating mechanisms for reverse communications are supplied. When increased pressure (in technical language, heightened initiation) is exerted from above upon a supervisory level (the comparable position being the teacher), there is an increase in action from the supervisory level upon the workers. These workers, in turn, have no place to direct their responses except inward on themselves or outward against each other, except to the extent that they vent their responses through organized protest in strikes, slow-downs, or other forms of resistance.

How widespread, for example, is the often stated observation that high school seniors, anxious and under pressure to prepare for college entrance examinations, show a deterioration in their capacity for performance? At least some teachers and parents have reported this situation to be a fact. The teacher who feels himself under constant scrutiny and who is measured by the performance of his pupils is bound to reflect the anxiety and pressure in his relations with the class. The principal is under similar pressures from the parents, who want to be assured that their children are getting the best education their money can buy and that, among the middle class at least, their children are being adequately prepared for college and can get admitted. The situation has some similarities to a cage full of squirrels.

The conclusion to which we come is that the realities of learning are variable and are only partially a function of the innate capacities of the learner. They are as much or perhaps even more a function of the image we hold of the child and his learning processes; of the perceptive system the child brings to the school from his subcultural system; and of the climate of the organizational structure in the relations among administrators, staff, teachers, and pupils, and the community of parents.

8. CULTURAL INFLUENCES SHAPING THE ROLE OF THE CHILD

It would have seemed unlikely at that time that anything new or different could have been added to the verbal and written outpourings of the 1960 White House Conference on Children and Youth. The conference organizers were thorough in their solicitation of the experts and the interested. Dozens of essays covering nearly every aspect of youth were submitted for deliberation and later publication in the proceedings. Their authors ranged the gamut of professional, religious, organizational, social, and intellectual segments of American life. Only one group seems to have remained unsolicited in this search for wisdom, namely, youth itself.

This type of oversight is not uncommon in the traditional American procedure of examining institutions and social problems. Those who are most directly affected by the preparation of a program are the ones most likely to be overlooked in the formulation of policy or of its instrumentation through organization. Patients, prisoners, or students are seldom consulted in the operation of hospitals, prisons, or schools. Perhaps this is as it must be, but then, again, perhaps those who suffer or benefit from the effects of the exercise of responsibility by others might also make a contribution, if it could be remembered to ask their participation.

That this remark is not completely gratuitous will become apparent as the analysis of the role of children in our society is developed in the next several pages. Possibly, an understanding of its relevance may well be the most important contribution that can be made to

"Cultural Influences Shaping the Role of the Child," *The National Elementary Principal,* Vol. XL, No. 1 (September 1960), pp. 18–32. By permission of the National Education Association.

those who are charged with the responsibility of formal education in the early childhood years. But first, it is necessary to establish at least some minimum justification to add one more statement to this recent flood of analyses and opinions by those judged most competent to speak to the subject.

An attempt to rationalize or clarify disagreements and confusion among the experts might serve as a legitimate excuse for further treatment. Actually, differences in interpretation are surprisingly minor. The confusion is more a matter of indigestion, due to the quantity of data, than of methodological deficiencies. For this reason, such justification as is offered must be upon conceptual grounds, that it is possible through reorganization and re-examination from a different set of assumptions and with different objectives in mind to extract more meaning from the available data than has yet been achieved.

The initial step in this process is to shift our focus away from the subject, in this case children, to the environment—physical, psychical, social, and cultural—that surrounds and influences the child in his development. This emphasis does not exclude examination of the subject; it simply recognizes the interdependency between the individual and the systems of which he is a part or representative. Precedence for this procedure has been well developed in the natural sciences. Within anthropology, for example, although culture constitutes the central focus of study, it can be objectified only as individuals are examined. Contrariwise, when we come to study personality, we assume that it reflects a mirror image of the cultural experiences of the individual.

Following these introductory comments, we can now turn to an examination of the role or roles assigned to children in our society.

FORCED ABANDONMENT OF CHILDHOOD

Although it is seldom stated in this way, the major role of the child *qua* child is to submit to and assist in the activities and processes that prepare him for adult status. The extreme dependency of early infancy permits no choice in the selection of the external environment in which the initial learning occurs. Later, when, presumably, the child has developed some rational discrimination in his response to demands placed upon him, it is too late for him to make effective protest. He has already internalized the emotional set of a system that requires that he eventually abandon the thought and habit ways of children and substitute those of the adult world.

However rewarding the culture of childhood, that of the grown-up world is continuously and persistently presented as more rewarding and desirable, and childhood is defined as a transitory and to-be-abandoned stage of life. No matter how entrancing, the never-never world of Peter Pan turns out to be just that, a fantasy in which childhood is forever threatened by pirates symbolizing demanding adults who must eventually win in the age-old struggle between old and young. Although James Barrie allows the illusion of a different solution, both child and adult know that his ending is founded in the realm of dreams.

This forced abandonment of childhood in which, if it is successful, the child is a willing participant represents the first of a sequential series of tragedies that each individual encounters on the road of life. No matter how sentimental or protective adults may be, the gradual and sometimes forcible destruction of the innocence of childhood is a necessary function of the relationship between adult and child. The latter is not the only one who suffers in this nearly abrupt destruction of childhood certainties. The transition also demands its costs of the adult. The mother's mixed emotion of anguish and pride when her "baby" first enters school is repeated later when her child, turned young adult, leaves home for marriage, college, or the world of work. She may also carry a sense of guilt because of the contradictory desire both to hold and to eject, and guilt because there can never be assurance that one has done enough or that what one has done has been right. There is solace in believing that one has done the best he could, but doubt may also nag the conscience.

The male response to these crises is different only in degree, and both parents share the knowledge that they have been parties to a failure, concealment, or perhaps even deception in communicating to the growing child what the world is really like. This conspiracy of silence is in part a function of the inability to articulate the realities; in part, it is an attempt to continue the protective role assumed during infancy; and, in part, it is a result of the parents' unwillingness or incapacity to face the realities of their own lives. The delusion they have perpetuated, the illusion they have lived under and passed on to their children, should not be assessed as deliberate. Not that adults and parents are blameless, for they are not. The offense with which they may be charged is the same one as the one that they first permitted and then prohibited, that of innocence.

The adult world is no more free of fantasy and illusion than is that of the child. The Walter Mittys are everywhere among us. Shaw's *Pygmalion* expresses a contemporary version of the Cinderella story. Our devoted adherence to romantic love as a necessary prerequisite to marriage and adult responsibilities of family and parenthood is real enough, but do we not deceive ourselves when we act as if erotic love is the panacea for the tough job of cementing relations between men and women in domestic functions?

These beliefs, and similar ones in other spheres of life, sustain us through bitterness, tragedy, and boredom. They are undoubtedly a necessary aspect in our kind of cultural world and as such should not, even were it possible, be either dispelled or destroyed. Our sin is that we let them delude us, that we insist upon maintaining an innocence of realities. Perhaps there is no simple way to explain why this is so, but probably these tendencies are linked with the generalized guilt our culture so successfully inculcates during that period of defenseless infancy. If so, then it is all the more apparent why we can understand the child's role only by examining the nature of the world surrounding him. In that quest, we turn to a brief look at the distinctive aspects of the American family in its metropolitan middle-class manifestations.

THE AMERICAN FAMILY SYSTEM

We can begin by examining how labels are used to describe and perhaps also obscure. There is some advantage, but also danger, in using such apt phrases or slogans as "the whole child." There is the tendency to treat such slogans as statements of objectives and to assign to the words themselves some magical quality that through their repeated utterance may produce the condition desired. There is also a failure to understand that, in most instances at least, the slogan—and the movement it represents—is an after-the-fact situation; that is, that the conditions that permit some approximate realization of stated goals called for in the slogan are, in fact, already existent. An example will illustrate the point.

The now shopworn label, "the family of togetherness," generated a profusion of slogans that served the special interests of varied groups. Some were self-seekers in their commercialization of this theme. Others were genuinely altruistic in their desire to promote the better life through encouraging praying together, playing together, learning together, and similar activities that, if performed as a family, might somehow enrich and fulfill life. The image of this family type is that of parents and their dependent children. The representation does not include grandparents, other relatives, or neighbors. In technical language, this is the "family of procreation," the biological and nuclear family typical of American culture. Neither slogans nor exhortations created it and the definition of the roles of its members has been set by conditions that do not include the effects of conscious propaganda. Its natural history and functions differ from and may be contrasted with other types of family systems, such as the stem, joint, or extended.

The succinct and penetrating analysis by Arensberg of the small family type—its historical antecedents, gradual modifications and evolution within the specific conditions of American society, and internal structure—permits one to establish a relation between scientific analysis and popular movements and their accompanying slogans. From his evidence, it is possible to demonstrate that what many conceive to be new approaches or discoveries are, in fact, only an emergent awareness by professional practitioners in education, health, and welfare of already prevalent characteristics of family life. Thus those who advocate democratic family life, togetherness, permissiveness, child-centered education, and individuation are less the creators of new progressive movements in family life and education than they are publicizers of an existing state of affairs. Of the American small family type Arensberg writes:

. . . The imperatives of our family system, basing the small household on the conjugal pair, isolating that pair to free them to command their own destinies and satisfactions and to confer on them nearly complete and untrammeled authority over minor children (except where the state and community limit them), are not easy ones. Nor is the task our educational ideal assumes a simple one: to prepare each and every man and woman to be in adulthood spouse, parent, householder, and family head all at once. These imperatives of our present small, conjugal type of family, with its minimum of kinship entanglement and support, ideally require each person to find a mate for himself, to love that spouse, to share the upbringing of children with him or her, to maintain a household with him, to find chief emotional identification in the little family growing up around this spouse and partner freely chosen and freely retained.[1]

Anthropologists know of no other family system that places such heavy responsibilities upon so few. In other times and places, the burden of obligations to succor and protect, to share and alleviate the tensions that arise from internal difficulties or external threat, are diffused through kin and the institutions of community. In contrast, the American family in both its ideal and actual state stands nearly alone. And if this imperative, rooted in historical continuity and contemporary conditions, applies to the family as a unity, it also applies to the individuals who compose the unity. They, too, have been taught the necessity of standing alone. Nor does the child in his period of dependency escape the requirement. If, by circumstance, he no longer contributes economically to the whole, as in an earlier agrarian period, his total burden is not thereby lightened in

[1] Conrad M. Arensberg, "The Family in Other Cultures." In *The Nation's Children* (New York: Columbia University Press, 1960), pp. 60–61.

some degree. The responsibility he now shoulders is, if anything, heavier and more difficult than before.

STANDARDS OF ADULTHOOD

The course that begins in infancy inevitably leads through childhood and adolescence into adulthood. This progression can be viewed in part as the result of natural processes, in part as the consequence of training received from parents, peers, and teachers, but in even larger measure as directed, purposeful, and at times aggressive activity of the child himself. If the question were asked, "Is not this the universal process of acquiring adulthood in all cultures?," the answer given could not be an unqualified affirmative. The major difference is found in the early inculcation in the American child of certain standards of self-performance, the full realization of which will be achieved simultaneously with maturity. Later on we shall show that this expectancy proves to be an illusion that is, nonetheless, also transmitted to each succeeding generation.

First, however, the problem of what these standards are and how they become internalized and are maintained should be examined. Simple observation establishes that a parent comforting a hurt child often urges that he behave like a little man and stop his crying. In hundreds of other instances in the life relationship of parent and child, each time the former holds up adult behavior as superior, there is implicit in the action a denigration of child behavior and an affirmation of superior adult standards. When boys are told, "Done like a man!," the implications of the praise for the action performed are quite explicit. Has anyone ever intended praise when he exclaimed, "You act like a child!"? And when older people do childish things, we call them senile or foolish.

Just when and where do we, in our multi-faceted relations with children, ever really judge their behavior except against the measure of progress they exhibit in the acquisition of adult standards? Irrespective of the steps by which the process is initiated, it is not difficult to observe the relentless insistence upon acquiring adult standards. If, by chance or intention, parents and teachers should abandon this aspect of their role, they would then have, to this extent, abandoned their function as adults.

The other part of the problem posed earlier, the question of what should be included under any listing of adult standards, was answered in large measure by Arensberg in his enumeration of the imperatives of our family system. Within this framework, however, there are certain specificities that need to be mentioned and their relevance elaborated if we are to grasp the role of the child.

It is generally accepted that family, school, and church transmit a greater portion of the cultural heritage to the child than do other agencies. What, then, among the many things adults expect the child to learn, may we count as significant? The broad categories include skills for handling, knowledge for understanding, and feelings for evaluating the things, persons, and ideas that are encountered in the business of living. These requirements are so universal, however, that their generality does not help us much. If we look at some of the requirements imposed upon the individual in the American cultural system and then examine these in their relation to the family and respective roles within it, we shall encounter those specific traits that have been idealized for all members of the society.

Commitment to Change

The central and perhaps most crucial commitment of American civilization is to the inevitability and, in most instances, the desirability of change. The activities and events of everyday life are interpreted through such terms as "progress," "advancement," and "development" within the context of the never-constant environment in which we live. If the individual is to be successful in this type of society, and the promise of success is one of the imperatives that moves him, he must at least keep up with the times. Even those not motivated by promises of success know that stagnation is penalized. For the individual, this imperative means that he must be continuously poised to take advantage of opportunities for advancement. In fact, he must actively seek and, if possible, modify the environment to ensure that situations favorable to him present themselves. Favorable chances and maneuvering avail nothing if there is resistance to working in new surroundings with new people and possibly learning new skills for new activities.

The successful meeting of new demands requires, first of all, readiness to abandon the present, whether it be locality, associations, or activity. Under such circumstances, it is unwise to invest too deeply either emotionally, professionally, or financially, for the wrench that change demands may require a sacrifice too great to make. The easy fashion in which Americans establish and abandon new relationships disconcerts Europeans, who accuse us of emotional superficiality. Their projection of values hardly explains the situation, nor are they likely to understand the necessity of such behavior as a function of our commitment. And they utterly fail to comprehend the more deeply imbedded guilt with its corollary of tragedy.

Self-fulfillment

These imperatives of mobility, independence, adaptability, and the capacity for continued growth represent, in one sense, subsidiary aspects of a more central requirement, that of self-fulfillment. Implied in the objective of adulthood achieved is the acquisition of competence, wisdom, and maturity. But fulfillment in the context of perpetual change contains a contradiction incapable of resolution. Final achievement is impossible because the objectives themselves are not fixed. They expand, recede, or are modified as the conditions within the system are changed, changes to which the individual in his progression also contributes. There can be no ultimate in the world view of those who adhere to the concept of an ever-expanding system. One might suppose that these circumstances would breed frustration and defeat, but apparently this occurs rarely since one is taught to accept striving as a lifelong necessity.

Perpetual Optimism

Finally, the role must be performed in a mood of perpetual hopefulness, a trait that has also been set by the culture. The extent to which this mood has been integrated into the events of daily life may be met in many contexts. The language of salutation reveals the extraordinary extent to which we have carried our insistence upon a positive and optimistic approach to the world. No matter how we really feel, we are obligated to meet the world with a sunny disposition. Our conventional "Good day" has no relation to the actual state of the weather nor do our replies to inquiries about our well-being have relation to the actual situation. The response of "Fine," or one of its many variations, expresses how we ought to be. Any other admission is incorrect. The child learns this ritual language and the accompanying values in his earliest years. He is taught to condemn whining, complaining, crybabies, and pessimists. We should also like to deny that pain, evil, and death exist, and, although we are forced to recognize them, we assign them only marginal status. We would like to believe that all beings are basically good and should be trusted, a character quality that sometimes causes others to accuse us of being naïve. These optimistic and positive traits found expression the 1920's in the ringing slogan of Coué, "Day by day in every way I am getting better and better!"

Our culture demands that we maintain this euphoric façade in our own perception of the world and our place in it. Furthermore, we demand that our children acquire and exhibit the same psychological posture. Obviously, at times, this optimistic perceptual screen through which we interpret the events of the world must lead to some distortions in our apperception of reality. The truth is that, on occasions, the situation we find ourselves in, individually or collectively, is damned bad. But our "natural" optimism carries us through with the belief that tomorrow or next year will be better, that all things work out for the best, it's always darkest before the dawn, and so on through the dozens of aphorisms that give expression to the same point of view. The fact that events usually do turn toward the better lends credence to the belief.

It is my contention that the configuration of beliefs we have been examining is a necessary corollary to the central value of self-fulfillment. To deny, in any degree, that societal conditions are not improving (through change) or that individual incapacitation prevents further growth is to admit that this keystone (self-fulfillment) upon which the structural unity of purpose in life has been erected is faulty—denies, then, the very basis of the American's conception of himself in his life role.

It should be apparent now why it has been necessary to examine these interconnections before we could turn to the direct study of the role of the child. The American small family, relatively isolated in its activities from other communal institutions, with the insistence upon the capacity for independence and mobility of its members, building and maintaining in each person the psychological posture of perpetual optimism with its corollary of self-fulfillment, taken as a whole and as functionally interdependent with other cultural systems, provides the conditions within which the role of the individual is defined.

Under such circumstances, the role of the child is as much central to the continued functioning of the whole as is the role of any other family member. A mutual dependence exists between children and their parents, since the latter seek some portion of their own fulfillment through their children. In part, they fulfill themselves by providing a sheltering environment that expresses and enforces a temporary dependence. The dependency relationship, however, contains both contradiction and conflict, for eventually, as both child and parent know, the independent and mobile condition must be claimed by or forced upon the child because adulthood is a necessary step for continued growth. This brings us to the point where we can more adequately conceptualize the child's role.

PROGRESSION INTO ADULTHOOD

Those who propose two alternative ways of viewing the child, namely, either as a miniature adult or as an undeveloped person but possessing the capacities for achieving maturity, may come to conclusions that distort reality. There is no intention to pose a conundrum by saying that the child is neither and both. For example, most children by the time they have reached the age of three or four have already learned a number of important adult skills. They walk, talk, control the elimination of bodily wastes in socially acceptable ways, and have developed habits, points of view, and skills around sleeping, eating, and their relations to a limited number of other persons. Childish ways may still adhere to some of their activities, but any realistic appraisal of the contrast between behavior in the first year of life with that of the fourth must grant that in some directions adult standards have been successfully transmitted. By six or seven, some children are judged precociously mature. For most children, however, the period of development coincides with physical growth, except that in our society the dependence is maintained for a much longer period because of the requirement for formal training through post-adolescent years.

Thus, at a very early age the child acquires some of the requisite skills of an independent individual. To this extent, he has cleared some hurdles that test for adult competency. In other areas, he remains dependent, undeveloped, and not yet capable of unguided mobility. We again restate the point made earlier that the fundamental role of the child is to become an adult. All his activities are either contributory or incidental to this end. The progression is partly a function of physical and neural growth, partly a function of the social and cultural environment within which the child learns, but it is continuous although uneven.

PRESSURES ON CHILDREN TO BE ADULT

The responsibility parents feel for converting their children into adults is so great that they impose a rigorous regime upon them during their dependent years. The intensity of parental concern reaches into every aspect of child behavior. It is expressed by an overconcern and overdirection of the child's activities. All types of special "opportunities" for developing skills are sought out. One manifestation has been the downward extension of formal schooling to pre-kindergarten classes.

The reality eventually became sloganized in the phrase "child-centered." Whatever excesses have been committed in home or school by adults who abdicated responsibility because of this doctrine, their behavior never violated the fundamental principle that children must be turned into adults. The freedoms given the child in activity or temperament were never justified on the grounds that these would permit him to remain a child; it was because this freedom ensured a healthier, better-adjusted adult. In effect, child-centered dogma was an unwitting device for putting ever-greater pressures upon the child. In its rationale, the adults deluded both themselves and the children they tended because it was never explained that this was a long-term transaction with an expected profitable pay-off at the end.

Perhaps we should be more explicit about the pressures to which the child is subject. The cultural context within which these appear is, of course, that children cannot just be allowed to grow up; they must be wisely directed. The justification is based upon the great latent "potential" in the unformed young that is waiting to be realized. Only as the potential is realized can the child fulfill himself, and fulfillment is a function of adulthood, not childhood. What is not made explicit to the child and is probably perceived by only a few parents and teachers is that their own role is dependent upon child accomplishments. Under these conditions, the child carries a heavier burden of responsibility in the proper performance of his role than that placed upon the young in any other society.

The child is expected to grow not only into an adult but into a successful one. The definition of the latter is, of course, adult determined. Success must be found in career, in marriage, in family, in community, and in one's personal life. The adult believes and the child comes to accept early that the route to these objectives can be reached through training. The apparatus through which much of this training is transmitted is the formal educational system. It is here that performance is judged by agreed-upon standards and a preliminary preview of the future seen. Hence, the parental pressures on the child for academic striving.

BARRIERS TO ADULTHOOD

Unfortunately, there are several conditions that inhibit and limit the child's efforts in acquiring that experience necessary for adulthood. The culturally isolating centripetence of metropolitan life reduces enormously the opportunities for significant cross-group experience. The capacity to make social adaptations cannot be learned in the severely limited urban enclave or homogeneous suburb. Emphasis upon personal adjustment is probably related to the narrow range of interpersonal experiences and the ultimate necessity to rely upon oneself. The poverty of cultural variation must have a serious distorting effect on capacities for comparative perception. Vicarious experiences provided by fantasy or documentary in television, cinema, drama, or literature are no substitute and cannot be truly comprehended unless there is a substantial comparative understanding from which these can be interpreted. Situations portraying romantic love, the vicissitudes of family life, or the struggle for power may be dramatized in African, Asian, or American settings, but the meaning is reduced to horizons found in Scarsdale, Plainville, or Little Rock.

In spite of our insistence upon cultural pluralism and the tolerance of deviancy, the danger of cultural diversity remains a powerful threat. Is it possible that the social isolation of the American small family intensifies the internalization of its values, manners, and behavior to the exclusion of differing standards? Forced to depend largely upon its own resources, as it is, this may be an expected consequence. In any event, family restrictions present another hazard in the child's struggle to grow up. These are found in the nature of the relationships between old and young and the sexes and exhibit emotional correlates. Informed observers agree that not all is well in our family system, and yet what degree of credence should we give to those who see our children as guilt ridden and hostile? [2] Does the American mother exhibit the black widow spider tendencies as described by Philip Wylie? To what extent have males abdicted their role in the squeeze of demands between wife and job and to what extent are they delinquent in claiming their sons for manhood?

Perhaps these questions really have no answers. Yet they have been repeatedly asked and answered by those with ready replies. The concern should be evidence enough that the child finds himself in a confused and hence difficult position. There seems little doubt, however, that there has been both an increase in pressure upon the child from home and school and at the same time a diminution in his opportunities and hence his ability to act independently. This combination is bound to produce serious trouble.

POSTSCRIPT

Parents and teachers are particularly susceptible to exhortations by "experts" on child rearing and child life. Their position requires that the specialist appear authoritative. And we should be tolerant of their necessity to change emphasis and direction from time to time. But parents and teachers cannot forgive themselves nor can they be for-

[2] William Line and Margery R. King, "Cross Cultural Research," *The Journal of Educational Sociology*, XXIX (1956).

given by their children for the consequences of following ill-advised fads of the moment. Our attitude toward the expert should be one of hesitant caution—once bitten, twice shy. The doctrine of the 1950's that extolled the virtues of the democratic family with its security through love, its togetherness, its permissiveness, and its equalitariansim is now being modified. Although the new doctrine of the 1970's has not yet been fully formulated, we may anticipate some of the line. The avant-garde has already abandoned the term "democratic" in its application to family life. Only those who lack sensitivity to the outmoded continue to champion what is dying, not family life but a style of exhortation about it.

Perhaps Bronfenbrenner is right when he suggests that he detects a cyclical trend toward "explicit discipline techniques of any earlier era" but adds that the most important forces redirecting "both the aims and methods of child training in America emanate from behind the Iron Curtain." Achievement has begun "to replace adjustment as the highest goal of the American way of life." He foresees that guidance counsellors, parents, and even youth itself will do their part to prepare "youngsters for survival in the new competitive world of applications and achievement tests." [3]

Sputnik may have provided the dramatic incident that focused our attention upon competitive achievement in education, but the seeds had been sown long before. Parental pressure upon their children in high school to compete through college entrance examinations for the scarce commodity of quality higher education is no new phenomenon. The bandwagon for this new party line of achievement is gaining momentum. Those who disputed adjustment as the central goal of child training were labeled "anti-democratic." Those who question achievement may be considered "anti-American." Such are the caprices of the spin of the wheels of future.

The serious question that should concern us all is that of the consequences of the compulsive pressures that are now force-feeding the process of turning children into adults but at the same time extending the period of dependency.

[3] Urie Bronfenbrenner, "The Changing American Child." In *Reference Papers on Children and Youth*, Golden Anniversary White House Conference on Children and Youth, Inc., 1960.

9. SOCIAL SYSTEM AND LEARNING

The educational process has always been a major concern of anthropologists. Transmission, diffusion, and innovation of culture are terms that refer to activities during which skills, knowledge, and values are acquired and transmitted from one individual or group to another. Explanations for the dynamics of cultural persistence and change have been sought by anthropologists within the mechanisms whereby one generation transmits its culture to another and modifies or innovates cultural practices—whether through borrowing from other societies or through the indigenous invention of new cultural practices.

When examined carefully, however, the transmission of the cultural heritage is no simple procedure, even among small, non-literate tribal groups. To seek out its particulars, one must specify who teaches what to whom, how, where, and under what circumstances. One must also observe the situations in which, although there is no apparent effort to teach, the youthful observers successfully imitate the behavior they have witnessed. We know that in the routine intentional and unconscious acts of parents and older siblings toward the very young, the bases for apprehending and interpreting later experience are laid. These predispositions, acquired during infancy, are thought to become the core of affective and cognitive patterns in maturity and are manifest through later life and passed on to their own children through the subtle processes of child rearing.[1]

"An Anthropological View of Social System and Learning," in Esther Lloyd-Jones and Esther M. Westervelt, Eds., *Behavioral Sciences and Guidance: Proposals and Prospects* (New York: Teachers College Press, 1963), pp. 11–30.

[1] Geoffrey Gorer, "The Concept of National Character." In Clyde Kluckhohn and Henry A. Murray, Eds., *Personality: In Nature, Society and Culture* (New York: Alfred A. Knopf, 1953), pp. 246–259.

61586

Nor do these infant learnings exhaust the range that can profitably be studied by anthropological methods. In play and peer-group activities a strange intermixture of conscious aping of adult ways combined with an apparently spontaneous, age-graded behavior is found. Behavior must be learned sequentially and then modified as the child moves inexorably through adolescence to adult stature and ultimately to old age and death.

Much of the approach of anthropological studies to learning in small, non-literate tribal groups seems fully applicable to the study of the educative process in contemporary America. One main and crucial difference in the two situations, however, must be taken into account. In tribal and agrarian societies practically all the child needs to learn in order to assume full adult status is obtained outside the purview of a conscious, planned, and deliberate educational program. Only among those groups that devote brief periods of instruction preparatory to initation ceremonies, or in the extended relationship of neophyte training to be a priest or medicine man, do we find a counterpart to formal schooling. By contrast, we hold our young dependent for many years in an elaborately contrived formal system that ostensibly prepares them to be adult participants in the society.

This system of education is the crucial and central instrument through which we gradually separate our children from home and family and equip them to establish themselves in the public world in whatever role and place their opportunity and ability may determine. Yet we may not be fully aware of its structural position in the counterpoise of the nuclear family and the complex of social superstructures. Education's pivotal position becomes clearer if we search for the linkage that unites the private world of the nuclear family and the public world of the great superstructures, for we then discover that education is the major connection between the two. The organizational patterns of the schools are in effect bridges and the educative process provides the skills our children must gain in their movement out of youth into full adulthood. Thus, in both its structural and functional aspects, we must view the school as unique among our great social superstructures.

That our formal, institutional organization of education is unique and essential in our society becomes clear when it is examined in the context of our other institutions organized for economic, political, religious, familial, or other purposes.

By way of contrast, the informal educative processes operating in family, peer group, and locality, and that mold perspective, shape character, and determine behavior, are one dimension of cultural learning that is found in all societies. Extensive, formal education, on the other hand, arises within the setting of a complex society and serves other purposes. It acts something like the locks of a canal—taking individuals by sequential stages from their family and friendship groups to the public world of work and social responsibility.

The structure and the function of the system of formal education will be molded both by the current demands of the other social superstructures and by the pattern of their development over time. Ours is now a cosmopolitan society, industrial in its technological orientation, pragmatic in outlook, and scientific in spirit. The Main Street towns and their symbiotically related rural neighborhoods, which for over half a century following the Civil War held the essence of the national spirit, have now become residual. With their decline has come the loss of the cohesive community with its internal status differentials expressed in social classes. In place of the cohesive community we now possess the sprawling metropolitan aggregate in which the central portion of the older cities is gradually reforming itself into a mosaic pattern of cultural enclaves, and, while dispossessed agrarians are feeding into and perpetuating older slums, the middle class is withdrawing to the sanctuary of the burgeoning suburbs.

Nearly all of our activity takes place within one or another of two principal types of social groupings—within the nuclear family of parents and children or informal clusters of peers on the one hand, or in one or more of the great corporately organized superstructures of education, business, government, industry, or health, on the other. It is through this latter series of interconnected, interdependent organizations that we discharge our public or societal responsibilities, and through them that we in turn receive those innumerable goods and services by which we sustain life, derive comfort and pleasure, and strive to fulfill our hopes and aspirations. We are all members of the great cooperative enterprises through which these tasks are accomplished and goals realized. It is the mission of the schools to prepare us for this membership.

CRITICISMS OF THE EDUCATIONAL ENTERPRISE

If we took seriously all that the critics have said about education in recent years, we might give over to despair. The effectiveness with which our schools fulfill their mission has been questioned at many levels and from many sources. Some critics have hacked at bits and pieces of the education edifice, exposing deficiencies and nonsense; others have leveled charges that are broad, sensational, and frequently ill-informed, if not irresponsible; others have struggled to evolve constructive reforms. All, however, appear unconscious either of the social issues that are currently agitating our society or of the relation between these issues and the process of cultural transformation that has generated them. They seem not to understand the interdependence between school organization and educational process, nor even, perhaps, the unique and solitary responsibility of the schools as the means of transition between the nuclear family and corporate organization.

In general, their narrow and completely erroneous assumption is that all we need do, to put our educational system in good order, is change what happens in the classroom. They further assume that what happens in the classroom can be changed simply by reorganizing the curriculum, beefing up the substance in subject matter, and modifying the methods of instruction. No one will deny that substantial improvement in these areas should be achieved, or minimize the thoughtful and sincere efforts of those who have directed their attention to the possibilities.[2] But no anthropologist could accept the implicit assumption that the educative process is divorced from its social environment. The learning situation is very far from being the atomistically conceived procedure implied by this approach.

RESEARCH AND THE EDUCATIONAL ENTERPRISE

It is logical to assume that, in a scientifically-oriented society such as our own, plans for modifications and changes in a system will be based on the results of research. A major difficulty with most of the available educational research until very recently has been that it has been as atomistic in conception as are the attacks leveled by education's critics. Innovations have been primarily trial-and-error responses to changing conditions, as these conditions were viewed by the innovators, and have included both wholesale borrowing and indigenous developments.[3] Research that might have placed these conditions and their implications for education in a clearer light, thus giving direction to change, and research that would have assessed the effects of innovation has, for the most part, not yet been undertaken.

The available research has tended to be marginal or superficial to the central problems of organization, pedagogy, and materials as related to learning. School surveys, statistical compilations, and attitudinal studies provide information of immediate usefulness, but little more. Psychological research, whose contributions outweigh those of any other field, has resulted in valuable findings that are, however,

[2] William VanTil, "Is Progressive Education Obsolete," *Saturday Review*, February 17, 1962, pp. 56–57, 82–84.

[3] Lawrence A. Cremin, *The Transformation of the School* (New York: Alfred A. Knopf, 1961), Chapter II, "Education and Industry," pp. 23–57.

marginal to the major problems of system, and the implications of which have not been carefully assessed. Thus, the tests and measurements that have been widely adopted for differentiating student capabilities and performances have come under heavy attack from many sources and the next ten years will doubtless witness radical changes in their form and use. Results of experiments in learning, perception, and reading have been applied in programing for machine teaching, in the construction of textbooks, and in teaching methods.

Until the last few years, the chief contributions of the other social sciences have been a brief splurge in the now moribund use of sociometrics and an awareness of the significance of social class background to school performance.[4] In addition, of course, sociology and anthropology have indirectly influenced the viewpoint of teachers and subject matter in ethnic and racial relations, socialization of the child, personality, cultural relativity, and so on. To the extent that these fields have broadened the perspective of teachers and enriched academic programs, the results should be counted as positive.

The significant areas of community relationships and functions, administration and school organization, curriculum, subject matter organization and content, social influences on perception and learning, are vital factors in the educational enterprise that have just begun to attract the attention of research in the social sciences. Most of such research is in the developing stages and sociological in orientation. It is too soon to assess its utility or its impact, and educators still seem disinclined to seek out social scientists to conduct research for or with them when they face problems in these areas. The collaboration of the social sciences with public health, agricultural extension, and industry has been far more extensive and richer in results than has similar collaboration in education.

AN ANTHROPOLOGICAL APPROACH TO
RESEARCH IN EDUCATION

Clearly we have not gleaned enough information from research to formulate a far-reaching program of educational change. We do possess, however, the conceptual tools to frame the problems about which research should be done, and the conceptual tools of anthropology are particularly well adapted to the formulation of problems that are fundamental to the educational enterprise.

Educational institutions and processes lend themselves to anthro-

[4] W. Lloyd Warner, Robert J. Havighurst, and Martin B. Loeb, *Who Shall Be Educated?* (New York: Harper and Brothers, 1944); A. G. Hollingshead, *Elmtown's Youth* (New York: John Wiley and Sons, 1949).

pological analysis because (1) they focus upon the intimate relationship between the social forms in which a people group themselves and the other aspects of their cultural system, an interdependence that is shown in the connections among technology, customs, beliefs, and even patterns of settlement and land use; and (2) there are available documents and other evidence to reconstruct the stages of transformation through which a society has moved for the purpose of elucidating the principles of change.

In the analysis that follows I propose to apply this approach to an examination of our educational system. Earlier mention was made of the rapid transformation of our society from rural-agrarian to urban-industrial. Between 1870 and 1920, the change was manifest in the rapid growth of cities, whose population increment resulted, in large part, from the arrival of millions of European immigrants; by the development and spread of a new technology in transportation, manufacturing, and services; by the spread of the factory system as the organizational form for production; and by the proliferation and growth of corporations as the system of managerial control and capital concentration.

The corporate form was an extraordinarily efficient and socially revolutionary way of assembling capital, skill, and manpower for production and distribution. It concentrated massive energies for the solution of problems; it developed and maintained orderly processes for achieving its goals; and it had a large degree of flexibility. Centralization of control and dispersion of operation through a hierarchy of differentiated positions, each charged with special but complementary functions, were the structural properties through which its results were realized. The capacity of the corporate system to evolve in response to a changing environment led to the expansion of its activities both in scope and size and to the exertion of its influence over other institutional arrangements, including education. Through the institutionalization of research it has stimulated rapid and continuous technological change, and there is an increasing attention to its problems of organization, all of which has important implications for education.

Even before 1900, the effect of societal transformation had begun to be felt in the public school system, especially in the cities. Expanding populations, higher requirements for work skills brought on by technological advance, universal education, and an increasingly larger proportion of students who continued their education into high school brought sharp increases in enrolments. These in turn created enormous pressures for new facilities, changed programs, and a suitable organizational structure.

The little red schoolhouse of agrarian America presented no problems of school administration and curriculum organization. This school was basically an extension of family and community and, as the subjects taught indicated, it had no need to prepare its students for participation in a large, complex, and changing society. As an educational enterprise, it was part of a unit that included the family and other community institutions, such as the church. It offered no pattern for meeting the educational demands of the emerging urban-industrial society.

Thus the sheer magnitude of the new educational task called for radical departures in educational organization. These took, in the public schools, the direction of an expanding departmentalized bureaucratic superstructure. The once direct relationship between teacher and a board of education representing citizens and parents gave way to a many-tiered line organization in which the pupil occupied the lowest level.

Although, since 1900, there has been a proliferation of personnel through the addition of supervisors, counselors, and specialists in more and narrower fields of subject matter and services, the educational structure as we know it today is essentially the structure that had been developed by 1900. The focal point of the system is the school superintendent, who acts as executive officer of the board of education, to which he is responsible as administrator of a departmentalized bureaucracy. The line of command runs from him through assistant superintendents to principals, and on down.

The development of higher education provides a remarkable contrast. The organizational structure of American colleges and universities did not respond to cultural transformation in the same manner as did the public school systems. Bureaucratization has been minimal in higher education and relegated largely to housekeeping rather than to pedagogical functions. Both teaching and research are functions of the faculty, which jealously guards its prerogatives against administrative encroachment through mechanisms that are well developed in most colleges. The principle of academic freedom remains firmly established. The structure of authority is diffused rather than centralized and horizontally segmented along departmental lines rather than vertically hierarchized, so that the colleague relationship is valued more highly than is the supervisory one. The area of student personnel administration may be more bureaucratized in higher· education than is the area of curriculum and instruction. This is a question that would lend itself well to anthropological or sociological research. Suffice it to state here that the retention of flexibility in an institution ensures greater capacity to incorporate new functions without disturbing either the central purpose of the institution or its form of organization.

How may we account for the sharp contrast between the type of organization usually found in higher education and the structure of the public schools, and what is its significance?

The answer lies in the response to a variety of factors: the divergent cultural tradition of each, their social roles, and their response to the social setting. Universities have now become connected with events and institutions on the national and international level and their personnel, organization, and functions reflect this.

How do we explain the organizational evolution of the urban public schools? It seems reasonable to suppose that public education, which has long been an adjunct of local government, has followed an organizational pattern similar to that of the other expanding municipal services in the big cities. We know that during the days of urban boss rule, and still today in some large cities, the school system has provided a source of patronage and graft.

The great corporations might have provided an alternative structural type, since their rise also coincided with the growth of the cities. It seems unlikely that the corporation served as the original model from which school organization was deliberately copied. On the other hand, the parallels between the bureaucratic structure of the two are sufficiently striking in their similarity that those who taught future school administrators, beginning in the second decade of this century, extolled corporate organization as a model to be followed. The corporate board of directors has been equated with the board of education, the stockholders with the citizens, and the executive officers with their counterparts in large corporations.[5] The analogy of teachers and students to foremen and workers has not always been made explicit, but the following statement, written in 1916, is quite clear in its intent:

Our schools are, in a sense, factories in which the raw products (children) are to be shaped and fashioned into products to meet the various demands of life. The specifications for manufacturing come from the demands of twentieth-century civilization, and it is the business of the school to build its pupils according to the specifications laid down. This demands good tools, specialized machinery, continuous measurement of production to see if it is according to specifications, the elimination of waste in manufacture, and a large variety in the output.[6]

That this point of view was not unique can be amply documented. By 1915 a number of the larger cities had already established "effi-

---

[5] Ellwood P. Cubberly, *Public School Administration* (Boston: Houghton Mifflin, 1916).

[6] *Ibid.*, p. 338.

ciency bureaus," which—through survey, measurement, and testing—were to apply the "lesson of the business world, from which we have much to learn in the matter of efficiency. . . ." [7] A determined band of pioneers, among them Terman, Ayres, and Thorndike, had already provided the educational world with tests and measurements. Industrial efficiency was being spurred by the principles enunciated by F. W. Taylor, whose *Principles of Scientific Management,* published in 1911, brought a surge of time-and-motion studies and rearrangements of work organization in factories. School administrators were urged to employ efficiency to bring about scientific school management.

Those who advocated that education borrow rational and organizational form from industry apparently perceived no dangerous incompatibilities. Efficient utilization of labor in machine production is clearly not the same process as the slow acquisition by the young of intellectual skills. In adapting mechanical processes to education, emphasis is apt to be laid upon rote learning and fact acquisition through repetition, including the inculcation of patriotism with flag drill. Stress on efficiency as the ultimate goal is apt to divorce education from human values.

In addition, the educational system does not have built into it those safeguards that limit corporate excesses in society as a whole—militant unionism and legislative enactments. Teachers have neither the tools nor the understanding to protect the cause of learning against bureaucratic regimentation. And citizens who are disturbed about the educational system direct their complaints not at educational organization but at practices and teachers. All these factors have tended to foster the persistence of our bureaucratical, hierarchical structure of public education.

As the urban school systems solve the problem of size through hierarchized bureaucracies, they also create a new organizational climate affecting the achievement of educational goals. When we seek to discover the consequences on learning, we move from the assumption that there is a relationship between the learning process and the environment in which it occurs.

Although a theory of learning based upon anthropological premises has yet to be explicitly formulated, such a theory is implicit and its outlines discernible in all descriptions of enculturation and socialization. Learning is a function of biological and cultural variables whose interrelations are so complex that in most instances they can only be inferred. Stimulus to learning can come from two sources: from the environment, and from within the individual. Each person, how-

[7] *Ibid.,* p. 335.

ever, interprets new experience through already established categories of understanding, and new learning consists of the modification of the old or creation of new categories. This psychic process patterns experience and gives to the individual his basis for comprehending the world and his place in it. Rote learning, or fact acquisition as an end in itself (the quiz-kid mentality), does not, however, require this patterned internalization, and, in a strict sense, such learning can have little meaning for the individual.

The educative process, to be effective, depends upon the learning process—the internalization and ordering of experience by the individual. Among simpler societies, where education is usually not institutionalized, this results in the repetitive recreation in each generation of those who resemble the preceding. In complex societies, in contrast, a formal system of education can and usually must be deliberately designed to produce successive generations that differ from their antecedents.[8]

Thus, although the learning process is similar in both simple and complex societies, the fact that in complex societies the child can learn *only* through *formal* education what he needs to know to become a fully participating member of adult society is of great significance. For this reason, the teacher-learner relationship is crucial in our complex society. When it is used to perpetuate the structure of the organization, then it has been corrupted. The danger of such corruption mounts with increasing bureaucratization of schools. This becomes clear through an examination of the functions of other types of relationships in institutional organizations.

In all line organizations, the directional responsibility from above to below is expressed through the supervisory relationship. Thus, the teacher who follows the instructions of a principal or his supervisory aide responds in a manner equivalent to that of a sergeant or foreman who obeys an order of his captain or manager. When the teacher directs students in their activities, she is supervising. In addition, the exercise of custodial responsibility in schools represents an extension of the supervisory relation. Of utmost importance is the fact that directional activity always assumes previous learning; any new learning is an accretion incidental to the event.

When administrators or teachers meet with their own kind to work out a common problem, we speak of a colleague relationship. In contrast, the businessman who serves a customer, or a lawyer who

---

[8] Margaret Mead, "Our Education Emphasis in Primitive Perspective," *American Journal of Sociology*, XLVIII (May 1943). Dr. Mead emphasized the discontinuities modern education engenders in contrast with the generational sequence of private societies.

offers advise, is in a client relationship. There are aspects of both relationships in the classroom, but it is in the dominance of the custodial and the supervisory relationships that the danger to learning activity is most acute.

Supervisory techniques can be used to demand and train for appropriate responses from children, from dogs, and from pigeons (à la Pavlov and Skinner), but such mechanically acquired responses barely challenge the human capacity for learning. Full human learning requires the use of cognitive processes in a relationship in which the learner retains autonomy for self-initiation leading to new insights. This potentiality is absent under strict custodial care and severely reduced in a supervisory relationship.

Teaching as an act of supervision may lead to successful achievement of rote learning and fact accumulation, since the system of rewards and punishments, tests and measurements, is geared to recognize and sanction such. But it is the development of the capacity for seeking relationships and dynamics of systems that is so badly needed and greatly rewarded in our type of civilization. This, I must reiterate, can be accomplished only within the context of formal education, since parents and peers do not possess substantive knowledge required for teaching. But as educators we possess no objective means for either discovering or rewarding the accomplishment.

What happens in the school today is crucial. It is the child's first experience as a participant in a corporately organized system. Whatever other qualities his earliest teachers may have, they represent for him the other world, the non-familial public arena toward which he has begun the long years of preparation for eventual induction. The success with which he masters his school environment—in other words, internalizes its learnings—foretells, in most cases, the degree of success with which he will master his public adult environment, although it has little demonstrable relation to the satisfactions he gains in his private life.

To this end we have dedicated vast efforts to the extension of professional competence to ever larger numbers of teachers. There may have been a real need for extensive supervision in the early decades of the century, when many teachers had little, if any, professional training—so that Cubberly could argue that the ideal school system had a superintendent who viewed his responsibility as similar to that of the principal of a normal school. But the urgency of such a procedure must have declined as the proportion of well-trained teachers has steadily increased.

More important, the supervisory system as we know it may defeat the goals of our educational enterprise—the development of the individual creativity and autonomy upon which the continuance of our complex, mobile, and dynamic society depends. We remain, it is true, fairly naïve about the learning that comes from participating in a complex organization versus what we label mastery of subject matter and for which we test continuously. Is the truant or rebel who evades or rejects the system protesting the controls or the academic requirements or both? Industrial research suggests to us that it is not the task, however difficult or onerous, that contributes to worker malaise—for work can be a challenge or it can be endured—but that it is the sometimes unbearable weight of a supervisory system that restricts the autonomy and creativeness of the individual.[9] This insight should give us pause, because in the educational hierarchy teacher and pupil are at the bottom of the system; they are the recipients, not the originators, of the messages that flow along the line of command.

We are not justified in charging that a supervisory oriented school system is disjunctive with its assigned educative function unless we examine all the dimensions of the society. But if the bureaucratic segment of the educational establishment is primarily concerned with its own perpetuation, then control of teachers and students becomes the implicit, paramount objective and the student is no longer in the position of a client-learner with a teacher. In the supervisory relationship, in contrast, the teacher socializes the student to respond as a subordinate. Such a situation is indeed a subversion of the transitional function of our schools and of the educative goal of developing intellectual and organizational skills and the talent potentials of the young.

It should be evident by now that the consequences of schooling are far more extensive than the process or results of the transmission or acquisition of knowledge. In fact, unless we take into account the environmental setting in which learning occurs, we cannot hope to understand the nature of learning, because they are interlinked. Unfortunately, most educators have entombed themselves in a professional tunnel that blinds them from seeing the problem whole. For them, curriculum has become the magic oracle whose pronouncements set the goals; the trinitarian syndrome of teaching, testing, and controlling constitutes the operating procedures; the assumptions about the learning process resemble those based on producing trained seals or feeding data into an imperfect computer.

This narrow perspective excludes much that is pertinent to the learning process. In particular, it ignores the social and cultural significance of institutionally organized formal education in the society, as well as the immediate human clusterings in family, peer group, or

[9] Chris Argyris, *Personality and Organization* (New York: Harper and Brothers, 1957).

locality. The school itself ferments its own distinctive social patternings based upon the multiple similarities and differences of its population. Learning arises, is extended, and modified within these social settings. For this reason, we cannot separate the learning process from the social process. As a social and cultural context, learning must be examined in the context of social system.

10. COMMUNICATION BEHAVIOR AS A FUNCTION OF SOCIAL STRUCTURE

As might be expected, there is some variation in the assumptions, research approach, and methods of analysis among those who concern themselves with communication. For example, Hovland, *et al.*, in *Communication and Persuasion* state: "Implicit throughout has been a definition of communication which may be more formally stated as the process by which an individual (the communicator) transmits stimuli (usually verbal) to modify the behavior of other individuals (the audience)." [1] It is clear from their treatment of the subject that they are primarily concerned with change in opinions and attitudes through the use of mass media. Their emphasis is almost entirely on what happens to the individual and ignores his social position and treats the cultural setting incidentally and casually. Their approach is basically atomistic and rational.

Hall, in *The Silent Language*, considers culture as a form of communication.[2] He develops an elaborate scheme based largely upon the model of linguistic analysis in which much attention is given to the style expressed in writing, dress, speech, etc. He says the communication system (culture) possesses structure, components, and messages. The duration of a message is an important consideration. Cultural

"Communication Modalities as a Function of Social Relationships," *Transactions,* Series II, Vol. 25, No. 4 (February 1963), pp. 459–468. By permission of the New York Academy of Sciences.

[1] Carl I. Hovland, Irving L. Janis, and Harold H. Kelley, *Communication and Persuasion: Psychological Studies of Opinion Change* (New Haven: Yale University Press, 1953), p. 13.
[2] Edward T. Hall, *The Silent Language* (Garden City: Doubleday and Co., 1959).

messages—such as the tone of voice—are brief, those that convey the personality of an individual take longer; whereas messages about political events—such as development of policy—may take years. His main objective is to establish an operational system that permits the analysis of messages. His insightful examination of space and time behavior exemplifies the specific application of his approach.

Ruesch and Bateson combine physiological process, psychoanalytical insight, and cultural concepts to produce a comprehensive approach to communication that they state "is the only scientific model which enables us to explain physical, intrapersonal, interpersonal, and cultural aspects of events within one system."[3] These events are part of and occur within a "social matrix." Their definition is quite inclusive and follows:

But communication does not refer to verbal, explicit, and intentional transmission of messages alone; as used in our sense, the concept of communication would include all those processes by which people influence one another. The reader will recognize that this definition is based upon the premise that all actions and events have communicative aspects, as soon as they are perceived by a human being; it implies, furthermore, that such perception changes the information which an individual possesses and therefore influences him. In a social situation, where several people interact, things are even more complicated.[4]

One useful organization of the mechanisms of communication is to separate the verbal and non-verbal. Let us agree that all things may serve as signals, and the act of perception constitutes an awareness of the signal that adds information to the receptor and may lead to a response. The non-verbal types of communication, according to Ruesch, include signs (gestures), action (walking, eating), and objects (the intentional or non-intentional display of material things), and these appeal to "different sensory modalities" than the verbal.[5] The signals of non-verbal actions are transitory, whereas objects continuously transmit signals. Ruesch calls them analogic in contrast with the digital alphabet and numbers. Ruesch does not make the point, but it is permissible to codify some types of verbalisms as pure gesture. Ritual forms of polite address seem no different from tipping of the hat or handshaking. The nonsensical football cheer carries meaning all right, but not semantically. The polite nothings those at teas, receptions, and

[3] Jurgen Ruesch and Gregory Bateson, *Communication: The Social Matrix of Psychiatry* (New York: W. W. Norton, 1951), p. 5.

[4] *Ibid.*, pp. 5–6.

[5] Jurgen Ruesch and Weldon Kees, *Non-Verbal Communication* (Berkeley: University of California Press, 1956).

cocktail parties address to one another represent standardized ceremonial vocal sounds, which Malinowski labels as phatic communion.

The meaning messages convey is of concern to all those engaged
in the study of communication. Hovland sees the effect of the message
as due primarily to motivation, credibility accorded to the source,
influence of others, and emotional state evoked. Basically, he relies
upon learning theory to explain communication effects. Ruesch and
Bateson emphasize the neurally-based perceptive system, which is a
consequence of the social matrix, and each message is interpreted
accordingly. All things emit signals, but communication occurs in social
situations. Hall posits three types of patterns, informal, formal, and
technical; the meaning of a message is dependent upon which one of
the three is used for interpretation. The differences among these three
approaches are not as great as casual examination might conclude.
They all assume learning theory and perceptive evaluation and differentiate approximately the same elements in the communication
process.

My approach accepts the validity of psychological and cultural
emphases and assumes their presence in communication processes, but
since my emphasis is upon the relation between communication and
the social structure and not that of personality or cultural pattern, my
analysis treats of a different dimension of the problem. It examines
communication variability as a function of a system of relations and
of categorical groups.

MODE OF COMMUNICATION

Cultural distinctions in style of verbal behavior, posture, and gesture
are accentuated in ceremonial and on public occasions. One recalls the
once customary orotund, mellifluous oratory of the Fourth of July
speaker, the exaggerated verbosity of the old-style politician, the im-
passioned fervor of the inspired revivalist, or the melodramatic render-
ings of Shakespeare. Such violent and colorful verbal and gesticular
exhibitions were expected fare by audiences, who accompanied the
presentation with their own form of partisan response. The muted
orderliness of today's public events, epitomized in the question-and-
answer television debate of candidates for high political office, provides a striking contrast.

All peoples possess their own characteristic styles of public
performance and response. These range from the arrogant bragadoccio
of the Sioux warrior publicly proclaiming his exploits, to the elaborate,
ritualized verbal maneuvering of the African palaver, or the intellectual exchange of a Socratic dialogue. Stylistic variability is also

found within each culture, depending upon group or situation. The occasional uproars of the Irish town saloon contrast with the arid politenesses of the salon and the intense chatter of the cocktail party. The quiet demeanor of the Navajo almost always pervades each of their gatherings, whereas among the Iatmul of New Guinea the fretful bombast of the males contrasts with the placid serenity of the women.

Enough instances have been adduced to establish a range of differences over time and between and within societies, differences that cannot be explained by temperamental differences among individuals but that we may assume are cultural patterns transmitted from one generation to the next. The various studies of child training practices have established correspondences between the modal personality of a particular tribe and the experiences of infancy. Thus, the contrast between aggressive Sioux and self-effacing Zuni have been attributed to differences in infant care. But to state the relationship in this way is to imply a causal and perhaps primary connection between the stylistic aspects of communication and personality formation that only further analysis can confirm. I prefer to start with the assumption that the mode of communication is a function of the social system and in this sense resembles the concepts of self and world-view in their conformance to spatio-temporal conceptualizations. The evidence to test this line of reasoning will be taken from the Bateson-Mead study of the Balinese.

These Indonesian people occupy an island just east of Java, with whose people they are culturally affiliated. They have gained world attention from their elaborate temple carving, religious dancing, and their beautiful and petite women.[6] Religion and social groupings reflect the effects of an early invasion by Hindus. The caste system they introduced is still operative, with descendants of the Hindus occupying the three upper castes, but with about 90% of the population being placed in the lowest or Sudra category. The Balinese are village dwelling agriculturists possessing hamlet-based, endogamous, corporate kin groups, who meet their community problems through a formal political organization and a series of voluntary associations. Each family usually belongs to several temple societies, through which its members observe an elaborate religious cycle involving dramatic reenactment of sacred themes. In addition, there are irrigation societies associated with each watershed, and a recently imposed territorial unit for administrative purposes. These groupings, taken together, constitute the "planes of organization" as designated by Geertz.[7]

    [6] M. Covarrubias, *Island of Bali* (New York: Alfred A. Knopf, 1936).
    [7] Clifford Geertz, "Form and Variation in Balinese Village Structure," *American Anthropologist*, LXI (1959), 991–1012.

The scientific objective of Bateson and Mead was to extend and test understanding of "ethos," defined as "a culturally standardized system of organization of the instincts and emotions of individuals." [8] Within the villages they studied, they discovered widespread consistency in "ethological content," although considerable cultural variability distinguished the simpler mountain villages from those of the plains. There were differences of wealth and poverty, of witches and no witches, of variation in agricultural practices and emphases, of elaboration or sparseness of ritual ceremony and observation, and of villages in which "trance is shared by all and those in villages where no one ever goes into trance." [9]

The authors remark upon the great similarity of attitude of mind and system of posture and gesture and conclude that there is no "apparent difference in the character structure" irrespective of the differences in cultural content. Thus the correspondence between the constancy of the "organization of the instincts and emotions" and their stylistic expression in posture and gesture, and the contrast of variability in cultural practices and content, is a fact of some significance. But how may this extraordinary fact be explained? It is abundantly clear that the authors believe the uniformity is a consequence of similarity in child training practices; and what seems important in child learning is orientation in time, space, and status. The child must learn to recognize and respond correctly in language and gesture to high and low, those of the ranked castes and those excluded from such distinctions, those with seniority and citizenship and those with something less. Between each hierarchical level there exists a tension the open expression of which is averted by observance of niceties of language and gesture. It is a tension comparable to that found between male and female, which is symbolically portrayed in enactments of Witch and Dragon plays, and in the courtship dance. In the first, the ferociously ugly, vicious, and destructive Witch is contrasted with the Dragon, who portrays the gentle and playful father representing health and safety. In the courtship dance, the male woos a princess but, having won her, discovers that he has wed a witch.

The ecological aspects of time and space are given little attention by the authors, and we may assume that they are not important. We learn that the rising and setting of the sun, and toward the coast and away from it, provide the basis for directional distinctions and that an agricultural and ritual calendar marks change in activity and enacts historical tradition. But the important spatio-temporal factors are those

[8] Gregory Bateson and Margaret Mead, *Balinese Character: A Photographic Analysis* (New York: New York Academy of Sciences, 1942), p. xi.
[9] *Ibid.*, p. xv.

related to human relationships. The significant time cycle is contained within the recurring rhythm of birth and death to reincarnation, each period of which contains its own perils. Space is divided into what is intimate and safe and what is unknown and fearful. There is the private, intimate world of house and courtyard, in contrast with the outer and public world of uncertain social and physical boundaries. It is not that the Balinese avoid the public world of crowds; quite to the contrary. Here one finds gaiety and joyful pleasure, but it is a mixing in the public world without sharing in it—the retention of an apartness or awayness. In public one avoids relationships that require commitment; such of those as are forced upon one are responded to with stylistic language, posture, and gesture.

Even within the boundaries of intimacy, one encounters somewhat comparable behavior. The authors report the lurking avoidance by which children skirt gatherings of their elders. If it is from the childhood experience that this type of behavior emerges, what are the specific processes that account for a form of personality that the authors report approximates "the sort of maladjustment which, in our own cultural setting, we call schizoid"? [10] They conclude that the pattern of behavior between mother and child, such as the encouragement given by the mother to the child to seek her in times of need or fear and who then rejects its approach by feigning indifference to its demands; the punishment of a child for its emotional outbursts, which have been induced by teasing; the handling of babies as if they were toys by women and girls who derive pleasure from this activity; and a style of infant handling that teaches identification and surrender by the infant to a host adult whose manipulation is primarily kinesthetic rather than verbal; that taken together these are the processes that are explanatory of the result. From such experience comes an individual whose body possesses fully "patterned physical movement (but) from which all emotion long ago withdrew." They point to the Witch drama as one in which the symbolic enactment of the pattern is expressed in the sequence of approach, rejection, and a subsequent turning in on oneself through trance.

It is an axiom of scientific research that the question or problem with which one initiates a project constricts his conclusions—answers are begotten by questions. The problem posed by Bateson and Mead was that of Balinese ethos, the "culturally standardized system of organization of the instincts and emotions of individuals." They solved their problem and gave us an answer in the revelation of those mechanisms in child training that give to the Balinese their distinctive

[10] *Ibid.*, p. xvi.

character structure irrespective of the variations in culture content they noted.

If we equate the manner in which parents relate themselves to children and the style of communication, then we would have to argue that variations in style of communication would modify character structure, but since the latter explains the manner in which parents relate to children, we are caught in the endless chicken-and-the-egg controversy, or else we must accept a causal, deterministic view of culture and of personality, which is equally circumscribed.

The escape from this ends-means trap comes if we ask a quite different sort of question based upon the assumption stated earlier that communication style is a function of social relationships. Hence our problem is to seek the nature of the relationship between social structure and process on the one hand and communication style as an aspect of cultural patterning on the other. If we can establish a meaningful relationship between the two, it will also explicate the congruence between cultural conceptualizations involving self, world-view (including the dynamics of change), and spatio-temporal definitions within the same social system. The analytical process ought, at the same time, to establish congruencies between cultural patterning and conceptualization. With the clarification of the relationship between these two and between them and the social system, we will have laid the basis upon which the analysis of any society, in whole or in part, may be dissected and its dynamics comprehended. This is indeed a rather startling claim. Whether we succeed or not we must still try, and our first step is to reexamine and interpret the Balinese data from the position stated above.

Bateson and Mead examined the relationship between the pattern of child training, within a given socio-cultural environment, and a specific type of character structure (ethos). We must not confuse their method of analysis with their findings, however. These portray Balinese society as a closed system of inherited statuses, the perpetuation of which is assured by the generational transmission of a distinctive type of ethos. The process could be viewed as a circular one if we assume a static situation in which each older generation inevitably shapes its young in its own image. This position is taken by those who are adherents of national character analysis, and there is evidence to substantiate their view.[11] If their chain of being permits no break, or at best only slight modifications from generation to generation, then the Balinese are trapped in a cultural cul-de-sac in which character struc-

[11] Geoffrey Gorer, "The Concept of National Character." In Clyde Kluckhohn and Henry A. Murray, Eds., *Personality in Nature, Society, and Culture* (New York: Alfred A. Knopf, 1953), pp. 246–259.

ture may be explained by child training practices, and vice versa. If, however, we look beyond this closed system and ask about the relationship between types of social groupings and child training practices, instead of treating the former only as the social milieu within which the practices occur, we arrive at a rather different interpretation. It is to this approach that I now turn.

The rigid divisions of status based on caste and seniority within Balinese society are manifested in the elaborate and precise arrangements that govern the spatial disposition of individuals at any organized event—rules that ensure the placing of people according to rank; by the stylized patterns of language, gesture, and posture that are observed when those of different ranks encounter each other; and by other cultural practices that give recognition to social distinctions. These relationships demand a mode of acting, not of feeling, and the outer calm but inner terror that is attributed to those meeting unknown situations is evidence of the intense necessity to meet each situation correctly, which is possible only if the emotionless "patterned physical movement" has been correctly learned.

Balinese culture emphasizes the form of behavior within relationships over such other aspects as emotional, economic, or spiritual. It is not the individual to whom one responds but rather the behavior that signalizes his position. Hence the training the child receives emphasizes his acting toward those in the outer world, not his feeling about them. Feelings are directed inward, the turning in on oneself, which is dramatized by those who go into trance, by the withdrawal or apparent stupor exhibited by those who have completed some ceremonial sequence, by the indifference of the mother to her suckling infant, by the societally observed cessation of activity (Njepi) at the beginning of each new year that contrasts with the activity (Rame) of other days.

Further evidence of the centrality of relationships vis-à-vis feelings is contained in a personal experience recited by Dr. Mead. As one device for establishing rapport with the villagers, she established a clinic to treat minor ailments of children. She experienced something less than full success until she learned that her assumption of a universal confraternity among women in their mutual feelings of warmth and concern for children was not shared by the Balinese and that her emotion-laden behavior was creating embarrassment, if not fear, among the mothers, a fear that was transmitted to their young. With this insight, she modified her behavior, making the overt expression of her emotions theatrical rather than real, resulting in an obvious beneficial consequence among the mothers, who could now relax. It is obvious that our natural tendency to link feeling and acting in interpersonal relations is a pattern of behavior that proved threatening to the Balinese, and in Dr. Mead's example did not communicate the intended compassion.

The theatricality of behavior in situations involving others and the deep psychic orientation to status is illustrated by another example. One of the recurring themes in the popular puppet shows is portrayed in a situation in which the etiquette of relationships between superiors and inferiors is caricatured by gross burlesque. The quality of the outbursts of laughter reminded Dr. Mead of the response evoked in other cultures by pornographic allusions, and she observed that "the restrictions surrounding personal relationships in terms of seniority, caste, and directions and levels, seem to have the same quality as the restrictions, which in many cultures surround sex." [12] These examples lead the logic of analysis toward the conclusion that one must look to the system of social relationships for the source of the pattern of child training practices and for the reinforcement and perpetuation of the distinctive Balinese personality system.

There is one further problem with which we must be concerned before our analysis is complete, namely, the coordinate relations between males and females, and in particular between husband and wife. Conceivably, the intimate world of family within house and compound could be a place of emotional expression and relaxation, a haven from the rigid requirements of the public world as it has come to be idealized in our society. The evidence does not support the supposition. The rigid sexual division of labor enforces a separateness in their respective contributions to the household. The playful handling of infants as toys by the women is paralleled among the men by an intense and absorbing interest in their fighting cocks. Although compatible relationships between husband and wife are not uncommon, they are not characterized by deep affective feelings of either love or hate. The treatment that the male as youth received from his mother is apparently fearfully expected from his wife, as portrayed in the courtship dance referred to earlier. Both sexes engage in transitory sexual adventures. In sum, there is no evidence to suggest any significant difference in personality pattern for coordinate relationships when contrasted with those of hierarchy. Nor should we expect to find any so long as the family must be the locus of training the child for activity in both the public world of hierarchy and the intimate one of family. If training for public participation were assigned to a separate institutional group, such as a priestly class or secular educators, then we might expect modifications in child training practices and

[12] Bateson and Mead, *Balinese Character*, p. 12.

resultant personality, a conclusion we are justified in making based upon the primacy of the social system and of the ensuing modifications in cultural behavior that come from changes within it.

Within any specific society, it is quite clear that, associated with each type of relationship, there is a modality in style of communication, sometimes expressed in language, sometimes in posture or gesture, sometimes by all of these. Nowhere is this more explicitly formulated than in behavior among kin. Among many peoples the oftentimes austere and formal behavior of a father with his children contrasts with the warm and relaxed posture of the mother. One may discover a separation based upon those with whom we may joke and those toward whom respect is enjoined. In rare instances, there is the denial of direct confrontation, such as is imposed by the taboo of avoidance upon mother-in-law and son-in-law. The analysis of kinship systems permits us to move from the particular, such as father-son relationship, to classes of relationship that group all those who resemble each other where, for example, one expresses a reserve toward one's uncles on the father's side comparable to that given to the father himself. Beyond the kinship system we find other categories of persons for whom we have set patterns of address and they for us. These include the opposite sex, those older, those younger, and those of one's age, the superior and the inferior, and those who compose the special categories of priest, doctor, teacher, and so on.

The principle that unites all these variations into some kind of consistent whole is derived from the fact that modalities of communication are based upon positional definition, upon the arrangements by which individuals are related to each other in on-going events. We could have arrived at this understanding by utilizing case material other than the Balinese. The examination of any kinship system or adequately described organization would have provided the necessary data. Our purpose was to seek the congruencies among the pattern of communication, the concept of self and world-view, the spatio-temporal realities of the socio-cultural milieu, and the psychic bases of personality. The Balinese data permitted us to examine all these aspects in their relation with each other and to establish, through inductive analysis, the ultimate paramountcy of the relational system. The meaning of child training, of personality, of cultural practice, and of communication emerged as we examined them in the context of a rigid system of caste, status, and sexual dichotomy.

But the analysis should also have given us a deeper understanding of the intimate connection that links modalities of communication with the whole psychic and social fabric. The manner in which we establish relationships with others, or order and respond to others, is no superficial idiosyncratic whim of the moment. It is derived from and expresses the process that governs the workings of our institutions and, through the family, molds the plastic infant into a participating adult.

The method of analysis and its conclusions pose some special operational problems relative to the study of the communicative process in some segments of the society, such as school, hospital, or factory. Is it necessary in a study of communication in these institutions, for example, to expose the origins of the psychic roots of the members of the group, to explicate their world view, or to determine the overarching time and space concepts within which they unconsciously work? The answer would depend in some measure upon the purposes of the examination, but in general no such elaborate data gathering and analysis are needed. But for those who possess the kind of understanding that has been developed here, there is an advantage in knowing that the immediate institutional behavior is deeply rooted in psychic, social, and cultural systems. It should prevent the kind of causal, deterministic conclusion about organization and its processes that is likely to be made by those who lack this comprehension.

11. INDIVIDUALISM AND THE FORMATION OF VALUES *

There is a general tendency among Americans to see the world from an individual focus. Such a view is particularly evident among some who currently write about alienation, loss of identity, conformity, and mass society. This emphasis has been given official currency in the report of President Eisenhower's Commission on National Goals, which concluded that the opportunity for *individual* self-fulfillment is the central objective of American civilization.

This focus upon the individual finds support in much of theology, historical interpretation, economic theory, and psychology. The historical development of psychology has provided scientific support for commonsensible observations about the primacy of the individual. In the early nineteenth century, Jeremy Bentham formulated his pleasure-pain theory. Later, William James gave us rational pragmatism, and McDougall posited an instinct-filled creature. They were followed by those who explained behavior as due to drives, needs, or tension-reduction responses. The most influential of these various theories has been the energy-laden libido postulate of Freud. Psychoanalysis became an interpretative scheme of world-embracing proportions. Even those who argue against psychology's one-sided emphasis upon the individual must grant, in all fairness, that one of its contributions has been to enhance the dignity and worth of the individual—of all in-

"Individualism and the Formation of Values," *The Journal of Applied Behavioral Science*, Vol. 2, No. 4 (1966), pp. 465–482.

* Originally prepared for and presented at the Institute for Religious and Social Studies of The Jewish Theological Seminary of America under the title "The External Origin of Values." Some minor modifications have been made in the present version.

dividuals—in a world in which autocracy in government, religion, or custom had relegated the masses to inferior status. In this respect psychology joined with those intellectual and political forces that were freeing men in other ways. But like its sister discipline, classical economics, which posited the rational economic man, it supported and contributed to a view of the world in which the social and cultural environment was either ignored or excluded.

My protest is directed against habits of thought that seek to explain the happenings of the world as ultimately based in the individual. This view underlies the emphasis upon individual self-development and is supported by the assumption of innate inheritance labeled instinct, drive, need, libido, or ineffable essence. In its extreme form it implies that, left to himself, the individual must inevitably grow into the kind of adult his innate stuff destined him to be. Although today there is an increasing acceptance of environmental influences in shaping the individual, we are still far from having worked out how these operate. It is my purpose to examine one aspect of the problem, namely, the relation between individualism and the formation of values.

I propose to examine the relation between the individual and the social setting within which individuals act out their lives. It is my contention that we may abstract from the behavior of individuals, particularly as it may be observed in groups, not only the distinctive social forms—the social system—but also a system of values. Furthermore, we should consider both social (interactional) and value systems as supraindividual; that is, we recognize them as operational generalizations that express the ordered relationships among individuals in groups and their valuing of things and actions.

I have carefully avoided stating that *society* creates values or that *society* determines and transmits the values held by individuals. Such reification of abstractions, the attributing to concepts of a consciousness and energy that no empirical experience can verify, is neither intended nor implied. This caution actually makes our understanding of the problem more difficult. If we could accept a supernatural origin of values or a secular counterpart in the "collective consciousness" of the sociological positivists, then we would have no difficulty in agreeing that a fountainhead of wisdom and energy transcends the individual. To this source we might then turn to receive the Word. It is just this procedure that those of the faith employ. But man is also a creature of reason, and in his probings of the processes of the universe he arrives at conclusions contrary to those currently prevalent, as for example, Darwin's formulation of organic evolution.

SOCIOLOGICAL POSITIVISM AND VALUES

Those who focused almost exclusively upon the individual gained wide acceptance partly because they were in one current of Western thought and partly because the spirit of the times favored this view. But, as always, there were counter positions. One of these is found within the French school of sociology led by Durkheim (to which contemporary American sociology owes so much) and in anthropology. The charge leveled against the French positivists that they denied the individual is, of course, ridiculous, but their emphasis upon the group and society was a welcome antidote to the extreme individualistic position.

A representative expression of their interpretation of values is made by Bouglé, who, following Durkheim, made a distinction between judgments of value and judgments of existence.[1] The function of the former, he declared, was "to formulate not the natural properties of things, but the desires of men living in society." He distinguished the judgments of existence as those related to reality and stated, "The will to be objective excludes, by definition, all other desire." Hence, he concludes that values exist only in relation to desires, and that "it is by transmission of evaluations that societies perpetuate themselves. . . ." Although he makes no attempt to explain the origin of values, he grants to them a primacy beyond other societal aspects and in their dynamics vests the power of societal change. "If we wish to make fundamental changes in institutions, we may well concern ourselves, first of all, with the hierarchy of feelings. The world of values is, as it were, the invisible workshop wherein are prepared the changes of scene for the visible world."

ANTHROPOLOGY AND VALUES

The position of most anthropologists is rather different. Concerned as they have been primarily with culture—the patterned behavior of organism, mind, activity, and group—they have been much less inclined to attribute to any one factor the explanation for human or social development. Instead, they have tended to approach their problems fully recognizing the relative contribution of physical, organic, psychic, cultural, and social aspects. Personality, for example, would be analyzed as a consequence of interaction between an organic individual and the enviroment—be it physical, social, or cultural.

---

[1] C. Bouglé, *The Evolution of Values* (New York: Henry Holt, 1926), p. 147.

Under this view, the psychic pattern (the habits of thought) arises from no determinate innateness, but is itself a consequence of social patterns. With this approach it is possible to describe the perceptual variations within and among different world cultures. The comparative study of values in different societies establishes the range of variation and can also force us to realize that values we may have assumed were universal are either absent or rejected elsewhere. Not many anthropologists, however, have addressed themselves to the specific study of values, although any listing of Americans who have been thus concerned must include Ruth Benedict, Dorothy Lee, Clyde Kluckhohn, and David Bidney. For example, Ruth Benedict shows that the pursuit of happiness as a major goal of human existence is repugnant to traditional Japanese. If we wished to extend the enumeration, we could proceed through all those qualities we value, such as honesty, justice, truth, love, equality, freedom, privacy, friendship, and so on, and demonstrate the sometimes radically different meanings these have among different peoples. The cultural diversity of values has been sufficiently well documented that it needs no further exemplification.

The anthropologists' concern with cultural diversity contributed to the questioning of beliefs about absolute standards of conduct and morals. It was readily observed that different peoples had achieved varied solutions to similar problems. The principle of relativity of culture gave dignity to the observed diversities. This principle has been so well publicized (and distorted) over the past four decades that it has now become a part of our intellectual equipment. But anthropologists have modified and extended the principle since its original formulation. Simple empirical comparison, through mere contrast, fails to deal with more fundamental questions of function and process, which would include attempts to explain why a given group holds certain values or of their relevance to the other aspects of the culture. The problem becomes even more complex if we accept the principle proposed by Whorf through linguistic analysis that Western modes of thought are not directly applicable in the interpretation of other cultures. Lee, for example, in her analysis of the principles of codification that shape the world view of the Trobrianders, and hence their interpretations, shows that for them "value lies in being," not in relationship or use.[2]

There is one further aspect in which anthropology can help to clarify our understanding. It is with the knotty problem of the relation between symbol and values and the sociocultural system, and that

---

[2] Dorothy Lee, "Being and Value in a Primitive Culture." In *Freedom and Culture* (Englewood Cliffs: Prentice-Hall, 1959), pp. 89–104.

of the process of valuation. Ever since Durkheim's famous analysis of the relation between religious behavior and the organization of society in his *The Elementary Forms of the Religious Life,* we have been provided with a theoretical guide not previously available for interpreting the function of religion. Although we may not wish to give unqualified assent to his conclusion that values are objective because imperative and imperative because collective, there is no doubt about the validity of the connections he traced between religious value symbols and tribal organization.[3] Such a neat one-to-one relationship as may be observed in static and simple societies does not seem to be completely applicable in our own complex and rapidly changing society, where such value symbols as "freedom" or "democracy" have a diffuse if not floating quality.[4] It is not that such terms are valueless; it is that their precise meaning can be made explicit only in a variety of situations. They possess many referents; in fact, it may be this quality that gives them their power.

Now this brings us to the problem of how value originates, is increased, maintained, transferred, or destroyed: the dynamics of the experienced value. One step toward solution is to examine the consequences that flow from acting by individuals in ordered relationships. An example drawn from the Bella Coola, and cited by Dorothy Lee, will illustrate the point. Briefly summarized, the chiefs of this tribe, in a series of public ceremonies at which they made gifts and exhibited a piece of thin copper, gradually increased the value of the copper in proportion to the number of exhibitions and the number of gifts distributed. When its value had been sufficiently enhanced, the owner broke it in two and flung it into the fire. By this act its value flowed into a dead relative, but the copper was now valueless. White traders who learned that thin pieces of copper were highly valued by this tribe flooded the market. Of these Lee comments:

But the new coppers neither had nor lacked value in themselves. They were symbols only in the sense in which the symbol has been presented here; they acquired and conveyed only the value inherent in the situation in which they participated. No one wanted to buy a copper unless he was ready to go through the long and expensive procedure of infusing it with value. So the flood of coppers brought no inflation; the value of coppers could neither rise nor fall through such manipulation. Being true symbols, they could acquire

---

[3] See W. Lloyd Warner, *A Black Civilization,* Rev. Ed. (New York: Harper, 1959) for an example of the application of Durkheim's theory to the sacred and secular life of a tribe.

[4] See Chapter XIII in Solon T. Kimball and James E. McClellan, *Education and the New America* (New York: Random House, 1963).

valid existence and value only through participation in meaningful situations.[5]

Lee rightly draws our attention to the culturally patterned process of value accretion and transference, in which the material object serves merely as the instrumentality of the process. What she does not emphasize is the value accrual to the person and position of the chief himself and to those who participated with him in the public ceremonies. The gift-giving feasts also reaffirmed the order of relationships among men. The chief, in the assistance given him in the preparation for the feast and in the bestowal of gifts upon those present, was acting out his part in the system of relations, and those who assisted or received were also affirming their own relationship to him. The point to be remembered is that any person who occupies a position must discharge the duties associated with it, and the value of a position will be judged according to its social validation, a process requiring both activity and interaction. The man crowned king must rule as one; those commissioned as officers must command; the teacher must teach. In these acts individuals validate themselves and their position, and in the response of subject, soldier, or student we find recognition and acceptance. The quality of their performance will be judged by criteria that involve their relationships with others.

From analyses such as the preceding, we seek understanding of the process of valuation. We look neither to some transcendental source nor to the attributes of an individual for that understanding. The assumption of fixity or absolutes for values is itself a denial of their dynamics. What we propose is that value may be enhanced, maintained, depreciated—even lost. It is as much external to a person, position, concept, or relationship as it is to a thin piece of copper. But it may accrue to any or all, depending upon the relationships and activities among men; these, in turn, are influenced by those factors we label the conditions within which events occur.

Before we attempt a fuller exposition on the formation of values, it is necessary to make an explanatory excursion to establish some points for subsequent analysis. In particular, I wish to examine the relevance of categories of understanding, canons of discrimination, and the relationship between values and character.

CATEGORIES OF UNDERSTANDING

It is widely accepted that communication would be impossible if we did not possess agreement about the meaning and referents of signs

[5] Lee, "Being and Value," p. 88.

and symbols. But we are also aware of the nuances and variations that accompany such abstractions as God, love, beauty, truth, or democracy —differences we may attribute to the life experience of an individual or group. Nevertheless, there are some areas in which deviation is held to a minimum as, for example, in definitions of number, order, class, sex, color, size, form, and so on. These are what have been called the categories of understanding. They constitute a universal minimum of agreement without which social life would be impossible. (Those who insist on private symbols become patients in mental hospitals, way-out artists, or both.) The symbols and their meanings are not subject to the whims of individual fancy, for they are ultimately supraindividual; that is, they are social, as Durkheim has insisted, and being social they are external to the individual.

Although categorization as a cognitive process and cultural device is universal to all mankind, the kind and substance of categories exhibit great variability from one society to another. Hence the mode of thought for each culture must be examined through its own logic. For example, we cannot accept, as have many philosophers, the universal applicability of Plato's categories of values—truth, goodness, and beauty. In fact, their conversion into static entities makes them worthless as tools of analysis.

The categories of understanding are instrumental. They are learned, utilized, verified, transmitted, even changed, but their persistence over generations establishes them as group phenomena rather than as idiosyncratic ones. Their meaning does not arise from any innate trait of the individual but comes from relationships with the environment, particularly from participation in social groups. They are cognitive formulations of man's perceptions of reality, and any attempt to argue their objective necessity is specious.

If there are some aspects of cultural life that are supraindividual, may this not also be true of other aspects, such as values? Although I believe the question warrants an affirmative answer, there are others whose discussion about values has been predicated on a different assumption. A representative formulation of this latter position is presented by Bidney, when he asserts:

Since the meaning of a culture is to be understood teleofunctionally by reference to the end, or final objective, which its adherents strive to realize individually and collectively, we must next consider the basic types of value which it is possible for man to pursue. Ever since the time of Plato, philosophers have recognized that there are three fundamental categories of value; namely, truth, goodness, and beauty. Truth may be defined as an attribute of thought by virtue of which the mind conceives the real nature of things. The good may be understood as a property of things and acts considered desirable. Beauty may be defined as an attribute of the forms of things which render them attractive.[6]

Quite apart from questions about the merit of Bidney's teleological orientation and the validity of Plato's categories is the ascription of an absolute and transcendental quality to truth, morality, and aesthetics. As illustrative of his position, Bidney writes,

The ideal truths of science and philosophy are products of cultural experience; yet they transcend the empirical limits of actual cultural experience. They are timeless, atemporal ideals, suggested by experience, but pointing to a metacultural reality which surpasses anything given in the context of historical experience.[7]

He then states that if the only reality is a cultural one

. . . then the concept of an ideal truth other than given cultural experience becomes meaningless. . . . Our conceptual and empirical knowledge of reality varies with our interests and experiences, but reality as an ontological existent independent of man is an absolute object to which our ideas progressively conform in the course of our pursuit of knowledge by scientific methods. Similarly, moral and esthetic values are real attributes of objects, although for purposes of physical science the former may be disregarded.[8]

The problem is not one of relativity versus absolutes, an argument from which anthropologists have retreated in the past decade, nor of universality as a euphemistic substitute for absolutes. Bidney defined the issue precisely when he stated it is a metaphysical one, although he incorrectly designates the cultural relativists as the protagonists. The intellectual issue is far more profound and involves the opposition between those who postulate "objective reality, independent of the observer," as does Bidney, and those who seek, not the definition of entities, but the explication of processes and principles within events. It is a difference between those who seek assurance through the search for wholeness, unity, integration, in the fixity of repetitiveness and those who, although granting man's capacity to discern a universal orderliness, direct their attention to the study of relationships in potentially limitless change. Objectivity, in the finite sense in which it has been used, becomes the illusion; reality is to be found in transformation.

    [6] David Bidney, *Theoretical Anthropology* (New York: Columbia University Press, 1953), p. 400.
    [7] *Ibid.*, p. 419.
    [8] *Ibid.*

CANONS OF DISCRIMINATION

Additional support for this position can be found in consideration of what we mean when we speak of "canons of discrimination." Enough studies have been made of the varying modes of thought among non-literate peoples and of the different epochs of Western civilization as well as of other higher civilizations to provide us with a rich literature for comparison. Sorokin, for example, has attempted to categorize the variations by such labels as sensate, ideational, or ideological. It seems unnecessary to comment further upon the fact that basic differences exist among scholars. Attention should be directed, however, to the gradual changes that may be traced within a given civilization and to their correlation with concurrent changes in other aspects of life. In particular, we should take note of the relationship between assumptions about the nature of the universe and the modes of thought. Contrast, for example, the static concepts prevalent in the medieval period with the later notions of continuous progress achieved through the operation of mechanical forces. Events are interpreted in each culture, or epoch, within the framework of the prevailing modes of thought. Under such circumstances, the specification of an immutable, objective reality seems hardly feasible.

Nor is it necessary for us to confine our analysis to the cosmic level alone. Each individual in each society learns to discriminate among the types of sensory experience he encounters, to categorize his activities and those of others, to identify objects, and to define his relationships to others. These discriminations presuppose categories of understanding, but they include a good deal more. They are based on patterns of perception, including shape, color, movement, and size, at the finite level; symbolic representation at the abstract level; and the experience of evaluation. Whatever the psychic process for organizing responses to stimuli appearing as sensation, item, act, or thought, these stimuli are sorted and judged by systems of mental action learned by the individual and are variable from one culture to another. When a Navajo Indian is in a state of hunger, he believes himself to be possessed by a supernatural essence—one of a triad with poverty and illness, which were not destroyed by the sons of Changing Women when the earth was prepared for man's habitation. Without these misfortunes, the people would never know the blessing of health, wealth, and repletion. For the Navajo, hunger is no punishment from benign or malignant gods, nor a consequence of economic law or personal ineptitude. Fasting is practiced by the Sioux youth, who seeks to induce a state favorable for a supernatural vision. For us

hunger is a consequence of failure in our social machinery, or of individual ineptitude, and is abhorrent. It is not the variation in the
meaning of hunger from one situation or culture to another to which
I wish to draw attention, however; rather it is to show the *range* of
discriminatory differentiation that is possible around a state that can
be described in such precise physiological terms.

Behind the act of discrimination lie not only the systems of codification (categories of knowledge) but also those implicit or explicit
modes of thought by which everything is evaluated or judged. In their
whole, we may call these the *canons of discrimination;* and, like the
categories of knowledge, they, too, are transgenerational and external
in origin to the individual. They constitute the filter through which
all experience is sifted and given meaning consistent with perceived
reality. It is for this reason that new learning, which demands an
altered perspective, is so difficult and oftentimes threatening. But
among the many possible modes of thought there is one that remains
wholly flexible in its capacity to make adjustments in categories and
canons. I refer to the concept of reality as transformation.

The relationship between codification and evaluation of individual
character should now be clarified. When we speak of an individual's
character we have in mind those personal attributes that are revealed
in his behavior—in his acts and in his relationships with others. What
we see is neither fortuitous nor random, nor is the process by which
we evaluate these. Our judging and what we judge both rest upon
learned canons of discrimination. Thus character represents certain
aspects of the individual's valuing system and is its manifestation.

CONDITIONS AND VALUES

There is one further aspect of the problem that deserves greater attention than has been given to it thus far. Simply stated, it is the
relation between the conditions (primarily social) that surround an individual or group and the prevalent values. We can postulate that
when there is a change in conditions, a change in values may also be
observed. There is little evidence that the reverse is true, although
many instances may be cited in which the conditions have been
changed because of prevailing values (for example, the conversion of
the wilderness into settled communities, the abolishment of slavery,
child labor legislation, and so on). In these illustrations, we are treating values in their normative function, that is, as the bases for making
judgments about behavior. The observation by Kluckhohn is in accord
with the position taken here. He states, "In common-sense terms, morals
are socially agreed-upon values relating to conduct. To this degree

morals—and all group values—*are the products of social interaction as embodied in culture.*" [9]

The question that is posed here is really crucial. All too often it has been phrased in the form of "the chicken or the egg" controversy, which is, of course, a false question. To deny a relationship between group behavior and values is, of course, fallacious. But to insist upon a priority between the two, based upon their order of origin, is to create confusion. In all stable, ongoing systems, there is a congruency between values and interaction—interdependent and mutually reinforcing. And commonsensible observation establishes that if you can instill the right perspective (values) into a group, then it will continue to function well. Hence, the belief that you can teach values, right moral judgments, and in the process create desirable character. The fact that we are engaged in such teaching all the time and that we seem to discover desirable effects flowing from our efforts lends further massive support to the belief that the results come from our efforts alone. This simple cause-and-effect logic betrays us much too often, primarily because we fail to account for all the variables involved, chief among these being the conditions under which the teaching occurs. Values are learned *only* if they are congruent with and referential to a situation in which they are tested.

The whole matter may achieve some greater clarity if we examine it within the context of some specific cases. Chester Barnard reports that one of the ideas that emerged from his lectures at the Lowell Institute in Boston in 1937, and of which he was not aware at the time, was

. . . that to a large extent management decisions are concerned with moral issues. Undoubtedly, long before recognizing this I had had numerous experiences exemplifying it; but I had never distinguished between decisions of a technical or technological character, subject to factual and reasoned conclusion, and those involving a less tangible sensing of values. But this idea of moralities in organizations was one of issues arising within organizations, *with little or no reference to prevalent moral conceptions in the great societies within which these formal organizations exist,* nor did it take into account the obligations of incorporated organizations as legal entities.[10]

Barnard's discovery was more than that of recognizing the inherence of morality in organization. "That cooperation among men, through formal organization of their activities, creates moralities was

[9] Clyde Kluckhohn, "Values and Value Orientation in the Theory of Action." In Talcott Parsons and Edward Shils, Eds., *Toward a General Theory of Action* (Cambridge, Mass.: Harvard University Press, 1954), p. 388. Italics added.

[10] Chester I. Barnard, *Elementary Conditions of Business Morals* (Berkeley: University of California Press, 1958), pp. 3–4. Italics added.

to me, in 1938, a startling conception." The insight Barnard gives us is clear enough. It supports the proposition offered earlier that there are changes in values (or new values arise) when there are changes in conditions. In this instance, the conditions are primarily those of the organizational forms in which men are grouped for cooperative action. Thus the locus of origin and the perpetuity of values must be sought in relationships, and we must understand them as processes rather than as entities.

As a final example, I propose to contrast briefly the agrarian period of late-nineteenth-century America and the metropolitan world of the present. In that earlier epoch of "Main Street" towns, with their agricultural hinterland, the Protestant ethic served their residents well. They extolled political liberty and personal freedom. Hard work, sobriety, honesty, prudence, and thrift were central virtues. Biblical precedent gave the rustic preacher ammunition for his exhortation against the sin and evils of the cities. Family and community, and a simple system of recognizing variants of success in what has come to be called social class, constituted the major social ingredients. The rewards of the society were believed available for all those who would struggle for them, and the belief in continuous progress was widespread. In sum, the way of life offered an impressive congruency between values and behavior.

By contrast, the social world today comprises massive and complex organizations carrying on economic, governmental, educational, health, and religious functions; the isolated and mobile family of parents and children; and a system of formal and informal voluntary associations that unite those of similar occupations, professions, and interests. These three types of social groupings engage the time and energies of a metropolitan population. But spatial separation and limited social identification prevent any meaningful face-to-face relationships beyond the orbit of these groups. The sense of community that comes from common participation in events embracing the whole is lacking because the events of this type no longer occur. Self-fulfillment, as recognized in President Eisenhower's Commission on National Goals, has become accepted as the ultimate purpose of our type of civilization. Such a goal should be viewed as a value judgment that reflects a change in the social milieu from that existing in an earlier period.[11]

11 My colleague, James McClellan, has noted that these changes require no significant modifications in the liturgy of religion, law, or education. The theologian, jurist, or educator can still retain the ritual language, although the original meanings have been drained away, to be replaced with new meanings. The process is so subtle that only the most sophisticated are even sensitive to what has happened.

If we accept the evidence from the preceding analysis, we must grant that the values and moralities that served one epoch are not necessarily the ones that will serve another. Some may persist; some are altered; some disappear; and others not previously envisioned, because the conditions necessary to produce them were yet to come, have arisen. What we must also accept is that the pace of change has not slackened and that the values of a decade or a century hence are likely to be different.

CONCLUSION

A restatement of the argument of the preceding pages should go about as follows. Although there are pervasive psychological systems that explain value formation as a product of the innate qualities of the individual, this view is one we reject. Nor can we accept the views of those who derive values from a locus of power external to the individual as do those who seek their origin in the collective consciousness of a reified society or in transcendentalism. All such explanations imply a substantive absolutism that the comparative study of cultures shows to be untenable. Some portion of the confusion in all these arguments is due to the tendency to treat values as if they were things and thus to isolate them and to attempt to define them through a listing of attributes.

The alternative approach presented here proposes that values and value formation are a consequence of the activities of individuals within a social setting. Such a position accounts for both the variability of value systems among peoples of diverse cultures and the changes that occur over time within a specific society. In other words, the meaning of things, of activities, and of relationships is a variable and arises out of participation and is affirmed in successive and repetitive events.

The meaning and form of human activity in events, however, must be understood within their context, one aspect of which is the cultural heritage. The cognitive tradition is found, in part, in the system of classification that gives order to experience—the categories of knowledge. But there is an additional psychic ordering that governs the responses of individuals to their experiences. This evaluative ordering I have called the canons of discrimination. In their use, the individual not only identifies the items that come into his sensory and cognitive orbit but responds to them in a predictable fashion, based upon his criteria of evaluation. He has been taught how to think, act, and feel, and to do so differentially because of the situational nature of learning. Hence the conditions of experience constitute another of the variables that affect evaluation and values. Since within each culture there is great uniformity in the cognitive and affective patterns of thought and feeling, a *sine qua non* for communication and cooperation, we can view both categories of knowledge and canons of discrimination as supraindividual. And although it is the individual who is their carrier and reflects them in his behavior, we must look to social processes if we are to understand their nature and process of formation.

Perhaps some brief reference to the implications of the perspective presented here in its relation to social science research and to programs of planned change would be helpful. For one thing, utilization of the concept of canons of discrimination should help in bringing a more systematic approach to the study of values. We now add the new dimension of the criteria of evaluation to those of what and how judgments are made and expressed. In our study of the process of the transmission of culture, we now have cognitive tools that are of a different sort from those that attempt to explain learning through imitation, repetition, association, or reinforcement. Instead of focusing entirely upon the individual, we now attempt to discover the cognitive and affective perspectives within which experience is presented and organized.

Although we have long been aware of the importance of values in either impeding or aiding programs of planned change, we have not been very successful in understanding why this is so. Now we should be alerted to watch for evidences of change in human groupings in events and of the relation of such change to ways of evaluating.

Finally, the message contained here has direct relevance for those who attempt to instill moral values or to build character. If admonition, lecture, sermon, or example were fully effective instruments in gaining compliance with codes of conduct, we would have reformed long ago the criminal, the delinquent, or the sinner. Verbal exhortation and exemplary conduct do serve a purpose, however, for a requisite of ordered human relations is the repetitive reaffirmation of the values associated with human groups. If those who attempt to teach values would see them less as entities and more as a function of the individual's participation in social groups, I believe they would have a more effective base from which to proceed.

12. THE TRANSMISSION OF CULTURE

If there is any aspect of human knowledge that is uniquely distinctive of education, and that can be claimed as the major prerogative of professional educators, it is to be found in the conditions and processes associated with the transmission of culture.

Ordinarily when we speak of education we have in mind the formally organized enterprise through which the teaching of subject matter and skills is accomplished. Presumably the purpose of this activity is to prepare the young to take their place in the society of adults. But the achievement of physical maturity, the acquisition of knowledge and skills, the development of moral judgment, and the learning of patterns of acceptable behavior are not restricted to the period of institutionalized and formal instruction. Infancy and early childhood furnish crucial experiences for the formation of the emotional and cognitive patterns the individual will carry into later life. In fact we can hardly expect to understand the consequences of directed teaching unless we know the personal and cultural antecedents the child brings with him into the classroom.

We are very far from knowing what can and must be known about these early years, in part because we have not known how to proceed. Study of the psychological aspects of child development has been helpful, but much of our energy has been directed toward accumulating those static data that tests and measurements render. This is not the stuff that reveals to us the intricate interdependencies between individual and environment. They do not lend themselves to a statement of the processes that explain growth and change. Furthermore, those

"The Transmission of Culture," in *The Body of Knowledge Unique to the Profession of Education* (Washington, D.C.: Pi Lambda Theta, 1966), pp. 45–70.

who are wedded to their use are trapped in an intellectual procedure that seeks orderliness through the categorization of the atomistic bits and pieces they have gathered. There is the temptation to label the results obtained as nonsense, since the reality they portray is not that of the world they examine but of the operations they represent.

Before we attempt to specify the ingredients necessary for a more rewarding approach to this problem, let us make certain that the objective toward which we are moving is clearly understood. If it is our concern to isolate what is unique to education, then we must extend our perspective to include more than is contained within the limits of formal education. In particular, we must view formal education as a special aspect of the socialization of the individual. Furthermore, we cannot say that subject matter, or that any one subject, exemplifies that to which we should pay special attention because knowledge is not in itself inherently related to the manner in which it is learned. We can similarly eliminate the acquisition of skills as the main point of emphasis, for, although skills can be taught, and their acquisition implies learning, these are only part of what the individual acquires in his movement toward adulthood. In essence, what we have been rejecting is a concern with the *consequences* of learning, the results of influences, direct and indirect, that shape the individual in his progression from birth onward. Instead, what we propose is that what is unique to education is knowledge of the conditions that affect the transmission of culture.

When we come to enumerate what should be subsumed within this area, we must include the relationship between teacher and learner; the cultural tradition and social environment within which learning occurs; the organic and psychic capacities of the individual to be modified through experience; and the dynamics of the learning process itself. Although we must examine each of these aspects in some detail, we can clarify and place in better perspective the ensuing discussion if at this moment we make brief reference to current learning theory.

The individual has been the focus of almost all of those who have been concerned with learning. This bias is understandable if we view it as stemming from a major theme of Western culture. It is exemplified by the attention given to the great and little in religion, history, and literature and to our interest in explaining their behavior. Traditionally, we have turned to such inner qualities as spirit, wisdom, character, or ambition to give us the key to the forces that have shaped their lives. These explanations are usually of two kinds. On the one hand, they seek a source of external energy such as God or Society for the locus of inspiration, and, on the other, they have turned to an innate force such as the instincts that create a property acquiring economic man as postulated by Adam Smith or the libido-driven patients and disciples of Freud.

In some cultures men are moved by acquisitive desires or by the need for love; but as explanations of pan-human behavior, these suffer from many inadequacies. Some portion of our willingness to accept such schemes can be attributed to our too easy acceptance of motivation as explanatory of the direction individual human behavior seemingly exhibits. In fact, we could be wiser to treat motivation as a psychological artifact than as a basic human variable. We might with equal cogency argue for the primacy of "guilt" or of "anxiety" or of "fear." These are terms that refer to recognizable emotional states, but we should not confuse the stimuli that evoke behavior and the behavior itself. Which is the motivant?

Those who seek for inner-state explanations of behavior implicitly assume a concreteness in the subject of their inquiry. If something can be treated as an entity, then its qualities or attributes can be made explicit through dissection; and presumably the mechanisms that control its functioning can be made explicit. Unfortunately for those who follow this course, neither "spirits" nor "instinct" nor "id" nor any of the other postulations lends itself to the kind of examination applied to substances. My objection, however, does not deny that under certain circumstances it is useful to speak of the needs of the organism, or that the designation of emotional states may have utility, or that cerebration is necessary for comprehension and insight. My objection is of a more fundamental kind. It is that the focus upon the individual has led to an inadequate statement of the problem and that, in consequence, the results of analysis have given us only partial, if not inadequate, answers.

In their search for the mechanisms that explain human behavior and learning, the psychological empiricists have made a great contribution in dispelling some of the metaphysical confusions. If we start with the simple pleasure-pain formulation offered by Jeremy Bentham over a century and a half ago, we can trace to the present the genetic links of a long intellectual and theoretical tradition. Its basic formulation is of utmost simplicity, the famous stimulus-cue-response. The focus is clearly upon the individual, but in its pure form it dispels any necessity to rely upon an ineffable "force," and it takes account of variables external to the individual. Among those we associate with advances in this field are Pavlov, Thorndike, Watson, and Skinner. But pleasure-pain, conditioned reflex, tension reduction, need-fulfillment, or reinforcement are still variations within the more general stimulus-response theory, and the question at hand is whether this theory is sufficiently inclusive to cover the range of empirical evidence with which we must contend.

The problem is an intricate and difficult one because if its solution depends upon unraveling the intricacies of the human neural system, it is far from certain that we can ever arrive at anything more than an approximate solution. The less complex brains and sensory apparatuses of dogs, rats, and pigeons are better subjects for experimention, but the transferability to humans of the results obtained is always open to doubt.

There is a second and even more valid reason for doubt, however. If we divide behavior into what reflects the responses based on conditioning, which we call "training," as one category, and classify behavior that is based upon the arrangement of experience in new combinations, which we label "cognition," as another category, then it becomes clearer why stimulus-response as an inclusive formula seems inadequate. As a simple example that distinguishes between the two, we can take the case of the student who learns by rote the answers to set questions. Irrespective of the complexity of either questions or answers, this type of learning falls within the category of training and offers no essential difference from the patterned behavior a Pavlov instills in his dogs or a Skinner in his pigeons. If, however, a student learns how to utilize experience to frame questions the answers to which express relationships, then we can say that the intellectual process has broken free of the limitations imposed by set responses to specific stimuli and exemplifies cognition.

The experimental problems formulated by Pavlov or Skinner represent cognitive behavior; and no matter how elaborate or intensive the training they give their animals, the latter can never create an experimental situation in which their erstwhile experimenters become the subjects. This does not deny the importance of training in the development of an orderly intellect. But the neural complexity of man's cortex permits the synthesis of experience into new combinations. Furthermore, immediate stimulus to cerebral activity may be apparent, and set stimuli may yield variable responses. Indeed, this may be what those who write of creative thinking have in mind. It is the process of cognition.

The distinction between behavior based on training and that based on cognition is a useful one, but it still leaves some tough questions unasked and unanswered. As yet, we have hardly touched upon the problem of the response as a function of the stimuli. I prefer to phrase the problem differently, although the intent can remain the same. Of what relevance is the relation between an individual and his environment to the learning process? In this formulation the emphasis is directed to relationship and process, and the individual and environment are seen as variables. Specifically, both of the latter are seen as undergoing continuous change of greater or lesser magnitude; hence the consequences of the interdependency between them continuously vary.

This formulation is one that avoids the trap of assigning fixed attributes or qualities to an individual and the danger of accepting an enumeration of these as expressing either process or relationship. Furthermore, I believe that the relationship between the individual and his environment is the crucial problem if we are to understand the transmission of culture as a function of conditions. Among other things, this formulation recognizes the cultural system as one aspect of the environment.

But there is much more that needs to be examined, and the remainder of this chapter will address itself to the task at hand. In the development of the argument, we shall range widely over several disciplines for our facts. Physical anthropology will help us to understand the relationship between the individual as an organic being and the culture milieu. We will then turn to some of the findings in the field of culture and personality, and to the problem of cultural perspective. Next, we shall seek an example in the socialization of the child to exemplify the operation of cultural patterning. This, then, brings us to an analysis of the mechanisms of culture and their relation to learning. Finally, we shall attempt a synthesis of the evidence to provide a new formulation of the processes of the transmission of culture.

MAN AS A CULTURE-CREATING ANIMAL

Among the characteristics that distinguish man from other forms of animal life is his capacity for culture. But we hold a quite erroneous perspective if we separate for analysis and description the physical attributes of *Homo sapiens* and consider them as developing according to biological processes quite apart from the influence of culture. If we did so, we would then attribute to the human organism the inevitable capacity to achieve full physical maturity outside of the environmental influence that human society provides. The evidence does not support any such assumption. Instead, we are forced to accept, in the spheres of both phylogeny and ontogeny, an intricate arrangement of intermeshing influences between the physical and cultural aspects of man. Each helped to shape the other, and the point in time a million or more years ago when this process began can be justifiably called "The Human Revolution." [1]

It is not our purpose, nor is it necessary, to recount in detail the inferred effects of man's tool-making-and-using pattern of skills, his social groupings, or the appearance of articulate speech with its system of abstract symbols. What we do need to understand, however, is that man represents a unique form of animal life in the creation of a nonphysical, that is, cultural, environment, which, in turn, affected the selective process that led to the appearance of modern man.

There are, however, several much commented upon consequences of this evolutionary sequence that need to be mentiond. The human infant at birth, and for a considerable time thereafter, is incapable of survival outside of an environment that provides him with nurture. This dependency of the young upon its mother, or other adults, which is not necessarily restricted to man, is necessary because of its physical immaturity. One consequence of the prolonged dependency is that the individual in his progression toward maturity is subject to an intense and continuous period of learning. Thus the extended period of dependency may be seen as a function of the immense amount of learning that must be acquired in the context of the minimally developed physiological processes that accompany the individual at birth.

The fact that infants do progress from an original immature condition to full cultural and physical maturity is significant. From this fact we can infer that, given the conditions of a cultural environment and of the stage of physical and neural development at birth, the infant does possess the capacities for responding to this environment. Furthermore, the fact that this process is successfully achieved in all known varieties of culture establishes that any existent cultural environment is adequate for the human infant.

We must also decide, however, whether mere physical nurture, that is, an environment lacking culture, is sufficient for the human infant to achieve full humanity. The evidence upon which we can reach a conclusion is provided from many sources, but the most dramatic instances are those of feral man. Reports of other children who have lived virtually isolated from human contact substantiate the overwhelming importance of the environment in the shaping of the human infant.[2]

The conclusion to which this evidence leads us is that the achievement of full humanity is not an inevitable attribute of the human

[1] Charles F. Hockett and Robert Ascher, "The Human Revolution," *Current Anthropology*, V, No. 3 (1964), 135–147.

[2] Kingsley Davis, *Human Society* (New York: The Macmillan Co., 1949), pp. 204–208.

infant. Minimal physical nurture can ensure the survival of the individual, but other patterned behavior is essentially a function of the environment. When this evidence is joined with what studies of child development have provided, we feel secure in accepting the almost infinite impressionability of the human neural system, an impressionability the development of which is itself a function of the environment. If this is the case, then how, we might ask, is it possible to understand the processes of learning or the development of the child if we focus our attention upon the subject, and not upon the influences that shape him? Such a procedure ignores the dynamic interplay between subject and his cultural environment and minimizes or even excludes variability within the environment as a significant factor.

When we come to seek an explanation for the failure to take culture into account as a significant variable, there are several reasons that come quickly to mind. Most of those who have been doing research in this area have been trained in psychology and are generally not conversant with culture theory. The minimum advantage that flows from acquaintance with anthropological materials is that, through comparison of findings in several cultures, the danger of assuming a universal application is reduced.

Cross-cultural comparisons, however, can be a trap for the unsophisticated. The assumption that apparently similar culture traits or patterns are identical ignores the possibly divergent meaning each carries in its original context. Some anthropologists are now attempting to overcome this hazard by developing more comprehensive models that are based upon cognitive comparisons in which they utilize linguistic and relational analysis.[3] Their approach has not yet been sufficiently tested, however, to judge if it solves difficulties in comparative analysis.

The most relevant contribution thus far has come from those studies in which psychological theory has been combined with the methods of ethnology in the field of culture and personality. The several studies by Mead, Bateson, Linton, Hallowell, Whiting, Hsu, Honigmann, and others have focused attention upon child training practices as a mechanism for the transmission of culture. Although these studies provide great insights into the variability in the patterning of emotions as a function of cultural differences, very little effort has been made thus far either to describe the cognitive environment within which child training operates, or to ascertain how cognitive patterns are acquired or expressed in the child. Until this deficiency

[3] A. Kimball Romney and Ray Goodwin D'Andrade (eds.), "Transcultural Studies in Cognition," *American Anthropology,* LXVI, No. 3, Part II (1964); Anthony Wallace, "Culture and Cognition," *Science,* CXXXV (1962), 351–357.

has been corrected, it will remain impossible to construct an adequate theoretical model of learning in its relation to culture.[4] Nevertheless, anthropological studies have confirmed the validity of one enormously valuable principle through clarifying the origin and variability of *perspective* and in demonstrating how the cultural perspective provides the screen through which experience is filtered and interpreted.

In its most comprehensive sense, the perspective system is synonymous with world view. This is the system of thought and feeling that explains the operation of the universe. It makes meaningful to man such natural phenomena as the seasonal rhythms of nature, earth, and heaven, and the origin and destiny of life. It provides the rationale for explaining success, failure, and tragedy. It identifies things and their attributes and expresses relationships between them through categorization. In essence, the world view provides the orderly system through which the aspects of experience are identified and interpreted.

Everyday experience easily confirms the point. Whereas the sheep rancher views the wolf as a predator, the conservationist sees him as one element in a harmonious balance of nature. Whereas we rely upon knowledge of the physiology of the body for diagnosing and treating illness, the Navajo sees illness as an active intrusion into the body of a spirit; and the removal of the spirit is accomplished through ritual means.

Even within the realms of science, world view may inhibit or advance the understanding of the processes of nature. One of the more dramatic instances is that of the great scientific naturalist, Louis Agassiz, who refused to accept the implications of his own evidence, and that of others, which supported the concept of evolution.[5] Agassiz believed in a Divine Intelligence, which through acts of special creation populated the earth with life forms that were immutable and fixed. From time to time this Divinity caused catastrophes that wiped out all life but in a succeeding epoch brought forth new life forms that were divergent from the preceding period. From this *a priori* conception it was unnecessary and, in fact, impossible to accept any phylogenetic connection between earlier and later species as they were revealed through the succession of geologic strata. Agassiz believed that in his discovery and classification of species he was fashioning the pattern of a great divinely inspired cosmic plan. He even utilized his theory of an Ice Age to support his view of divinely inspired catastrophes.

[4] Solon T. Kimball, "Communication Modalities as a Function of Social Relationships," *Transactions of the New York Academy of Sciences*, XXV, No. 4 (1963), 459–468. (See Chapter 10 above.)

[5] Edward Lurie, *Louis Agassiz: A Life in Science* (Chicago: University of Chicago Press, 1960).

It seems unnecessary to aduce further examples to establish the point. A part of each culture is a system of identifying and interpreting the things and events that constitute experience. In fact, without the culturally induced perspective, experience is meaningless. Furthermore, we may posit that each such system operates within a framework of logical consistency and that it is possible to extract from the behavior of individuals those rules that explain categorization.

Perspective or world view, then, is more than the specific content of culture. It also contains the unstated premises that order thought and feeling. For those who would attempt to make these explicit, the problem they face is to develop those techniques that expose the structural logic of the culture they examine. Some of those who are working in the symbolic analysis of language, as did Whorf, are attempting to do just this. Their results will eventually be of great assistance in examining the transmission of culture, but in the meantime we must explore the problem with such knowledge as we possess.

Understanding of perspective and its variability does have direct relevance, however, for our central problem. It alerts us to the fact that we cannot understand the process of learning by a mere recounting of the sequence of stimuli the individual receives in passing through infancy to adulthood. Stimuli cannot be viewed as bits and pieces that somehow add up to a whole. They come to the subject from a cultural environment in which the perspective has already colored their meaning, and somehow they are received by the subject in the same manner. Otherwise we could not speak of cultural transmission at all, and an individual would present an idiosyncratic personality. Observation readily establishes that this is not the case, but until we know more about the relation of neural and cultural patterning, we cannot know how one may mirror the other. This should not deter us from seeking the consequence of this process as it is manifested in the behavior of the individual, nor from examining the pattern of the culture that has been embedded in a physical base.

CULTURAL PATTERNING AND LEARNING

It would seem that this is an appropriate time to examine what we mean by the patterning of culture and its relation to the socialization of the child. It will be remembered that considerable attention was given to the overwhelming importance of the environment in developing those capacities that make possible the physical, psychic, and cultural maturation of the child. It should also be remembered that variations in environment are reflected in the child's development. This being so, it would seem completely logical that examining the cultural environment itself could make explicit the learning process. This is, of course, what we must do because we must not rule out the possibility that the subject patterns his processes of learning from the influences exerted by those around him.

Although this proposal does not contradict our normal assumption that the infant is already prepared at birth to receive and organize stimuli, it does assert that the pattern of the organization of experience is a variable and is external to the infant in origin. What we insist on is that all the evidence supports the view that we cannot look to any innate neural tendency to fashion the impact of the cultural environment in a given direction. The restrictions imposed by the neural system upon the newly arrived, cultureless creature are minimal and give to the infant the capacity to cope with sensory experience of a limited kind only. The higher nervous centers are not yet organized; in fact, they are not fully developed. Only in mythology do we find godlike creatures, not humans, springing fully developed from their progenitors.

In humans, a determinate period must elapse before the child can respond to stimuli on other than a physical basis. Such a proposal does not deny, however, that all the stimuli flowing to the infant from its mother or other persons, as well as the type of physical environment provided for it, are not highly charged with cultural significance. The methods and rhythms of handling, suckling, cleaning, and comforting have been shown in study after study to be culturally variable and presumably significant in personality formation. (This latter supposition would be on much sounder ground if we knew what would happen if we transferred the child to a culturally different environment immediately preceding the appearance of the sense of self.)

The point I wish to make is that child-rearing practices impose upon the infant the necessity of adjusting to a particular set of stimuli and, by implication, to the distinctive cultural patterning they represent. Specifically, the infant must learn how to learn, an argument advanced by Gregory Bateson some time ago. This line of reasoning adds further support to those who have protested the validity of intelligence tests on the grounds that they are culturally biased, although in this instance the objection is advanced from a different basis. We would argue that the learning process, once acquired, varies from one culture to another, and in each instance organizes experiences differently.

Our understanding of the relation among culture, the mode of its transmission, and learning can be enriched and deepened if we turn now to empirical evidence provided by a study that is relevant to our focus. Most such research has been primarily concerned with the affective aspects of child rearing, and the failure to look at cognitive processes represents a real deficiency. With this limitation in mind, I have chosen a study of the Hopi Indians by Dorothy Eggan for illustrative purposes.[6] Her immediate concern is with "the emotional commitment involved in the socialization process." She contends that the Hopi were experts in the use of *affect* in their educational system, and that the results continued to be effective throughout the life span of the individual as a "reconditioning factor." She also argues that the internalized code of right behavior served as an effective social control for a society that lacked institutionalized means of individual restraint and punishment, and also added stability to the personality structure and to the society.

There are many aspects of Hopi life that need to be known if we are to understand the particular form in which their culture has been cast. We should know that the semi-desert environment in which they live imposes a precarious balance upon their ability to gain a livelihood through agriculture and some livestock grazing. The little villages in which they cluster atop the high mesas probably originally provided some protection against enemies, but also permitted them a better position from which to exploit the meager resources of their habitat. They are grouped in maternal clans, which regulate the obligations of their members and provide rules of residence and descent. They possess an elaborate calendar of religious observances; the participation in ceremonies is practically obligatory. When their children come to puberty, they are subject to initiation rites. Although this quick summary barely touches the richness and complexity of the cultural life, particularly that related to cosmology, it hopefully contributes some sense of the situation.

The emotional commitment of the Hopi is contained in the concept of the "good heart." It means a heart at peace with itself and one's fellows. There is no worry, unhappiness, envy, malice, nor any other disturbing emotion in a good heart. In this state, cooperation, whether in the extended household or in the fields and ceremonies, is selfless and easy. Unfortunately, such a conception of a good heart is also impossible of attainment.[7] But the Hopis also recognized the "bad heart—Kahopi," and when an individual was in this state he was threatened by imminent retribution manifested in illness or death, or other misfortune. But he might also cause harm to others

---

[6] Dorothy Eggan, "Instruction and Affect in Hopi Cultural Continuity." In George Spindler (ed.), *Education and Culture* (New York: Holt, Rinehart, and Winston, 1963), pp. 321–350.

[7] *Ibid.*, p. 338.

and even to the group as a whole. One who was not in a proper state of "grace" when ceremonies were performed and prayers offered might prevent rain and cause the crops to fail. For those who attempted to achieve or maintain the "good heart," the *burden* was enormous, not alone an individual one, but affecting the welfare of the universe, since they believed that the Hopi way of life had been bestowed when the world began, and only as it was perpetuated could the world continue.

The duality of good and evil, and the sense of burden, gain further significance when we add to them the concept of the "wall of Hopiness." We can think of it as a bounded area within which Hopiness prevails and expresses the separation of inside and outside. The tight relationships that bind a kin group might also be conceptualized as the wall that separates one clan from another. It reflects the sharp sense of identity that has been built on a commonality of origin, residence, and way of life. It would seem that we would be justified in viewing this cultural centripetality as a force of great potency and in harmony with the other concepts.

The origin and meaning of these concepts must be sought in the environment provided by the family, and in participation in religious practices. In the maternally organized household, usually including more than one generation, the infant learns to make distinctions among those who are his caretakers, distinctions that include the terms, obligations, and feelings toward those who are in one's kin group, toward the outperson or stranger, and also toward oneself as a reciprocally participating member of a group.

Implicit within these learned distinctions, feelings, and behavior are the categories, stated and unstated, that the cultural system provides. These include the dichotomy contained within sexual separation, ordination expressed in generations, the polar duality of good and evil, the inside-outside division based on the distinction of the right and familiar versus the strange and uncertain, the categories by which things and qualities are arranged, and a way of perceiving time, space, and process. These distinctions and arrangements constitute the cognitive pattern. They provide the logical framework upon which world view rests, and, when combined with the affective overtones that accompanied their acquisition, they provide the perspective within which all experience is seen and interpreted.

It would still be useful, however, to look at some of the devices that shape the child in the image of Hopi culture. Eggan emphasizes that the effect of the teaching effort was to inculcate in the child a sense of interdependence. Even the act of weaning, which in many societies is a beginning step in creating independence for the infant, among the Hopi led to a different consequence. Her apt statement follows:

He [the Hopi infant] was in no way *forced to find satisfactions within himself;* rather these were provided for him, if possible, by his household or clan group. His weaning, then, was from the breast only, and as he was being weaned from the biological mother he was at the same time in a situation which increased his emotional orientation toward the intimate in-group of the extended family which was consistent with the interests of Hopi social structure. Thus, considering weaning in its wider implications, a Hopi was never "weaned"; it was not intended that he should be. For these numerous caretakers contributed greatly to a small Hopi's faith in his intimate world and conversely without question to a feeling of strangeness and *emotional insecurity* as adults in any world outside of this emotional sphere.[8]

It is quite clear that the instruction was deliberate and persistent. What was relevant to kinship behavior was learned within the context of the event through patient and unceasing explanation and admonition until, by the time the Hopi was an adult, his "kinship reaction patterns were so deeply ingrained in his thinking and feeling, and in his workaday life, that they were as much a part of him as sleeping and eating." But any occasion could be utilized for the recitation of stories, adventures, journeys, or other experience that could illuminate for the child ". . . what it meant to be a good Hopi from a wide variety of determined teachers who had very definite and *mutually consistent* ideas of what a good Hopi is."

But the base upon which all instruction could be effective had been laid in the earliest years. The simplest acts were responded to from the polar reference of the Hopi definition of the "good heart." Offenders soon learned that their acts would evoke the condemning term "Kahopi" and serious offenses brought forth a stern isolation, the most severe of penalties in a world that rewarded interdependence. The desire to want to learn and to observe right behavior was further reinforced by the use of fear. Children were told that their misdeeds might attract the evil spirits, who either harm them or take them away. Thus, in these and other ways, an emotional base was laid from which all acts, theirs and those of others, could be judged against the ideal of the "good heart." What we must remember, however, is that, irrespective of the physiology of the human neural and glandular systems, their response to each stimulus, to each item of experience, was the consequence of a patterned learning that had its origin in culture.

[8] *Ibid.,* p. 329.

What is learned in childhood, however, nowhere completes the education that must be given if the cultural heritage is to be transmitted. In one sense childhood should be viewed as the period of preparation for the important knowledge that is still to come. Among those people who practice formal initiation ceremonies, usually at the time of puberty, we have the opportunity to observe the dramatic fashion in which the new learning is conveyed.

The analysis by Hart [9] of the differences between prepubertal and postpubertal education has helped enormously to clarify some of the problems related to learning and the transmission of culture. He argues that in most primitive societies the educational vehicle and its purposes in those two periods are clearly distinct. Education in the prepubertal period is provided primarily by one's intimates—the members of his family and the associates of his place of residence. He notes the variations, the wide latitude in practices, and even laxness in the insistence that learning occurs at a given time or place or under the supervision of designated personnel. It is true, of course, that a basic commonality exists within and between cultures in the practices observed by the nurturant group in bringing the infant to increasing stages of physical independence and in the training of bodily functions, but this constitutes only a small portion of the skills and knowledge that are learned from peers and adults.

Postpubertal education is an entirely different matter. Among those peoples who observe formal initiation ceremonies, and such practices are found among most primitive tribes, the pubescent members of the group are separated from their intimates, oftentimes forcibly, and subjected to periods of formal instruction that may last from several months to several years, depending upon traditional practice. Hart makes the significant observation that the personnel responsible for this period of instruction are different from the intimates of childhood because, among other reasons, the material of education, the manner of its preservation, and the urgency of its acquisition require a type of relationship and a type of knowledge that the group of intimates could not provide.

Hence, this responsibility is vested in "strangers," who, even though they may be known to the initiates, represent a different, sometimes hostile, segment of tribal organization. Where such internal divisions do not exist, and intimates carry out the initiation practices, the fiction of strangers is created by the use of masks.

Deeper understanding of the relevance of initiation ceremonies

<hr/>

[9] C. W. M. Hart, "Contrasts Between Prepubertal and Postpubertal Education." In George Spindler (ed.), *Education and Culture* (New York: Holt, Rinehart and Winston, 1963), pp. 400–425.

can be gained through a brief excursion into the theory of *rites de passage*.[10] Over a half century ago, van Gennep noted that those occasions on which an individual was in transition from one status or category to another were marked by ceremonies. These included the universal life crises of birth, puberty, marriage, and death, but also included other situations in which changes in behavior or group identification were involved. In many of these ceremonies there was a ritually enacted simulation of death and of a subsequent rebirth into the new condition. Van Gennep also noted a structural arrangement of the sequences into three phases. The initial phase, in which the connections with a current way of life were severed, he called *separation*. The individuals, or, in the case of puberty ceremonies, the neophytes, then found themselves in an intermediate stage, in which they were neither of one group nor another; they were *not-beings*.[11] This liminal condition was labeled *transition*. In the final stage of *incorporation*, the individual returned to the group, but into a different social niche and with altered behavior.

From a societal point of view the most significant *rite de passage* is initiation into tribal membership and adulthood at puberty. The ceremony marking this event may be quite brief, but it may also extend over a lengthy time period, depending upon the nature of the instruction that must be given. Even among those groups that do not have formal observance of physiological puberty as the point in time for initiation, there are other occasions or educational devices that serve the same purposes and incorporate the basic ritual and instructional aspects. The important point is that each society does have ways to *claim* the young.[12]

In those societies in which the origin and operation of the universe is viewed from the perspective of supernatural forces, instruction in and revelation of religious mysteries constitute a major portion of the knowledge that is transmitted during the period of initiation. In contrast, instruction is not in the mundane matters of how to make a living or to build a house, nor even in the private magical practices that accompany so many activities. This useful knowledge is gained elsewhere. In Australian tribes, for example, the neophytes are taught theology—the mythology that explains the origin and meaning of life,

10 Arnold van Gennep, *The Rites of Passage* (Chicago: University of Chicago Press, 1960) (Paris: 1909).

11 Victor W. Turner, "Betwixt and Between: the Liminal Period in Rites de Passage. Symposium on New Approaches to the Study of Religion." *Proceedings of the 1964 Annual Spring Meeting of the American Ethnological Society* (Seattle: University of Washington Press, 1964), pp. 4–20.

12 Solon T. Kimball and James E. McClellan, Jr., *Education and the New America* (New York: Random House, 1962), chap. x.

the sacred songs and prayers, and the ritual and dances of world-renewal ceremonies. Much of this knowledge must be acquired so precisely that, in theory, there is no deviation from generation to generation in ceremonial performance.

Hart interprets postpubertal education as preparation for citizenship and argues,

Citizenship training in these societies . . . means exposing the boy under particularly stirring and impressive conditions to the continuity of the cultural tradition, to the awe and majesty of the society itself, emphasizing the subordination of the individual to the group at large and hence the mysteriousness, wonder, and sacredness of the whole individual-society relationship.[13]

If we turn once again to the particulars of Hopi culture, we can not only exemplify the relevance of the analysis but also extend our own perspective. The induced striving to achieve the "good heart" and to learn to follow the Hopi way of life is not an individual goal in our sense of the word. Our perspective could readily equate the individually centered orientation, as it has been described, with the ultimate goal of self-fulfillment, which our own culture emphasizes. The similarity is a superficial one and to treat it otherwise would lead us astray.

For the Hopi, self-perfection serves a larger purpose. Their mythology posits a preestablished universal order, but in order that this cosmic orderliness be actualized it is necessary to have man's cooperation. In such a formulation, we are again witness to the *interdependence* of basic Hopi thought and social behavior. Man is also a necessary aspect of the universe and without his contribution and only through the fulfillment of his part can what might be exist. The responsibility constitutes a cosmic burden that can only be properly discharged by those whose moral rightness is manifested in the striving for the "good heart." Hence the linkage between the private life of the individual and the public life of the society. Hence also the distinction between the instruction and training received from one's intimates in childhood and the formal education that begins with a first initiation between the ages of six and ten, and a subsequent initiation ceremony eight to ten years later. The learning of the values, mythology, and ceremonies of the society is further extended in the years that follow.

It is true that the initiation ceremony marks the separation of the individual from his childhood and from other children, and his entry into the public and adult world, but it is also much more. When the

13 Hart, "Prepubertal and Postpubertal Education," p. 420.

Katchinas—the gods—are unmasked and the realization breaks through that these are mortal men among whom are some you know, there follows the destruction of the illusion, the loss of childhood innocence, the final separation from childhood, but also the realization of man's part in a great cosmic scheme.

Before we begin the next part of our analysis, it might be well to recapitulate briefly our original objectives and the relevance of the description and analysis to these. The search for an understanding of the conditions affecting the transmission of culture constitutes our primary goal. Toward this end we have, first of all, argued for the validity of the distinction between affective and cognitive learning. The stimulus-response paradigm appears as adequate to explain affective and skill learning, although it is not realized through simple, additive repetition. It seems, however, that we must look to some other mechanism to explain cognitive learning. We were also interested in establishing the cultural fashioning of the how and what of learning and to show that the stimulus-response connection is itself a variable of the cultural environment.

We wanted to show next the distinction in the educational approach and personnel for prepubertal and postpubertal education and to relate this to subject matter and objective. In particular, we wanted to draw attention to the fact that the stuff of the deliberate and highly patterned instruction of the postpubertal period was knowledge, although we cannot exclude the influence of the affective context within which it was imparted, nor the affective disposition the individual carried into the situation from childhood experience.

But the preschool learning includes much more than the organization of instincts and emotions—the ethos, as described by Bateson and Mead.[14] It also includes the acquisition of the tools with which the world can be apprehended symbolically, the facility of language, and the patterns of differentiation of things, events, relationships, and processes. These are the intellectual tools that can be used quite apart from any affective predisposition. They constitute the basic *sine qua non* of intellectual efforts in learning the knowledge or subject matter of formal schooling. The instruction may focus upon mythology and sacred ceremonies as exemplified by initiation rites, or it may be organized in formal courses under the rubrics of mathematics, grammar, logic, and science.

There is, however, a basic similarity in the instructional content of either "bush" school or classroom. In both, not only is there trans-

[14] Gregory Bateson and Margaret Mead, *Balinese Character: A Photographic Analysis* (Reprinted 1962; New York: New York Academy of Science Special Publication, 1942).

mitted knowledge and a way of thinking about such, the whole of which we may call world view, but also there is transmitted the criteria by which events may be analyzed and judged. The use of these criteria in the understanding process represents the epitome of cognitive learning. Among the Hopi, for example, everything ranging from simple good fortune to catastrophic drought can be placed in the interpretive reference of individual behavior or of cosmic process. Let it be said now that the problem is not one of testing the validity of such interpretations against our own explanations of the workings of the laws of nature. It is quite certain that each contestant examining a specific event from his own perspective would inevitably be guided by his own rules of evidence, logic, and process in rendering a decision. How else can we understand an Agassiz, a Darwin, a Hopi priest, or a Murngin elder? Nor is the problem of who is right or wrong ours to consider; it leads us astray. The problem is to make explicit the criteria and the mechanisms that explain cognition and ultimately to examine these for their relevance to formal education. It is to that problem that we now turn.

CULTURE AND COGNITION

There are several approaches to the study of the relation between culture and cognition that promise fruitful results, and eventually all of these should be used. The analysis of the internal structure of language, as developed by Whorf,[15] has yielded early rich rewards. His procedure shows that certain thought processes are derived from the structure of the language employed by the speakers. Language may also be examined as a tool in communication or studied semantically as a system of symbols. But its study may also be approached from the more purely cultural perspective, in which it is treated as one aspect of culture.

The approach used by social anthropologists introduces a rather different perspective. Their intellectual tradition stems from Comte through Durkheim and Radcliffe-Brown, to those contemporary anthropologists who are seeking the processes of change through study of the structure of human groupings and their relation to other aspects of the environment. From this perspective, all symbolism, of which language is a significant part, may be understood as a hypostatization of social reality. Warner utilizes this approach in his analysis

[15] Benjamin Lee Whorf, "Language, Thought, and Reality." In John B. Carroll (ed.), *Selected Writings of Benjamin Lee Whorf* (Cambridge: Technology Press of Massachusetts Institute of Technology, 1942).

of Murngin totemism.[16] Patterning of behavior as a function of culture
has been utilized constantly. The specification of these approaches
here recognizes their contribution and shows the breadth of the conceptual base from which this analysis proceeds. They will be implicit
in much of what follows.

In this chapter, I have consistently insisted that the learning
process must be viewed as an aspect of the cultural milieu. Since culture is transgenerational, we should find in culture those clues that
could explain both what and how the child learns. But our effort must
also be transcultural if we are to abstract what has universal relevance.
Since it is the screen of cultural perspective through which experience
is received, ordered, and acted upon, our problem is to identify those
commonalities that encompass all cultures irrespective of their substantive divergences.

There are three such commonalities that I believe to be universally present; namely, the categories of knowledge, the canons of
discrimination, and process as a function of relationship between
variables.

Each individual who has participated in the full range of cultural
experiences appropriate to his sex and status possesses a set of categories that permit him to distinguish and classify individuals, things,
qualities, events, and processes. The language he speaks contains the
verbal referents for all such distinctions and may itself be analyzed
for grammatical structure. Among such other commonly agreed upon
categories are those of order, class, number, shape, time, and space.
These *agreed upons,* not just the label they carry but the basis upon
which groupings of similar and dissimilar may be made, are part of
the cultural heritage, which is transmitted in a multitude of ways, and
which makes possible meaningful communication among cultural
similars. In our society, those who operate from private symbol systems
are often institutionalized or, if they are artists, may be considered as
avant-garde and tolerated in the hope that they may be expressing
something significant.

The social base of such categories is readily apparent in the terminology of any kinship system and in the acquisition of identifying
terms and appropriate behavior easily observable in parental teaching of the young. In the acquisition of such knowledge, the child
also learns implicitly the more inclusive distinctions based upon sex,
age, generation, descent, and sequence through birth order. For example, in the kinship terminology used by Navajo Indians, all those

16 W. L. Warner, *A Black Civilization* (New York: Harper and Row, 1937).

who use the reciprocal term of "sister" for each other are called "mother" by their children. The extension of the principle contained within this system of categorizing means that you apply the term "sister" to all those who are daughters of the persons you call "mother." The further fact that both classes of persons (mothers and sisters) are sexually taboo excludes them from the group from which one may choose a marriage partner. When categories and the process of categorizing are extended to all experience, we can see how extensive, comprehensive, or orderly is the cultural framework. We should also note its stability, since it is embedded in the language, expressed in mythology, and governs the thought processes.

If the categories of knowledge are supraindividual, so also are the canons of discrimination.[17] Here we are concerned with two aspects, each one of which must be treated separately, although they are related. The learning of identities is only one step in acquiring a cognitive framework. The individual must also learn the criteria that make identification possible and permit classification of the item of experience in the larger whole. Not only must each individual learn the basis upon which items are classified, but he must also learn the criteria that permit him to evaluate and hence to respond.

From our knowledge of how cultural interconnections exhibit an internal consistency, we can infer that evaluative responses are expressions of a coherent system. Our analysis of Hopi affective patterns supports this view. Our goal, then, is not only to discover the canons that order the system, but also to make explicit the criteria upon which these are based. Being unstated assumptions of behavior, their exposure will not be easy. Knowledge of them cannot be gained by blunt question and answer approaches; they must be pried out through processes of inference utilizing linguistic, mythologic, and behavioral data. Only with the appearance of the conscious questing of the practitioners of science has it been possible for us to even begin to discover these wellsprings of human thought. We cannot assume, however, that they lie buried in the unconscious of the human psyche or that they spring from an assumed inner force. Rather, we shall gain knowledge of them from culture itself. If we accept the supraindividual sources of discrimination and of the canons that govern their use, then we must accept cultural variability in the criteria by which one identifies and evaluates. What is culturally universal is the process by which canons and criteria are transmitted.

This brings us to the consideration of process as the third member of our group of cultural commonalities. We have defined process

17 See Chapter 11 above.

as a function of change in the relationships among variables. Sometimes these changes may be seen as a consequence of modification in the magnitude or quality of variables, and sometimes they may be due to changes in the conditions within which a system operates. Further elaboration of this terse statement is necessary.

Relatively little attention has been given thus far to the analysis of the internal dynamics of culture as viewed from the internal vantage of a specific cultural perspective. The task would be far from easy, since it would require two sets of intellectual tools. It would require, first, an adequate general theory of social and cultural change; and, secondly, a theory of change, or process, viewed from within each culture. Few people would grant that a general theory now exists, although Marxian and Freudian theorists make such claims. Such a theory could be the base from which cultural data would be probed for the purpose of yielding another theory of change specific to the culture under study. It is quite probable that we shall win through to such a model only through the slow, laborious process of inductive empiricism. It *is* possible, however, to designate some of the data that must be examined and the direction in which we can proceed.

The simplest formulation of what we are seeking is contained in the question, "How do things happen?" Now the mythologies of the various cultures of the world provide an explanation to their members of how the universe came to be. In content these creation myths vary widely. Some specify set stages of development with the appearance of man in a culminating epoch. Others see the tension between natural forces as essential to creation. In some, a transcendental power effectuates a divine plan, or a mythological culture hero prepares the way for man and lays down the rules of life. There are some cultures in which their myths express only a feebly developed sense of beginning. The direct comparison of the contextual material of differing cultures has been tried time and again and does not yield much, but there is another approach that holds great promise.

The difficult problem, of course, is to hit upon a method of analysis that will yield results of a kind we are seeking. If we could examine mythological events of a given people within their context of time, then we might begin to make meaningful the pattern of rhythm and sequence as they see it. If the cycle of birth and death, or the succession of the seasons or of other recurrences, are contained in these accounts, then we can compare them to seek for the framework of repetition. But we must also examine the explanations that accompany the descriptions. In these we must search for the relationships that explain emergence, becoming, being, and ending. Hopefully, this approach will yield the principles of process for which we seek.

The activity suggested above, however, is only one phase of our quest. We must subject the ongoing communal life to the same kind of examination, seeking out the time patterning as men join and separate in activities. And finally, we must see what the structure of language reveals. Hopefully, we might some day be able to establish the connections among all of these. The rich rewards garnered by the few who have begun the exploration give great promise.

Let us not forget that the same purposes are to be served in the applicability of this approach to modern science, philosophy, or theology. We must make explicit the pattern of the process by which we interpret events. We seek the processes of nature in the cyclotron, in experiments with substances and animals, and in the observation of plant and animal life in their ecological settings. But we must also make explicit the process by which we achieve results, for this is the essence of education. These are the tools of cognition. In the systems of categorization and discrimination and their associated criteria and in the conceptualization of process, we find cognitive commonalities that are transcultural.

CONCLUSION

If we view the primary function of education as the transmission of culture, then what is unique to education are the conditions that govern its process. Process is a variable relationship of two systems, the social and cultural environment, which prescribes the method and content of education, and the individual in whom experience is organized and internalized.

From each segment of the culture comes knowledge of a different sort. Within the family the child is trained in bodily functions, kinship behavior, and household skills. In institutionalized schooling the child is taught by strangers. In both, the child learns body skills and affective and cognitive behavior, although the emphasis will vary from one to another. Presumably, experience is cumulative, but the differential of the limits for performance between training and cognitive development remains largely unexplored. It is possible that the affective disposition of most persons has been set in early childhood, particularly so if there are no changes in the conditions of life. Certainly one of the conditions that affect the transmission of culture is the nurturant environment of the infant. It is here that the individual is prepared to be culturally acquisitive. Since what happens here is apparently so crucial to what happens later, and because the content and method of education in early childhood are substantially different from that of formal schooling, knowledge of the process of the preparation of the infant for responding to cultural experience is a basic concern in education.

We must turn to the social and cultural environment itself to discover the other applicable conditions. We should distinguish, however, between those we call operational and those we call conceptual. The former includes all those informal or institutional arrangements that a society provides for instruction. It should also include the organization of the presentation of subject matter and, as a separate category, the relationship between teacher and learner. In essence, the operations in cultural transmission subsume the how to do it.

Although the conceptual conditions that affect the transmission of culture are of far greater significance, because in these are found the stuff of full humanity, they have been left largely implicit in educational theory. From these conditions comes the perspective that is reflected in world view. The rules that govern the organization and evaluation of knowledge and explain the processes of change are to be found here. In them are the oftentimes unstated assumptions that make experience meaningful. In them are the guideposts for learning itself.

All of the conditions that affect the transmission of culture constitute a proper, if not exclusive, concern of educators. It is my belief that in the study of the mechanisms of cognition, seen as functions of social and cultural reality, educators can gain the understanding that is essential to the process of education.

PART III

Development
Through
Education

13. INTRODUCTION: INTERNATIONAL COOPERATION AND EDUCATION

National development, broadly defined, encompasses much more than progressive government policies and economic productivity. It should also include humanistic goals that guarantee to all men the opportunity to lead full lives in harmony with nature and their fellow men. Its achievement is primarily an educational responsibility and the task is an urgent one because, if we cannot solve the problems of environmental destruction, resource conservation, unchecked population growth, and international aggression, there is small chance that we shall survive long.

Each epoch has its own prophets of doom. Only recently, however, has total world devastation, through atomic war or pollution, become potentially real. The prescience of Lewis Mumford is most remarkable. In 1938, in his *The Culture of Cities*, he wrote:

> Today our world faces a crisis: a crisis which, if its consequences are as grave as now seems, may not fully be resolved for another century. If the destructive forces in civilization gain ascendancy, our new urban culture will be stricken in every part. Our cities, blasted and deserted, will be cemeteries for the dead: cold lairs given over to less destructive beasts than man. But we may avert that fate: perhaps only in facing such a desperate challenge can the necessary creative forces be effectually welded together.

Little did Mumford realize, when he wrote these words, the extent of the power of destruction that was to appear within a decade. But for our world, fear and hate are destructive forces of even greater

"Education: The Foundation of International Cooperation," *Teachers College Record*, Vol. 56, No. 5 (February 1955), pp. 252–254.

magnitude. These evils are rooted in ignorance, and our effective weapon for their defeat is to extend the understanding of the common purposes of mankind. Only if we achieve victory here can we convert to productive goals the knowledge of physical energies that now threaten total destruction.

The creative forces of which Mumford speaks are found ultimately in men as they join together to meet problems, the nature of which they understand and the solution to which they believe attainable. It is at this point that the world must turn to education, for only through the process of learning can man hope to overcome his difficulties. And the knowledge must extend to the relations among nations.

International cooperation is both an ideal and a necessity. The requirement is based upon our need to survive. From one viewpoint we are already living in the "One World," which Wendell Willkie extolled. Industrial technology has swept away the space barriers that once separated nations and continents.

The age-long search by man for knowledge that will permit him to provide the essentials of the good life through the utilization of the world's resources has, for all practical purposes, been solved. But new techniques for resource conservation and use must be developed and accepted. We are alert to the problem, however, and there are many programs by public and private agencies to bring advanced techniques of production, health, and education into operation.

The serious and as yet unsolved problem is to bring order into the relations among men. It is all too apparent that the world does not yet possess those devices that permit the constructive solutions of its social problems. The newspapers provide a daily record of tensions arising from population dislocations, cultural antipathies, economic stress, nationalist sensitivities, and the crumbling of traditional beliefs and customs.

We are in a period of deep-seated and radical change. Toynbee and other historians have labeled the period as one of world revolution, the source of which is the shift from an agrarian to an urban-industrial civilization.

During the past five hundred years there has been continued acceleration in the process of change. The growth of cities has been accompanied by industrial advances, which have enormously expanded productivity. Water power, coal, and oil have provided quantities of energy immensely greater than could be derived from men and animals. New institutional arrangements have been devised to coordinate the complexity of technical processes. Cultural beliefs and practices have been modified.

The penetration of technical processes, social forms, and concepts of the new Euro-American civilization has only begun to reach the older civilizations of Asia. Most of the people in such countries as China and India continue to live under a cultural tradition that extends back several millenia. There are serious dangers that the response to accelerated change will produce regressive reaction.

It is an awful thing when the certainties of traditional ways are seen to be illusions and the cry for security drives men to accept political tyrannies that represent an enslavement far more deadly to the human spirit than is the parochial world-view of an agrarian civilization. Nor has Western civilization been immune to the sickness. Totalitarianism has had brief but terrible flights to power in Italy and Germany, and is a built-in aspect in Communist countries. Unfortunately, the United States has harbored a few whose tormented minds have driven them to deny the dignity of human spirit in their demand for conformity.

These forces of reaction and despair seem to appear when education has not had an opportunity to function, or has failed. Education has already proved that it can open the way for peoples emerging from an agrarian civilization to grapple with new economic and social problems. In the United States, the development of industrialism was accompanied by a great popular movement that included the ideal of universal education and in a few decades resulted in a nation-wide system of public schools and state colleges and universities. Through this educational system has come a broadening of the horizons that may lead to an understanding of problems and peoples of the world.

It is inevitable and proper that each country should develop the distinctive institutional arrangements that give expression to its cultural forms, and that these will vary from our own. It is reasonable to expect, however, that as traditional beliefs and customs continue to crumble among agrarian peoples, there will arise increased demands for systems of education that meet the new needs. It is indeed doubtful that these needs are now being adequately met anywhere. The emphasis upon development of technical skills must be balanced with social skills and a point of view that provides the basis for understanding the necessity for world cooperation.

Universal education is a requirement of a high energy, complex society. But the question that still remains to be answered is, what kind? It is a universal responsibility to make certain that the content of education meets the needs of a world in which no portion can longer remain isolated.

A listing of the specific functions of education would include the transmission of the cultural heritage. In itself this is not enough. Tribal groups and village peoples have preserved their cultural views and practices from generation to generation with considerable success. The modern world demands that education interpret and translate the advancing knowledge within the arts, sciences, and humanities to the contemporary generation. This task is vastly more difficult than that required when our civilization was agrarian based. And educators who work in predominantly agrarian countries face additional problems as they attempt to reconcile the traditional world with the one that is emerging.

The assumption that the spread of technological skills alone can be the answer of the free world to the solution of stress within our own or agrarian societies is narrow and naïve. If we continue to choose this field as our battleground, we are almost certain of defeat. The task is much broader.

Education must bring to all peoples the understanding of their relation to nature, to each other, and to other cultures. It can provide insights into the sweep of world forces and interpret change. It can demonstrate the immense creativity of mankind when faced with new problems. Finally, through education can come the understanding of the basic dignity of man and of the universality of humanity. It is on this broad base that the solution of international problems through cooperative effort may be accomplished and it should be to this goal that we dedicate ourselves.

14. COMMUNITY STUDY AND APPLIED ANTHROPOLOGY IN INTERNATIONAL EDUCATION

In the decades following the end of World War II the world has experienced a vast cooperative effort in nation building. The Marshall Plan, the first of several major efforts, was designed to rebuild the war-ravaged countries of Western Europe. Equally dramatic results were achieved under military government in the occupied countries of Germany and Japan. In the Third World, in Asia, Africa, and South America, the new countries that had emerged from the collapse of colonialism and older nations that had lain economically dormant for a century or so also began to clamor for the capital and technology that would assist them to become modern states. The response to this need came rapidly in the creation of new agencies and programs and the invigoration of some older ones. The more active ones are well known and include UNESCO, the International Bank for Reconstruction and Development, the Point Four program of the United States (now known as the Agency for International Development), and a few private foundations.

The Western nations, with their advanced technology and high standard of living, provided the model of aspiration. Initially it was believed that large infusions of capital accompanied by industrial equipment and technical know-how were the ingredients necessary to overcome economic backwardness. But the planners soon learned that the engineers, agriculturists, and economists, which this simple formulation called for, were insufficient to achieve the goal. A modern nation is much more than its productive capabilities. It also includes personnel possessing a vast range of organizational, technical, and in-tellectual skills, and these become available only through a modern educational system. The building of such a system is a slow and costly undertaking and it is not surprising that many of the underdeveloped nations turned to UNESCO, the United States, and other Western nations for assistance.

The host nations represented extraordinarily diverse cultural and educational traditions. For example, Korea still clung to the classical form of Chinese scholarship; in Afghanistan and the Middle East, one encountered Moslem instruction based on the Koran as well as modern academies; in most of Latin America, nineteenth-century French pedagogy and scholasticism were dominant; in Africa, the school system of each new nation was an attenuated version of the one that the colonial overlords had imported from the homeland.

With rare exceptions, the educators recruited to serve in these various countries were not only unacquainted with the specifics of its people and history but had had no training to prepare them to work in a cross-cultural setting. Furthermore, they were incapable of recognizing their own deficiencies. They were primarily educational programers operating from a set of culture-bound principles that, however appropriate these may have been for the tradition of their own society, were usually ill suited for another. Such a cast of mind excludes the necessity for both research and experimentation. They neither knew, nor if they had known would have considered the knowledge of any consequence, that the forms of cooperation and the styles of learning vary from one culture to another and that educational procedures, as is true in other fields of endeavor, must be adapted to the situation. Nor should one be surprised that the reaction of some host countries to these efforts led to charges of cultural imperialism—in truth an unwitting arrogance of superiority cloaked under the guise of helpfulness.

Unfortunately, there have been few resources in the pedagogical tradition that might act as an antidote to cultural narrowness. The subject matter of comparative education would have been helpful if it had been utilized. But its traditional emphasis upon the formal, legal, and institutional variations in national educational systems conveyed little about the connection between education and other institutions in a society and nothing about the processes of planning and innovation. The need to bring educational advisement into touch with reality was of some urgency. In some instances economists and sociologists were included in the survey teams that developed national plans. Even a bit of the anthropological perspective began to filter into considerations of problems. As the awareness arose of the need to break out of the restrictions of educational ethnocentrism, there began to emerge a new breed of professional educator, one whose interest was cross-national and cross-cultural and whose training encompassed both pedagogy and social science. The breed is still struggling to acquire a certified pedigree and there is still no agreement among them on a patronym, whether it is to be called comparative, developmental, or international education. It is still too soon to draw the sharp boundaries of method and subject area as a separate discipline, and the definition by Bill Sayres of international education "as a kind of bastard son of education and the Holy Grail" seems apt enough.

In the metaphor of eugenics the mixing of breeds is chancey. The offspring may be a nondescript mongrel or it may reaffirm the principle that mixed ancestry creates hybrid vigor. The immediate task before us is to specify those aspects of anthropology that will strengthen the heritage. Initially, however, we should inform ourselves of the dimensions of this new specialization if our recommendations are to be wise ones.

Professional activities of practitioners in the field of international education are many faceted. They may elect a career that encompasses the traditional academic functions of teaching and research or they may utilize their skill in some appropriate governmental or private agency. At some one time or another, however, they are almost certain to be asked to cross cultural boundaries and to develop programs that involve the modernization of existing educational systems or to plan new innovations. In this cross-cultural setting they may be employed as consultants, as planners, or as administrators.

Granted the variety of interest and practice prevalent among those who are international educationists it is possible, nevertheless, to delineate three major areas of concern and activity. It may be viewed as a body of subject matter organized in a curriculum; it is an area of professional training and practice; and it may be considered as a procedure or working method to be utilized in educational development. Stated differently, its three components are those of knowledge or subject matter gathered through the methods of survey and research; the teaching and training of students; and the formulation of programs and their implementation. With this formulation as our operating framework, we can now turn our attention to examining those aspects of anthropology that have relevance for the future development of cross-cultural education.

Community-study method and applied anthropology are the two branches of anthropology that offer immediate basic assistance in the growth of international education. The former includes a perspective of human behavior, concepts and procedures for research, and permits comparative analysis between peoples of divergent cultures. As a method it provides the means by which knowledge about educational

organization and process can be examined within the whole of surrounding institutions and practices.

The growth of applied anthropology in the past several decades has
been concurrent and parallel with that of community studies. In fact,
only from understanding the interdependencies that permit us to see
communities as wholes has it also been possible to anticipate the consequences of planned innovations or those that flow from modifications
in the conditions that affect humans in organizations. Its theoretical
focus has been that of the processes of change, the professional focus
has been one of strategies and tactics for planning and implementing
change.

Both of these fields are important to the development of international education, since they will help to solve some problems that are
inherent in it. For example, the programmatic and professional orientation of education has not, until recently at least, evidenced any major
concern for educational research or experimentation and only to a
limited extent through comparative education has it developed any
cross-cultural perspective. Furthermore, international education cannot achieve the stature it seeks if it is to perpetuate the ethnocentric
blindness and institutional parochialism that hobbles its parent, professional education. Hence it must turn elsewhere for its perspective,
its research method, and even the style of its programmatic planning
and procedures. Let us examine first the matter of perspective.

Belatedly, and much more as rhetoric rather than as practice,
educationists have come to recognize that cultural differences affect
the response to educational programs and the consequences that flow
from them. Such a view challenges two linked assumptions that have
prevailed previously—that it is possible to achieve an embracing and
universal philosophy of education, and that psychological research can
unravel the mysteries of learning and lead to the formulation of a
pan-human learning theory. Anthropological findings challenge both
of these beliefs as ethnocentric and monolithic. The evidence indicates
that in the world view of each of the distinct peoples of the world
there can be found an implicit philosophy of education and of learning
appropriate to each specific culture. And furthermore, all educational
innovations must pass through the cognitive and affective perceptual
screen of the recipients and hence become modified through incorporation, and can be understood only within a preexisting context. Moreover, the assumption that educational organization and processes can
be transferred from one society to another and be expected to achieve
the same effects in the recipient culture is utterly ridiculous. Such an
assumption is equally invalid in the United States and other Western

nations, where regional, ethnic, and social class differences furnish a welter of sub-cultural variation.

These sub-cultural variations are even more pronounced in many non-Western nations of the world, particularly in those that have recently emerged from colonial status and whose territories reflect an administrative unit of a former political master and do not constitute a culturally homogeneous one. Even in nations with a much longer history of political independence, such as Mexico or Peru and others in the New World, the cultural distinctions between separate indigenous tribes and the descendants of the migrants from the Iberian peninsula are sharp. Even the homelands of the colonizing nations were far from homogeneous, as the long history of conflict among Welsh, Irish, Scot, and Saxon of Great Britain so readily attests. Such obvious cultural variability causes us to raise a question about the very usefulness of the rubric "international education" if that term assumes an equivalence of political boundary and educational process. Descriptive summaries of educational institutions and practices, interpretive evaluations, or innovative programs even among long established nation-states must be considered highly suspect unless they make explicit the variabilities. It is here that the conceptual and research tools of community study and area delineation in anthropology can be of such value.

COMMUNITY STUDY

In ethnographic reports, the anthropologist describes the forms of human organization—their social organization—the behavior of people, and the shape and distribution of their settlements. From these he can specify the boundaries of a contiguous culture area. He knows, for example, that Nigeria holds such diverse peoples as the Tiv, the Hausa, the Ibo, and the Yoruba, and because of this he also has some clearer understanding of the internal stresses between distinct tribal groups, which in the Nigerian instance led to tribal slaughter and civil war. A plan for national educational modernization that does not take into account such cultural distinctions can be little better than a pious statement of generalities and aspirations.

The intensive study of sample communities within a culture area provides us with overview of the social and cultural characteristics of an entire population. Julian Steward, who affirmed that anthropology's major contribution to area research was through community study, had this to say:

The purposes and methods of community studies are extremely varied, but their importance for area research is that they all apply a cultural or ethnographic method to contemporary society. This method was developed by anthropology in the study of primitive peoples, and it is being applied to modern societies by anthropologists and by sociologists who have some knowledge of anthropology. . . . Applied to primitive tribes, this approach has three distinctive methodological aspects. First, it is ethnographic: the culture of a tribe, band, or village is studied in its totality, all forms of behavior being seen as functionally independent parts in the context of the whole. Second, it is historical: the culture of each society is traced to its sources in ancestral or antecedent groups or among neighboring peoples. Third, it is comparative: each group is viewed in the perspective of other groups which have different cultures, and problems and methods are used cross-culturally.[1]

Very considerable advances in theory and method have been achieved since 1950 and community-study method now stands as one of the major instrumentalities of social science. The method has been described in detail elsewhere along with exemplifying case studies.[2] It should be remembered, however, that the purpose of such study is to use the community as a setting in which the interconnections between social and psychological facts and processes are examined *in vivo*. It should also be remembered that in this view community presents a model or "master system" linking culture and society. An extract from Arensberg's analysis follows:

First, to be specific, a social scientist using the community-study method must choose a community which is a "whole," a "full round of local life." He must try to find a community in which he can at least hope to take a "cross-section" or a "sample" of the society and the culture of the person showing the social and psychological behavior or problem he is interested in. A community study is thus necessarily comparative, at least implicitly, since one such whole of human social and cultural experience must be alike or different from another. . . .

Second, and again specifically, a social scientist using community study must choose many, not just a few, techniques of observation and data collection. To date depth interviewing, participant observation, sociometrics, collecting genealogies, house-to-house canvasses, collecting cases, content-analyzing documents, to name just a few techniques usable under the community-study method, have been used quite widely. For it is the material, not the problem, that requires a manifold and flexible use of techniques. . . .

The reason is simply that a community study is nothing if not "multi-

[1] Julian H. Steward, *Area Research: Theory and Practice* (New York: Social Science Research Council, 1950), p. 21.

[2] Conrad M. Arensberg and Solon T. Kimball, *Culture and Community* (New York: Harcourt, Brace & World, 1965).

factorial." To explore the natural, living setting of a problem necessarily involves concurrent attacks upon all the relevant factors at a single time, the moment of observation. . . .

Third among the special and specific characteristics of community study is the need to reject and rework data already extant describing the community under study or its facets. . . . It means not that the student ignores extant information but rather that he cannot accept it as it stands: too many false or irrelevant assumptions incrust it.

Particularly where the community studies have been made upon complex modern literate societies is the need to rework acute. In such studies authors have quite rightly drawn heavily upon existing economic and statistical data, on local records and histories, and on court records and newspaper files. But they have had to do things with them other than their compilers have either yet done or even intended. . . .

This fourth and last specific and special characteristic of the method (structural, qualitative, topographical) goes back, of course, to one of its origins, to the anthropological attempts to describe unknown cultures and social "wholes." Here again clarity in social science seems only slowly to be emerging, and controversy is still rife. Where a "whole round" of local life, patterning human interaction, human expression and aspiration, human evaluation of experience, in a way comparatively different from that in another time and place, is to be understood and described, the first order of business, as we have said, is a working model.[3]

The question of model building can be a particularly sticky one in community studies unless we keep distinctly in mind the difference between the conceptual framework of research and analysis and the community as object of study. Unlike those in other disciplines who create abstract models whose validity is then tested through research, much of which is experimental in nature, the anthropological tradition and that of community study are derived from the natural-history method of the natural sciences. Rather than starting with hypotheses, which are then tested, the researcher starts with a general problem and focus and then lets the accumulating facts lead him in the direction of general statements about the object of study. It should be obvious that such a procedure is required where little or nothing is known initially about what is being studied and research is for the purpose of replacing ignorance with knowledge. The model of a community that emerges from this approach is best labeled a "living" model rather than one that is hypothetical or confirmed. As such it may be seen as the conceptual organization of a perceived reality.

The conceptual framework, or "model," if we might label it as such, is something quite different. Primarily it is a method of thinking about facts, organization, priority, and relevance. It is empirical, inductive, and examines behavior through events in time and place. It is concerned with the qualities of items or traits and their relationships with other traits within the stable or changing conditions of the several environments—physical, cultural, and social—within which they appear. It utilizes the concept of system in its organic rather than mechanical or statistical sense, and through the recording of interaction within events abstracts principles of homeostasis and change.[4]

The specific applicability of community-study method to the purposes of international education becomes more apparent when we turn to the analysis of a specific community. There we can see the relationship between the social groupings and their accessibility and response to schooling. We can also note the congruencies between educational organization and that of the community. For my exemplifying materials, I shall go to the town of Ennis in County Clare in west Ireland. It was there that my colleague Arensberg and I became immersed in the life ways of a town and also learned the process through which a community might be understood.

When we began our studies in Ireland in the early 1930's, that country had enjoyed only slightly more than a decade of political freedom from its centuries-old political domination by England and the economic and social domination by a landlord Ascendancy whose way of life was largely alien to the native Irish. It was not that some remnants of the old Protestant Ascendancy did not then persist, but they were no longer a viable factor in the life of the country. In the counties of west Ireland, including County Clare, where an overwhelming proportion of the population was of native Irish descent, the Norman-Saxon influence had eroded further than elsewhere. Stark reminders of the past could still be found in both countryside and town, where the abandoned shells of once stately mansions stood as forlorn sentinels over a countryside that had been reclaimed by small farmers as their own. In the towns the empty symbols of British rule stood as massive grey hulks of barracks that once garrisoned alien troops, the workhouses that had sheltered the derelict poor and the old, and the once pretentious Protestant college or secretive Masonic Hall.

The main current of Irish life of that day paid little attention to these remnants of the past. The national government strove to broaden

[4] Conrad M. Arensberg and Solon T. Kimball, "Community Study: Retrospect and Prospect," *The American Journal of Sociology*, Vol. 73, No. 6 (May 1968), pp. 691–705.

the industrial base beyond the predominantly agricultural one dominated by a population of small farmers, promulgated schemes for social amelioration, and extolled all things Gaelic. The few large cities demonstrated some vitality even in the face of a depressed economic situation as evidenced in their slow population growth. But market towns and the countryside were still in a slow decline of population that extended back nearly a century. The economic stagnation that then afflicted the rest of the world had been in progress in Ireland for a much longer period of time. All of these factors operating in concert contributed to preserving the status quo for the nation as well as for Ennis, seat of county government for Clare and a market town for the surrounding area.[5]

When we first came to know Ennis, it claimed a few more than six thousand inhabitants, down nearly a third from a century earlier. In addition to its governmental and economic activities, it was also the residence of the Roman Catholic Bishop of the Diocese of Killaloe, whose responsibility included supervision of the education of all Catholic children under his jurisdiction.

In the heart of the town stood a statue to Daniel O'Connel, the great Catholic emancipator of the previous century, and from this vantage four streets radiated. One of these led across the Fergus river to the Georgian residences of upper-middle-class families. The other three were narrow, winding arteries lined on both sides by tightly packed small two- and three-story shops with upper-level living quarters. As these streets reached the outer limits of the town, the shops gave way to the one-story cottages of laborers built in end-to-end fashion along both flanks of the roadway. North of the center of town were the massive, grey stone buildings of the convent, but elsewhere behind the shops and in the backstreets there were dense concentrations of simple dwellings housing both laborers and artisans, broken by an occasional clustering of small shops. There were, of course, other buildings such as warehouses and former mills along the river, the centrally located Catholic church, the Franciscan Abbey, the court house and other public buildings, most of which were on the outskirts of town, and a scattering of private dwellings whose lawns were enclosed by an ornamental iron fence or masonry wall.

We are now ready to turn to the life of the town to demonstrate how community-study method contributes to understanding the educational system. In particular I want to show that only with knowledge

[5] For an analysis of Ennis see Conrad M. Arensberg and Solon T. Kimball, "Part Two: The Town," in *Family and Community in Ireland*, 2nd edition (Cambridge, Mass.: Harvard University Press, 1968).

of human groupings, and their associated values and behavior in context, can statements about the educational structure and process become meaningful.

The educational facilities of Ennis were not equally available to its youth in either theory or practice. In fact, those deeply embedded cultural attributes arising from differences of sex, age, social class, and religion also provided the rigid framework around which educational distinctions were built—in fact, they permeate all social behavior in Ireland. For example, the children of Protestants, a tiny minority, and of Catholics were kept rigorously separate from each other. Among Catholic children, strictures against mixing of the sexes were observed with equal strictness through the secondary school level. The convent school, staffed by nuns and a few secular female teachers, provided both elementary and secondary education for girls. Boys attended either the Christian Brothers School or the National School. These two schools differed in a number of respects. The former was staffed by a celibate teaching order, the later by secular teachers who were free to marry if they so chose. But there was also a difference in the student clientele based upon tradition and economics. Parents who sent their sons to the Christian Brothers were required to pay tuition. No such fees were exacted for attending the National School, with the consequence that the latter was populated almost entirely by children of the laboring class. It is probable that even if fees had been abolished the differences in clientele would have continued.

These distinctions based on religion, sex, and social class were continued at the secondary level. Protestants sent their older children to church-operated boarding schools elsewhere and of necessity had to bear the financial burden. Affluent Catholics oftentimes also sent their children away—to church operated schools. But the families of the middle class who sought further education for their children usually enrolled their daughters at the local convent school, whereas the boys attended the local diocesan college. Both schools were also boarding schools that accepted students from elsewhere. The combination of tuition payments and successful completion of an entrance examination effectively excluded all children except those from affluent families and a few of the very bright who managed to win county council scholarships. These, however, seem to have been awarded largely to the children of farmers, teachers, and some from the respectable poor, artisans, clerks, and the like. The National School did not seem to prepare the children of laborers for advanced scholarly achievement.

Educational achievement in Ireland validates one's social standing and facilitates advancement much as it does in other countries of the world. The Irish system is as successful in this regard as any other. The schooling provided the children of laborers ensured the generational perpetuation of their social and occupational position. The extended period of schooling for higher social classes has comparable results. The differing types of schools are both symbol and reality for children and their parents of the system and their place in it. As an example, orphaned young girls or those who have been taken from unwed destitute mothers, because of a feared deleterious effect upon their moral development, are given into the custody of the convent. There they are housed and educated through the elementary grades but not beyond, even though they may remain resident there until early maturity. The explanation offered was that they should not be educated beyond their station in life. But neither are girls whose parents come from the laboring class educated beyond their status.

Further insight into the congruency of education as a part of the social system can be gained from a look at the sub-cultural variations of social class and the differential values associated with each one. The residents of Ennis defined three clearly demarcated social classes. The relatively small upper-middle group included lawyers, bankers, physicians, land-owners, merchants, and those occupying high level governmental posts. Shopkeepers, publicans, and middle-level civil servants, including school teachers, formed another clearly recognizable group. Then there were the laborers. Above the laborers was an interstitial group of artisans, clerks, and those with occupations demanding some skill, a marginal group that constituted the respectable poor. Although these latter showed similarities in their style of life, they exhibited little social cohesion compared to the other three. Mention should be made also of the wandering Tinkers, who were at the very bottom of the prestige ladder, and, in sharp contrast, a shattered remnant of an Ascendancy at the top, the children of both of which were outside the formal schooling system.

Each of these several groups possessed a life style and associational pattern that were different from the others. What is of particular relevance for us, however, is the recruitment of members to each group, the natural history of the family in each, and the values about education and social position. The Tinkers and the Ascendancy can be disposed of quickly. For both of these groups status was inherited and perpetuated. For them schooling as a device for advancement was of no relevance except as it validated a style of life. But the situation for the town's laborers was almost identical. When we traced family genealogies for this group we found that, over generations, the same families perpetuated themselves without change in occupational designation. Whatever success the children of laborers may have achieved elsewhere in the world, there was no chance for advancement open to them in the town in which they were born.

The situation for shopkeepers and the upper-middle-class professionals was quite different. There we discovered that the former were recruited as young men and women from farm families of the surrounding countryside. They first served an apprenticeship in some shop, moved then to the status of shop assistant, and by the age of thirty-five most of them had married and established their own shops. The brighter of their children were encouraged to advance along the educational ladder beyond secondary school to the universities and toward professional goals; some of these then returned to the town in a new and enhanced status. In this group, three generations completed the cycle, not of shirt-sleeves to shirt-sleeves, but of migrant country youth to commercial success, professional standing, and eventual dispersion to cities in Ireland and other parts of the English-speaking world. There was thus renewal through continuous recruitment from the country combined with generational advance that could be realized through successfully clearing educational hurdles. Advancement for the children of the respectable poor was much less certain. But with determination and ability, they too might win the coveted scholarships that paid for post-elementary education.

No such process of recruitment and educational linkage applied to Ascendancy, Tinkers, or laborers, nor was there desire for or expectations that one might change his social standing. The middle group, however, sought favorable social achievement and also held in their hands the mechanism through which their children might advance. Laborers experienced no such changes in their closed world of generational perpetuity.

When I returned to Ireland in 1968, three decades after our initial study, I encountered some new developments that have begun to modify the pattern described above. Opportunities for the laboring class are greatly enhanced due to new industries, the general prosperity, and a government-sponsored program of new houses and other benefits. Together these factors have eliminated the abject poverty of the laborers, and the once near impregnable educational barrier that kept the respectable poor and the laborers in their class generation after generation has now been breached. The vocational education program now includes academic subjects that can carry one to the doors of the universities. Even the lowly Tinker has felt the assault on the barrier of caste as he finds his children being forced to attend school.

The basic pattern of education, however, has not changed in over three decades. The separation of Protestants and Catholics is rigidly observed, and the Catholic Church, through the Diocesan Bishop, retains undisputed control over the education of the more than 95% of the population of that faith. Only the sons of laborers in the towns are taught by secular teachers; the Christian Brothers and Convent are staffed by those bound by vows of celibacy. School organization continues to reflect values and social divisions of the community in the separation of the sexes, and in the differential accessibility to education based on social class. The level of educational attainment continues to validate the social position into which a child has been born, and no more nor less. In this respect the educational system could be viewed as an extra-familial instrumentality of socialization that perpetuates the status quo.

There is no intention to imply that the situation has remained on dead center. Residents of Ennis are justly proud of the attractive new buildings at the convent school and facilities for vocational education, and educators are forever tinkering with the curriculum to modernize it. Furthermore, the expanded vocational program opens up new avenues for advancement. But this latter development must be viewed as an extension of the central government in response to a national policy of industrial development, and not the consequence of local, internally-generated change.

Although the general welfare of the laboring class has been greatly improved since 1930, there has been no other significant change in social structure or life style in Ennis since then. The expanded vocational program extends the opportunity for social mobility to the children of laborers and is a consequence of the central government's program for economic development. It should be remembered, however, that both the expanded educational program and the industrial emphasis were generated external to the traditional community. As institutional additions to an agrarian-focused way of life, they enrich the social complexity and also create new social tensions.

The important point to remember, however, is that the base-line knowledge of community system is essential to understanding both stability and the consequences of innovation. It permits us to see the congruencies between educational organization and practices and other structural and behavioral aspects. We learn something about the relation between the present and the past and we can see the groupings of population based upon differential life styles of social classes. Furthermore, we can interpret the effect of influences arising from externally based sources, or those that spring from internal regroupings. In effect, educational significance emerges only as an interconnection with the community matrix.

APPLIED ANTHROPOLOGY

Once research has given us knowledge of a community system, there still remains a gap between this knowledge and its use in constructing a working program of educational development. With the problem phrased as a question, we ask: In the need to unite knowledge and program, what specifically can anthropology contribute to the process of policy making, program planning, and implementation? This problem logically connects with our examination of the use of the community-study method, and its consideration brings us to the field of applied anthropology.

It might be argued that program and development are matters that should best be left in the jurisdiction of educational specialists. After all, all of the essentials of educational practice are encompassed by organization, management, facilities, pedagogy, curriculum, and materials. However comprehensive such a listing may appear to the pedant, the detail of activity that accompanies each of these facets is little more than a bag of tricks, rule of thumb gimmicks, if they are not imbedded in guiding principles of learning, behavior, and organization. And anthropology has a great deal to say about all of these, as I have written of them in other chapters of this book.

Obviously the experienced educator does know a great deal about professional practice and the anthropologist has learned some things about social process, so our problem becomes one of joining the experience of the anthropologist in social and cultural change with the special skills of the educationist.

During recent decades, some anthropologists have been directly concerned with the application of their knowledge to a wide variety of human endeavors; a brief account of this activity should indicate some of the potentialities for educational usage. In the middle 1930's, a handful of American social anthropologists, joined by a few from other disciplines who were stimulated by the infusion of new ideas about the relations among organization, behavior, and the individual, and challenged by the opportunity to apply their knowledge to the solution of practical problems of policy and program, laid the base for what has now become a well-developed branch of the discipline. Although information supplied by anthropologists about native peoples had been utilized at an even earlier date by Dutch and British colonial administrators, the role of the applied anthropologist became defined rather differently in their colonies from what eventuated in the United States. In this country, individuals assumed a more activist role, either as consultants or as employees of established agencies.

In the latter category they contributed to policy making and program planning. The Bureau of Indian Affairs, the Soil Conservation Service, and the Agricultural Extension Service of the federal government and a few private industrial corporations provided the initial openings.

During World War II, the range of opportunities increased enormously, as did the number of those who were actively engaged. The War Relocation Authority, the Office of War Information, military intelligence, and the administration of occupied and trust territories were only a few of the agencies and activities that enlisted the special skills anthropologists offered. Subsequently there was an expansion into the field of professional training for health and education, as well as participation in some foreign aid programs.

This brief résumé of the background of applied anthropology can serve several purposes. It shows the diversity of areas in which activity occurs and that the demanding conditions of front-line problems have tested knowledge and skills. It does not mean, however, that these ideas and methods have been widely utilized in administration, professional training, policy and program formulation, or planning. Quite to the contrary, utilization of ideas and processes has been limited, oftentimes either rejected completely or grudgingly accepted. Limited recognition has been won in industry, the health professions, and some foreign aid programs, but very little in education. Probably only in rare instances have these ideas and methods been fully comprehended as a theoretically based and tested means for creating the conditions to modify human behavior rather than as an insightful gimmick that serves some immediate end. When the complexities of the operational dimensions are stated, it becomes easier to understand some of the barriers to acceptance.

In most of these engagements, the practical problem was a social engineering one. As such, they called for developing programs and specifying procedures that should be followed to incorporate successfully a new practice or to modify existing ones to achieve some stated objective. The goal might require a limited innovation only, or it might involve thoroughgoing modernization. Irrespective of the magnitude of the task, however, there were always sequential stages that ordinarily should have been followed. These included the initial studies, planning, implementation, and devices for continuous evaluation and readjustment thereafter.

Empirical experience in social engineering, moreover, has led to the formulation of guiding principles that explain the reasons for the rules or procedures. In addition, there is a body of theory, in part drawn from traditional anthropological concerns with social structure and culture and in part newly formulated from observing the consequences of attempts at innovation. Explanations of the process of change originate from direct experience. Together, principles and theory constitute the necessary intellectual tools that support and focus research, planning, implementation, and reassessment.

Let me illustrate the point by referring to a basic principle involving capability, responsibility, and participation that affects the acceptance or rejection of an innovation. We know from biology that every organism learns to cope with its environment from its continuous responses to a stream of external stimuli. (It may also perish if these exceed its range of capability.) When the same principle is applied to child rearing, we say that a child cannot learn to solve problems unless the opportunity is present for him to do so. The over-protective parent teaches the child to depend upon others for answers to his problems, but once this paternalistic covering is withdrawn, the inability to cope is readily observed. The same principle applies to individuals grouped in institutions and communities. Capability to solve group problems develops only as its members forge the relationships among themselves that permit them to respond in an organized fashion to the conditions of their environment. This capability is not acquired either by desire or by fiat. It comes from slowly acquired and often transgenerationally transmitted patterns of human cooperation.

The social ability to act cooperatively is only one of several aspects that must be learned. Another is the substantive skill (cognitive, affective, motor) that must accompany an activity such as planting a field, constructing a building, operating a machine, or teaching a class. The principles that explain the acquisition of these abilities to act through acquired social and technical skills are comparable to those of individual growth and development. Modification in condition, either internal or external to individual or group, create tensions that evoke adjusting responses. Ultimately, new learning must be incorporated by doing.

This explanation of growth and change, which implicitly incorporates responses to innovation, ought by now to have become part of our conventional wisdom. When you observe what actually happens in educational planning and administering, however, you are made aware that other and quite contrary assumptions frequently form the basis for deciding programs and procedures. The rhetoric of rationalization may be quite varied but the meaning is all too clear. The phrasing comes out something like the following: "They are like children and for their own good need to be told what to do," or "they lack the education or the knowledge to make the kind of decision this situation requires," or "they respect authority, and like to be told what to do." Such a perspective justifies the retention of authority and control by those who already possess it and the perpetuation of a system that keeps the subjected in their inferior position and validates their incapabilities. When programs are prepared without consultation and imposed from above, it should be easy to understand why recipients should receive them with lack of understanding, passive resistance, even rejection, and why administrators and professional practitioners who consider themselves liberal-minded should become so frustrated. The cynical have already decided that helping others brings no rewards and the important objective is to get all you can for yourself. In truth, direct help may diminish the capability to act except in a dependent relationship.

What then are the implications of this principle for application in education development? Fully accepted and understood, it means that provision must be made for all of those who are affected by the modification of an educational system to share in planning and implementing change. Opportunities, sometimes requiring new learning, must be opened for those who have a stake in what happens to take part in the assessment of existing conditions, in the definition of needs and future goals, in planning the kind and sequence of changes, and in implementation. But the process does not end there. In addition, provision needs to be made for continuous evaluation and modification as the plans are carried into effect or as new evidence is acquired. This principle of multiple responsibility and participation is only one of those that has been empirically proved as essential in social engineering.

Educational development has not utilized this approach in any systematic manner in this country and only fortuitously elsewhere. The failure may be attributed to several factors. For one thing, except for the nuts and bolts of school operation, the institutions that train professional educators have, in the past, largely ignored educational planning. Their preoccupation has been primarily with transmitting professional competence and the training of experts for specialized fields. It was assumed that such a cadre of personnel would have the answers to educational problems. Even a limited evaluation of existing conditions should convince us that concentration upon skill and subject area is an approach that has failed. The value of such training is not being questioned, but its divorcement from human behavior and the processes of change ignores the significant dimension of the context of the human groupings in which educators must work.

Unhappily, there is nothing in the training of most educators that makes them aware of the measure of their own deficiency, a deficiency that becomes even more marked if they are called upon to work in a cross-cultural situation. A report by the mission director of the Agency for International Development in a Latin American country illustrates the point. An educational institution in the United States agreed to furnish a team of elementary education specialists, under contract with AID, to advise on educational development. Soon after their arrival, they were told that fifty percent of the children who enter school do not advance to the second grade. They were asked to discover the reasons for this lamentable situation and to prepare proposals that might remedy it. After a year of study, they reported to the mission director that the introduction of a system of education resembling that of the state from which they came would solve the problem. Their solution failed to take into account the cultural conditions, and, even if attempted would not have worked.[6] A Brazilian educator-sociologist, concerned with the same problem, suggested that some improvement in the proportion of children attending school might be realized if the level of an acceptable test score for grade advancement was lowered. His suggestion was followed in one of the provinces with the result he predicted. This simple measure did not correct, of course, the basic problem of an elementary system of education that had been designed in the previous century to educate only the children of an elite and which did not meet the requirements of universal education in an industrializing country. It did make the statistics look better, however.

The evidence clearly demonstrates the hazards, difficulties, and even undesirability of attempting to transfer institutions and practices from one culture to another. Such attempts ignore and violate what we know about cultural integrity and institutional congruencies. But what steps need to be taken to improve the situation? The necessities have been succinctly put by William Sayres, it seems to me, in a report on the development of an international education program at Teachers College, Columbia University. I quote his statement.

It is also recognized that basic and advanced preparation in professional education is not enough for effective performance in international development programs. The expatriate consultant must be able to adapt what he has learned to the special requirements of different social systems and cultural patterns. He must be sensitized to the ways in which the traditions, values, customs, sanctions and outlooks of other people shape the provisions they make for educating their children and limit the channels through which changes, if they are not to be transitory, must be introduced. He must have insight into the varied dimensions—e.g., historical, social, economic, political, psychological—of educational development in a comparative and cross-cultural frame of reference.[7]

[6] See Chapter 15 below.
[7] William C. Sayres, "Field Notes on the Subculture of a New Program," mimeographed, New York, 1967, pp. 13–14.

Dr. Sayres is himself a practitioner of his own prescriptions and has experienced the results that arise from their application. In 1964, as a member of an Alliance for Progress team of educational advisors to the Ministry of Education in Peru (subsequently Chief of Party), he initiated, in collaboration with Dr. Adrico Via Ortega, Peruvian anthropologist-educator, a program of community development centered around teachers and schools. Titled CRECER, an acronym for Campaña para la Reforma Eficaz de las Comunidades Escolares de la Republica, the program initially enlisted the voluntary services of several score teachers in widely scattered communities who were then assisted in the techniques of gathering and analysis of data and their utilization in school and community betterment.

Since it appears unrealistic to insist that all educators acquire cross-cultural competence, however desirable that might be, we are faced with finding intermediaries who can advise the culture-bound educator or with creating a new type of professional educator. Perhaps both avenues should be utilized. Where available, anthropologists could instruct on relevant cultural practices and advise on socially acceptable procedures of innovation. But the magnitude of the demands actually calls for a more regularized solution. We need a cadre of trained personnel whose specific focus is on international, cross-cultural, and development education. They may either serve as intermediaries who can translate, interpret, and explain the relevance of cultural differences or operate as practitioners in their own right.

By whatever rubric the practitioners in this new sub-discipline may eventually come to be labeled—comparative, international, development, or anthropological educationists—the present narrow mold that now constricts preparation for professional practice must, in my judgment, be broken. Some part of the liberation will come only as there is a search for and adaptation of theories and techniques from various disciplines. What is needed most urgently is a cross-cultural perspective, a research methodology, and theory and techniques for planning and innovation. Anthropology is a fertile territory from which these needs may be met with its comparative approach, the community-study method, and the social engineering of applied anthropology.

15. PRIMARY EDUCATION IN BRAZIL

Brazil resembles, in some ways, other underdeveloped countries that are struggling to free themselves from the suffocating grasp of an agrarian past through the slow but steady adoption of the technology of industrialism and the transformation of its institutions. The changes, however, are not progressing evenly on all fronts. For example, its newly introduced factories and network of air transport contrast sharply with still existent primitive agricultural practices. Its traditional political processes yield slowly to new demands. And its conservative educational system, partly from neglect and partly from indifference, has failed miserably to meet the needs of an emerging industrial society.

The goal of Brazilian educational leaders is to provide a system of universal and obligatory primary education. It is also their hope to modernize teaching methods and curricula, to stimulate enthusiasm for professionalization, and to bring the salaries of teachers to a level commensurate with their status and needs. A complete program of educational reform would include many other measures, such as administrative decentralization, development of citizen participation in educational matters, the construction of new facilities, and provision of classroom texts and materials. Unfortunately, any ideal plan for educational reconstruction has little chance of success. Inertia, opposition, and lack of resources are barriers sufficiently formidable to discourage even the bravest.

Such sweeping statements need qualification and explanation. Over the years there has been a gradual extension and modification of

"Primary Education in Brazil," *Comparative Education Review*, Vol. 4, No. 1 (June 1960), pp. 49–54. Addendum written especially for this volume.

the educational system. Many men and women of good will and intelligence have devoted their energies to the task. Through training programs, experimentation, and research, the basis has been laid for modernization. But Brazil presents a curious contradiction in the acceptance of cultural innovation. There is great freedom to attempt the new, the novel, and the dynamic. But indifferent tolerance is very different from serious examination of new ideas and procedures and their eventual acceptance or rejection. Probably the politics of vested interest becomes the determining factor in social change. For this reason the incorporation of modern educational methods has been quite slow and it is doubtful if they have kept pace with other social changes or with the needs of the country.

It is necessary to know something about Brazilian culture and society to understand the reasons for existing conditions in education. A full description represents a task of great magnitude and is beyond the immediate objectives of this report. Brief comment should be made, however, upon industrial development and the system of social classes. Both of these aspects are of major significance in understanding the educational situation.

The process of incorporating industrial techniques and organization is progressing differentially in the several regions of Brazil. For example, the economy of the Amazon valley remains almost exclusively extractive. The Northeast, with approximately one-fourth of Brazil's population, is at a colonial stage of development and retains a subsistence and plantation agrarianism that has persisted with little change since its inception in the sixteenth century. Although cattle *fazendas* and sugar plantations have adopted some new practices, they are very far from approximating scientific and industrial agriculture. The cities of this region are primarily administrative and commercial centers. In contrast, São Paulo and, to a lesser extent, adjacent states form the core of modern Brazil with industrial cities, some modern agriculture, and developed public services. In general, the level of educational development corresponds to the economic picture. In the rural subsistence areas of the Northeast, illiteracy may reach 80 percent. In the city of São Paulo it is negligible, and in other cities of the south has rapidly declined.

EDUCATION AND SOCIAL CLASS

The problem of education is also related to social class. Although it is a common practice today to speak of a middle class, the basic Brazilian pattern was a two-class system. The upper group was and is composed of the descendants of the great land-owners, members of the professional classes, the higher governmental officials, and those engaged in certain types of commercial activity. The lower group included the slaves and later their descendants, agricultural laborers and marginal rural renters or proprietors in the country, and the mechanics, artisans, laborers, and shopkeepers in the towns. Expanded occupational opportunities and a higher standard of living through urbanization and recent industrialization have tended to modify the system and favor the appearance of a middle class. Although there is no study that gives the relative proportion of the population in different social classes, some rough approximation of the distribution is necessary for our purposes. Probably not more than 20 percent of the population should be included in the middle and upper classes; in the Northeast and other agrarian areas, this percentage could be halved. At least three-quarters of the population are in the lower classes and at least half of these are marginal or outside the productive system. Understanding the system of social classes is basic to understanding the educational problem. For it is in the 70 to 80 percent in the lower classes that we find the lack of formal education as well as the great failure in educational methods.

The statistics state clearly the stark reality. Of the 12,700,000 children between the ages of seven and fourteen, 6,900,000 are in primary school, 150,000 have completed the primary course and ended their studies, 500,000 are in secondary school, and 5,150,000 are not in attendance. Of the 8,200,000 children between seven and eleven, 2,500,-000, or 30 percent, are not attending school. Of the 2,900,000 who matriculated in the first grade in 1957, only 1,200,000, or 44 percent, remained in school in 1958. More than half of the pupils abandoned their studies in the course of the first year. Only 18.2 percent of those who matriculate in the first grade finish the four-year primary series.[1]

The problem is clear. Many thousands of children are denied access to education through lack of schools or fail to enter because of parental neglect. Over half of those who do enter never get beyond the first grade. Less than one-fifth finish primary education.

Secondary education has had an exceptional growth during the past quarter century. In 1930 there were 60,000 students. Today the number has reached almost a million. Even so, less than 10 percent of Brazilian youth between the ages of twelve and eighteen years have access to these schools, and only 7 percent of those who enter finish the course.[2] Statistics do not classify students on the basis of social class, but simple observation and common knowledge establish the

[1] Juscelino Kubitschek de Oliveira, *Mensagem ao Congresso Nacional* (Rio de Janeiro, 1959), p. 216.
[2] *Ibid.*, p. 220.

fact that secondary school students are drawn almost entirely from the
middle and upper classes. The fact that a majority of these schools
are fee-charging institutions almost automatically eliminates children
of the poorer classes. The children who enter the secondary school must
finish the primary school successfully. Thus, the requirements of the
primary school are not barriers to children of the upper classes. As
some Brazilian critics have pointed out, the almost complete academic
orientation of the primary school may be explained by its emphasis
upon preparation for further education.

But it is also certain that factors other than the content and
orientation of the primary curriculum may be held partially accountable
for the lamentable situation. The middle-class environment of the
school may be both strange and punishing for lower-class children.
The reports by Pearse [3] and Consorte [4] in Brazil, as well as that of
Allison Davis in the United States, support this assumption.

The deficiency in number and professional training of teachers
constitutes another problem. Within the whole of Brazil, only 55 percent of primary school teachers are normal school graduates. But the
extremely favorable educational situation in the state of São Paulo
heavily weights the national average. Nearly one-fourth of all teachers
and students are found within this one state; of these, over 95 percent
of the teachers are normal school graduates. Only Minas Gerais, Bahia,
Espírito Santo, and the Federal District have more than half their
teachers professionally trained. The proportion in other states varies
considerably, with the worst conditions in Rio Grande do Norte, where
only 20 percent are *normalistas*. The situation in the private schools [5]
is actually less favorable than in the public schools, for here we find
that only 42 percent have completed normal school training.

Politics and the family system create additional problems in the
formation of the spirit of professionalization among primary school
teachers. The study of these teachers in Rio de Janerio shows that
teaching is considered as a part-time job through which the woman,
if married, contributes to family income or, if single, has taken temporary employment while awaiting marriage.[6] Under these conditions
and with a large proportion of married teachers, it is to be expected
that family obligations take precedence over those of the school.

[3] Andrew Pearse, "A Formação de Atitudes para com a Escola em Migrantes
do Interior," *Educação e Ciências Sociais*, Vol. III, No. 8 (August 1959), pp. 9–54.

[4] Josildeth Gomes Consorte, "A Crianca Favelada e a Escola Publica,"
Educação e Ciências Sociais, Vol. V, No. 11 (August 1959), pp. 45–60.

[5] Ministry of Education and Culture, *Sinopse Estatística do Ensino Primário
Fundamental Comum* (Rio de Janeiro, 1958).

[6] Consorte, "A Crianca Favelada."

Family needs demand occasional absences, and pregnancy requires a much longer interruption. In Bahia, for example, an average of one-fifth of the primary school teachers take four months' annual leave because of pregnancy. Parents and children complain of the disturbances such interruptions produce.

Another problem with which education must contend is that of politics. Political activity may be either harmful or beneficial. It may interfere with the discharge of professional duties, demand appointments and dismissals, or it may focus attention upon educational problems and create public concern. Undoubtedly, education both benefits and suffers from political activity, but there is no study that gives any measure of its impact. Educators, however, may also use the methods of politics to advance their objectives.

The problem is further complicated by a system of federal, state, county (*município*), and private primary schools. The total number of all types of schools in 1958 was 82,963. Of these, 267 were federal, almost all of which were in the remote nonfederalized territories. State schools numbered 33,073, county schools 40,730, and private 8,893. Simple observation confirms the fact that the *ensino municipal* (county school) is more likely to be found in rural areas and that on the whole its facilities are often inadequate. Its teachers are the most poorly paid and trained. For example, 73 percent of the teachers in state schools, but only 23 percent of those in the county schools, were normal school graduates. County schools also fail to retain as large a proportion of pupils beyond the first grade. In the state schools, 70 percent of all primary school pupils are in either the first or second grade. But for every 100 students in the first grade one finds 48 in the second. In contrast, in *ensinos municipais*, 85 percent are in the first two grades, and for every 100 in the first grade there are only 30 in the second. In both instances the first grade serves as a major barrier to further education, but its effect is more pronounced among *ensinos municipais*.

CULTURAL ASPECTS

No fully satisfactory explanation of the failure of more than half the children who enter the first grade to reach the second can be offered until we have additional research. The study by Consorte on *favela* (slum) children gives us some important clues. Her findings show indifference or misunderstanding on the part of some parents, the absence of a home environment that provides homework assistance or incentive to the child, the critical attitude of middle-class teachers toward the lower-class behavior of their pupils, inadequate preliminary preparation for entering school, and a system of school organization that permits frequent changes in teachers, and does not hold them individually responsible. An additional important item has come from the recent research by Seguin.[7] He discovered a high correlation between verbal skills and school performance and that, in general, lower-class children are markedly deficient when compared with those of the upper classes. This finding suggests a cultural deficiency in the background of the child, or, as an alternative interpretation, the curriculum and procedures of the elementary school favor children who exhibit a higher degree of verbal facility.

To these factors that militate against the success of the lower-class child, we may tentatively add some others. The graded system of education in Brazil is used as a device for the progressive screening of those who are unable to perform satisfactorily on examinations that test academic learning. There is an implicit philosophy that it is desirable to eliminate, as early as possible, those who show no aptitude for academic achievement. Those who succeed will have been prepared for entrance to secondary schools and eventually the university. In this sense the primary schools serve as a proving ground for eventual access to higher education, and the academic requirements of the secondary school and university determine the orientation. Such a system obviously works to the detriment of the lower-class child, whose aspirations seldom go so far, or whose financial capacities do not permit such advancement.

Whether centralized administration contributes to malfunctioning of the educational system is not clear. There is an undoubted failure to adjust to local conditions because of uniform requirements in curriculum and examinations. Local administration of the schools, however, does not appear to be a solution for the entire problem. The locally financed and administered municipal schools are less successful in terms of student achievement than are the state schools. These latter are better supported financially, have a better trained staff, and undoubtedly attract more students from the better situated families.

On the other hand, the traditional centralization of governmental functions has worked against the development of a type of local responsibility and civic consciousness that has characterized local communities in the United States. But there are evidences of a local vitality that might be strengthened. The hotly contested elections for local political office, the exercise of certain municipal functions, the

[7] Roger Seguin, "Promoção e Aprendizagem na Escola Primaria," *Estudos nos Fatôres Sociais,* Part II, Centro Brasileiro de Pesquisas Educacionais (in manuscript, 1959).

appearance of voluntary associations such as Rotary, and the old, self-regulating "brotherhoods," which function in connection with religious festivities, are all evidence of local initiative and cooperation. With rare exceptions, however, the conceptualization of an educational program as a function of community is not common.

The unconscious linkage of education with social class and family values, and to a lesser extent with religion, is a major factor in the present situation. The spirit of individual liberty that permeates Brazilian culture can operate as a deterrent to enterprises that require communal effort. Under such cultural circumstances it is not surprising that education has been viewed in the past much more as a problem of private decision and action than as a proper concern of either community or state. Certainly, the experience of the Jesuits and the educational system of the colonial period would support such a conclusion. Furthermore, there is consistency in other areas of personal behavior, such as that of the code of honor, which demands of the individual that he settle his problems with others directly and oftentimes apart from the restrictions of law and order.

Whatever the relevance of these aspects of Brazilian personality and culture to educational problems, the fact remains that the traditional educational system in Brazil has worked fairly well for the requirements of a semi-aristocratic agrarian civilization. It has provided education for a select minority that prepared its members to take leadership in political, economic, and cultural activities. But the statistical and other evidence leads to the conclusion that it is not the type of education that can be successfully extended to the less favored segments of the population.

If Brazilians really desire universal primary education for their children, the obvious solution is a reform of the existing system. But those who have led the fight for better education in Brazil can testify that changes come very slowly indeed. The combination of vested interest, tradition, and just enough success of the present system to serve the needs of the upper classes does not create the feeling of urgency among those who hold the power of decision. The restricted influence and indifference of the great mass of Brazilians is a contributing negative factor.

There is another possible course of action. It is to create a new system of primary education for the 70 to 80 percent of Brazilian children for whom the present system does not work. Such a policy is not nearly as radical as the present one, which attempts to force the values and cultural aspirations of a dominant class upon a lower one through the use of formalized education. The slow evolution, or disintegration, of the academically oriented system might continue undis-turbed, without the calamity of imposing it upon a group that is hardly culturally prepared to receive it.

THE CONTRIBUTION OF ANTHROPOLOGY

The use of anthropological knowledge in the development of a system of education for the educationally deprived offers several possibilities. Basically, there is need to understand the culture of the "common man," his characteristic forms of social grouping, and then learn how to construct an educational program that, although it requires exten-sive changes in the existing system, can be accepted and understood by those for whom it operates. In this instance, we cannot separate the school program from the system of family, from institutional ar-rangements, nor from the place of Brazil's common man in the com-munity, whether urban or rural. Special difficulties arise because the lower classes have been outside the tradition of literacy; in the rural areas, at least, formal education has been little valued, in contrast to the type of learning that came from adult members of the family for work in house and field. There is indifference, inertia, and even hostility to be overcome. An example based upon the use of indigenous patterns of cooperation will illustrate a specific contribution as well as the dif-ficulties inherent in such a proposal.

Although traditionally the common people in Brazil have looked for protection from a *patrão* to whom they gave unwavering loyalty, there are also some cultural devices that permit cooperation among equals. These appear within the system of extended sociological kin-ship, the *compadresco*, and in the system of mutual help, the *mutirão*. In the plantation areas, the *compadresco* united those of high and low status through implicit obligations that resembled the relations be-tween extended kin. But the *compadresco* system also extended laterally and, although one's peer might not provide the same protection as would a powerful *patrão*, the network of relations across generations and between families provided security in individual crises.

There is a reported decline in the incidence of *mutirão*, but in its original form it represented the cooperative labors of a neighborhood group that, to a certain extent, cut across status factors. The fact that a traditional system of cooperation different from the vertical structure of the sugar, coffee, or cattle *fazenda* could bring peer groups into con-certed action is of importance. Although cultural forms fall into disuse, they may also be revived. In fact, existing and comparable forms of cooperation may be observed in the culturally old *irmandade* (Catholic religious brotherhoods), in the equalitarian Protestant minority sects, and in recent labor unions. More infrequently, charismatic leaders such an Antonio Conselheiro win fanatic devotion. Their contemporary may be the popular demagogue.

These illustrations give emphasis to the capacity of the common people, urban and rural, for self-organization. But it should also be noted that the ruling classes, through civil and religious authorities, have viewed such movements with suspicion and on occasion have used force to suppress them. An additional negative aspect is that such spontaneous groupings have served religious, economic, and personal ends, but not those of education. Thus, even before experimentation in the adaptation of these cultural patterns to educational purposes could be attempted, the approval of the ruling classes would be needed. This one illustration demonstrates that what appears to be a simple problem may actually be very complex. Nevertheless, if Brazil is to meet the educational needs of its people, its leaders must rely heavily upon planning based on social and cultural analysis, for the problems are as much sociological as they are pedagogical.

ADDENDUM 1971

More than a decade has passed since the material for this analysis was first gathered. During that period, the record of Brazilian development has been an uneven one. The constitutional government was overthrown by a military coup in 1964 and a military dictatorship is firmly entrenched in power. Population growth accelerates and Brazil's women hold the dubious honor of being among the world's most fertile. Industrial production mounts, but the contrast between the poverty gripped Northeast and the progressive South deepens. The problem of growing adequate foodstuffs to feed the population has yet to be solved.

The educational outlook, however, continues to brighten, especially in the areas of secondary and higher education. A governmental decree in 1965 ordered the restructuring of the Federal universities along lines similar to those of the University of Brasilia. If successful, this plan would strengthen the social sciences, education, and technical training and provide a more flexible organization for future development. A new project to reorient the middle-level school from its academic focus to a vocational one has been initiated, and money was provided for building 300 new GOTs (ginasios orientados para o trabalho) for 280,000 students in four states in 1969. In the early years of the decade, a new basic law of education was enacted after many years of controversy among the various vested interests.

Brazil, however, still faces the problem common to all developing nations that are attempting to catch up. The variety of claims upon the limited resources restricts its ability to construct and staff sufficient schools to provide basic literacy for all of its population and in the allotment of a disproportionate share of money to secondary and higher education continues to favor the middle and upper classes in contrast to the laboring class. Furthermore, there is no evidence of significant reform at the primary level, which acts as a fine-meshed screen that permits only a small fraction of students to advance to secondary education.

Some measure of the changes in recent years are contained in the officially published figures. A serious search was made for statistics comparable to those utilized in the original analysis, but unfortunately the effort was only partially successful and hence item-for-item contrast is prohibited. Nevertheless, the data do give us a sense of the direction and magnitude of change.[8]

Primary education during the 1958–67 period shows an important numerical increase in all categories. The number of schools increased by 54 percent (82,953 to 127,813); the number of teachers doubled (197,423 to 395,149); the percentage of teachers holding certificates rose to sixty percent, a one-third jump in only four years; students enrolled increased by 65 percent (6,775,791 to 11,182,746). These gains are somewhat illusory, however, since the total population of the country increased by one-third in the same period. Furthermore, the distribution by grade shows little change. Half of the total numbers of students were enrolled in the first grade in 1966; if we calculate the number in the first grade in 1963, and the number in the terminal fourth year four years later, only twelve percent of that group remained in school after four years.

The secondary school picture is somewhat better. Between 1959 and 1967, the total number of secondary schools increased by 66 percent (6,931 to 11,522). Private schools continued to dominate this sector of education, in contrast to primary education, where more than 90 percent of the schools are public. 62 percent (7,084) of the schools were listed as private in 1967 against 65 percent (4,388) in 1959. Enrolment jumped significantly. In 1967 there were 2,816,440 students in contrast to 1,050,000 in 1958, a 169 percent increase. A significant change appears, however, in the proportion of students enrolled in public institutions. In 1958 there were 35 percent (366,769) in public schools against 52 percent (1,466,205) in 1967. This could probably be interpreted as an increase both in availability and quality of public schools and in the proportion of bright youngsters from the

---

[8] *America en Cifras 1967* (Washington, D.C.: Pan American Union, 1969).

working classes who are remaining on the educational ladder. When we examine the numbers of secondary school teachers, however, we find that their number rose more slowly, 126 percent (80,472 to 181,581), than did either students or schools. The Brazilian custom of secondary school teachers' holding more than one job, often teaching in two or three schools, may account for these figures.

Higher education in 1958–1967 outstripped all other segments in a phenomenal increase of 250 percent (86,365 to 215,322) in student enrolment, even though the total remains less than one percent of the age group because of successive examination hurdles for secondary and higher education.

The Brazilian educational system, in the severe attrition in primary grades and the subsequent examination hurdles for entry into secondary and higher education, still reflects its aristocratic origins in restricting formal education to a small elite. If it should become a policy of the Brazilian government to democratize and modernize education, the centralization of control in federal and state ministries ought to facilitate a rapid change. That such has not occurred in the past makes one wonder if these bureaucracies do not first place their own interests ahead of those of the schools. Furthermore, any expectation that the schools might become a community function, a suggestion that was offered in the original analysis, remains pure fantasy. We should expect that change, if any, will continue to be initiated from the pinnacle of administrative power and will reflect political objectives as much as educational ones. Under such adverse conditions, it is no small miracle that teachers and students do as well as they do.

16. EDUCATION AND CHANGE IN A TRADITIONAL SOCIETY

Peru resembles many of the other countries in Latin America and elsewhere in the world that have only recently begun to experience accelerated internal change. Influences flowing from industrialized societies and those generated from within are contributing sources. The change thus far, however, is much less evident in the transformation of an older way of life and its associated institutions than it is apparent in the introduction of new technology and human groupings in industry and agriculture. But Peru and these other countries differ from one another in their distinctive combination of such factors as topography, climate, resources, demography, cultural tradition, institutions, and history. These are the factors that shape the pace and direction of change.

Lima, the capitol, reflects more fully than elsewhere the impact of internal forces and external influences. It is a bustling commercial and industrial city that now holds more than a tenth of the nation's twelve million inhabitants. As the seat of the viceroys in the days of Spanish hegemony, and later as capitol of the nation after independence was won, it has always exhibited the grandeur that comes from being the ecclesiastical, governmental, social, and cultural center. Only Cuzco, high in the Andes, the seat of Inca rule before the conquest, could challenge its preeminence. But life here, as in most other provincial capitols, is also beginning to reflect some of the winds of change, although the basic social and institutional pattern continues much as before. There are several factors that contribute to this stability. The circulation of people, ideas, and goods has been impeded by a rigid social layering, differences of language and custom, and terrain.

201

The physical contrasts include coastal deserts, the rugged mountains of the interior, and the dense jungle of the tropical eastern provinces. These environmental barriers have been intensified by the cultural divisions based upon ethnic distinctions. Indians comprise nearly half of the population, with Aymara and Quecha found at the higher elevations and a congeries of small linguistic stocks resident in the jungle. Mestizo, a designation used primarily for those who speak Spanish and with greater cultural than racial implications, applies to those of Indian or mixed Indian-European ancestry but whose speech, dress, and customs are in the European tradition. This group is somewhat greater in number than the Indians and continues to receive a trickle of members from the latter through the acculturative effects of education. Finally, there is a numerically tiny elite, sometimes labeled the "forty families," in whose hands the traditional wealth and power reside. Over generations, these great land owning families have dominated the country through ownership of great estates with their resident Indian and Mestizo laborers.

The cultural divisions in Peru do not form a system of social classes in any sense that we know or understand what is meant by that term. There has been no true middle class whose members strive for higher social status and who can fashion a favorable environment for themselves and their children. Prestige comes from ancestry, which is derived from the accident of birth; it cannot be won. The plantation agrarian system barely provides a minimum for subsistence, and surpluses are drained off in ritual or family obligations or for the benefit of the landlord. Neither opportunity, nor aspiration, nor reality, promotes a situation in which mobility has any meaning.

The rigidities contained in cultural and economic factors are equally operative in the functioning of religion and government. Although the staffing of lesser positions offers some opportunity for the appropriately educated, the control of these institutions is held firmly in the hands of the elite. Even shifts in political power, from conservative to liberal, may bring new faces, but the recruitment for varying levels of governmental posts strictly follows existing social distinctions. Although bureaucratic functionaries may be the intelligent and educated children of artisans, petty shopkeepers, or clerks, and may rise to positions of responsibility with years of service and age, they are still barred from joining the ranks of the oligarchic elite, which reckons its membership through family lineage.

The simple rigidity that such broad generalizations convey fails to catch the incidence of variety and deviancy. The generations do not replicate themselves in exact similarities. Individuals or families prosper or decline, and social forms change in response to new influences. For example, there has been gradual expansion of public services with broadened opportunity for individual employment and beneficial consequences for the public recipients. As modern methods of agriculture, commerce, and industry are introduced, largely as a consequence of outside influences, these new enterprises offer additional opportunities, and older social arrangements become reshaped.

Segments of Peruvian life are now experiencing such a transformation, and new social alignments become evident. The process is one that favors the emergence of a vital middle class, but the outward manifestations of change should not delude us into believing that vested interests will readily yield their favored positions nor that time-honored institutional arrangements can or will quickly make those adjustments that the emergent conditions require.

The tensions that appear may or may not be most evident in the educational system, but for those nations that have set a course of modernization, the capability of the educational system to provide qualified personnel for new functions is crucial if they are to succeed. For this reason, those who seek to reshape Peruvian society need to know in detail how their educational system now works in order to prescribe the steps that must be taken to bring it into step with the other phases of national development.

Before we get further involved in such analysis, there is a need, however, to state a general proposition. In Peru, and in other comparable countries, the educational system reflects the social ordering found in social class and other institutions. It also expresses the cultural values and practices characteristic of these diverse and divergent social groupings. In this sense, education exhibits a marked congruency with other aspects of social life and culture. This view is one that affirms the interconnections between institutions and behavior, but it does not assert either determinancy or causality.

Formal education differs, however, from other institutions in its distinctly crucial responsibility to transmit, consciously, designated segments of the heritage. In the fulfillment of this role, then, education helps to perpetuate the system. The conditions under which the education system fails either to reflect or to perpetuate the existing system must be very unusual, and perhaps possible only under conditions that permit the imposition of control by some alien government or agency. Such a situation does not now exist in Peru, nor is it likely to appear. But with this double tendency both to reflect and perpetuate the status quo, how can education ever become an instrument for change? Possibly change appears only as other aspects of the society experience transformation. This problem, however, is one that we can reserve for later consideration. For the moment, we return to the quest for understanding of the present system.

The relevance of the proposition formulated in the preceding paragraphs should become evident in its specific application to the Peruvian situation. In fact, only as we comprehend the relationship between the social order and its cultural patterning can we appreciate the organization, philosophy, and practice of formal education.

We must remember that in a traditional society the career expectancies have been largely determined by the social position of the family into which one is born. Under such circumstances, the inculcation of a spirit of achievement in which individual aspirations and efforts are encouraged and rewarded has little meaning. The range of choice is greatly limited, as are the alternatives. Thus formal schooling and the learning that comes from such exposure are seen primarily as a validation of inherited position and not as instruments for mobility. The degree of literacy, or its absence, is a badge of social position, and, however important as an occupational skill, does not contribute significantly to what are considered the essential learnings. These are derived from within one's family and its connections. It is in this distinctive counterpoise, between school and family on the one hand and adult career on the other, that we uncover a fundamental contrast between our evaluation of education and what one obtains in Peru, perspectives that have roots in the social system that distinguishes each.

Most accounts of educational systems describe the legal structure of administration and policy with little or no attention to the interdependencies with other aspects of the society. Our concern is with this ordinarily neglected focus. For that reason we will restrict description of formal structure to those parts that seem most cogent to the questions related to social and cultural congruency.

Public education in Peru is a responsibility of the national government and is lodged in a Ministry of Education, which is directed by an appointee of the President of the Republic. The Minister and his top aides are usually drawn from the elite so that change in government does not threaten continuation of control by the group that traditionally governs the country. The concentration of all aspects of management in the centralized ministry requires a complex and inclusive bureaucracy staffed by functionaries of varying degrees of skill, some of whose jobs are subject to changes in the winds of political chance. These employees do the immense amount of paper work associated with preparation of reports, allocation of funds, employment and assignment of personnel, and distribution of supplies. Policy, planning, and program have been determined by legislation or by ministerial edict, and there is little leeway for modification in any established procedure.

Theoretically, the centralized authority held by the Ministry of Education might facilitate rapid adjustment to new conditions. In fact, its organization and operation favor the status quo. The concern with minutest details drains all energy into observing the routine of precedent. The pattern of personal encounter, which resembles that between landlord and tenant in obeisance given and received, injects capricious components into what, for us, should be rational decisions. There is also the tendency to link innovations with the personality of the innovator and hence to view each major proposal as a monument to its initiator; continuation thus is not incumbent upon successors. Thus can we understand not only the endless planning among the professionals of the Ministry, but a predictable failure, even lack of intent, to carry proposals into realization. To consider this perpetual but essentially non-varying whirl as a mark of organizational or cultural deficiency is to project our own culture-specific values to a situation where they are not applicable. Instead we must view the social form and the activity within its own setting. From this perspective we can recognize the self-stabilizing congruency that the educational enterprise shares with other aspects of the society.

The divisions within the formal structure of education resemble those found in other Latin American countries. Children may enroll in a pre-primary sequence of three years at age four, but in 1965 only 50,000, a small fraction of the whole, were enrolled. Primary education is a five-year sequence, preceded by a year of schooling called "transition," which the child enters at age six or seven. In 1965 there were 18,839 such schools (87 percent public) with an enrolment slightly over two million, but this represented only 65 percent of the population between 5 and 14 years of age. Even so the total number in school had increased from 1,234,000 in 1957.

A student may enter a university after completing his secondary education and passing an entrance examination. Most normal schools require only three years of secondary schooling.

Education in Peru cannot be understood without some comments about privately operated schools. These may be sponsored by religious groups or they may be profit-making enterprises. The fees they charge provide an effective barrier for children from poorer families. Recruitment based on other criteria also serves to ensure students from a select background.

Advancement within the elementary school and entrance and advancement in secondary and normal schools and the university is

TABLE 1. EDUCATIONAL UNITS AND ENROLMENT BY LEVEL
AND PUBLIC AND PRIVATE, PERU—1965.

	No.	Public	%	Private	%
Primary					
Schools	18,839	16,372	87	2,467	13
Students	2,054,021	1,862,622	91	191,399	9
Secondary					
Schools	1,376	973	71	403	29
Students	379,575	299,734	79	79,841	21
General	310,857	237,079	76	73,778	24
Vocational	68,718	62,655	91	6,063	9
Higher					
Schools					
Universities	28	21	75	7	25
Normal	95	71	75	24	25
Students	71,611	61,733	86	9,878	14
Universities	56,893	53,022	93	3,871	7
Normal	14,718	8,711	59	6,007	41

Source: America en Cifras 1967. Situacion Cultural: Educacion y Otros Aspectos
Culturales (Washington, D.C.: Union Paramericana, 1969).

strictly regulated by a series of examinations. These not only measure
student achievement, but they also prevent further advance on the
educational ladder for those who fail. Theoretically, they are objective
measures of acquired knowledge and presumably of ability. In effect,
they are screening devices along ethnic and class lines. There are many
ways in which such results are assured. Almost all children of the
elite, including those from the leadership positions in the Ministry of
Education, attend privately-operated elementary and secondary schools,
which are generally conceded to provide a better education, although
some of the urban public schools are also excellent. If special tutoring
is needed, and the important entrance examinations to secondary
schools or the universities are usually preceded by periods of intense
study, the better-off families have the means to pay for such assistance.
These factors in themselves give the children of favored families an
advantage that, when combined with a home environment that values
formal education, practically assures educational success. Except for a
few bright and ambitious children of the poor who hurdle all obstacles, the educational system validates their inferior status by failure
and rejection.

Evidence of variability and accessibility of formal education as
manifestations of cultural and social distinction may be seen in other
statistics. In 1961, nearly 40 percent of the 5,617,000 over 14 years of

age in Peru's population were illiterate. Of these, Indians, who constitute 45 percent of the entire population, have among them only 38 percent who have had enough schooling to read and write.

The persistent attrition in student numbers at each higher level is revealed by a simple statistical count. In round figures, 660,000 children entered the primary grade in 1965 for the first time. It is expected that 31 percent of these will graduate and that three-fifths of these will enter secondary school. Approximately half of these will be graduated. Stated differently, over ninety percent of an entering primary class fail to complete ten years of schooling. Three-fifths of those who do, however, go on to higher education, a percentage greater than that in the United States, but total numbers in 1965 were only 71,600. (Two years later enrolment had risen to 88,100, a healthy 23 percent increase and indicative of the rapid growth of higher education.) Such a quantitative statement gives us some sense of the availability and results of the school system. Comparison with earlier periods would show that there has been a gradual expansion in the proportion of the population reached and in level of schooling achieved. In particular, there has been rapid growth in secondary school enrolment.

But how do the pressures for change manifest themselves in the educational establishment? There has been a great deal of reform rhetoric, but advances have been largely limited to some aspects of higher education—agriculture, medicine, and engineering—and to technical programs related to industry. These modifications are a response to new conditions, not a restructuring of the basic educational system. For apart from the practical problems of financing and staffing new or expanded activities, there is a deeply imbedded philosophy, structure, and practice of pedagogy that is fully congruent with the values and structure of Peruvian life and will not readily yield to modification. As we come to understand school organization and practices, we will also see how they reflect world view and behavior and help to perpetuate them.

Peruvian educators emphasize that the ultimate goal of education is to instill moral values. These values provide the code that governs the individual's behavior and his relations with others. They are eternal and unvarying and they exist apart from the individual. Violation of the code can bring either supernatural or secular retribution, sanctions imposed from the outside for wrongdoing, but the individual may also suffer shame as he senses the condemnation of others for his transgressions. Internal agony may be great, but it arises from the anxiety about what others will think of you, and not from the self-condemnation of internalized guilt. In this respect the goals and consequences of influences exerted by family, church, and school are similar.

They attempt to shape the child into an idealized moral person. Note that this conception assumes a more or less initially unformed and receptive individual who, lacking the innate capacities for moral growth, acquires morality from external sources. For Peruvians and other Latin Americans, the term that embodies this educational philosophy is *formacion*. As a term, it appears again and again in educational writing and speech. As a concept, it directs and justifies the activity in the classroom and expresses educational objectives. Although it is not fully synonymous with the term "to educate," it is the essence of education. Obviously, schooling also seeks to impart technical skills of reading, writing, and doing numbers, but does so in a rote style and instances have been reported of Indian children being capable of reading parrot-fashion from a book, but with no comprehension of the meaning of the words they enunciated. The spirit of inquiry, experimentation, or analysis is notably absent. When the essential aspects of the universe have already been determined and man needs to learn only an appropriate moral posture toward events and things, then of what use is an inquiring, or, worse, a doubting, mind?

Some comments about pedagogical practices will be helpful in understanding the philosophic view and the extracts from school observations that follow. These also illustrate how practices are linked with social and cultural distinctions. Instructional method requires that the child learn set answers to specific questions. What must be remembered is that neither answers nor questions may vary. Some kind of authority, either supernatural or secular, has already determined both the questions that are to be asked and the answers to be given. In this regard instruction resembles exactly the traditional way in which the catechism is taught and learned. The insistence is upon learning the right answer. There is no need nor desire to explore the problem to see what other questions might be framed, or to let the data direct the course of inquiry. Under this system the successful student is one who excels at rote memorization and the capacity of perfect recall. The notion of variable or contingent answers or of possibly alternative solutions is utterly alien to such an approach. Repetitive drill is the device that teacher and pupils alike use to accomplish these ends. It is ironic that the Ministry of Education decreed an end to rote teaching more than a decade ago, but only rarely can one encounter a teacher who has learned how to utilize other methods than those by which he or she was also taught.

This generalized overview of the social setting and educational characteristics in Peru has prepared the ground for the next step in analysis. Now the evidence we need to substantiate the congruency among world view, social structure, and the organization and operation of the schools must be derived from the detail of careful observation in specific educational settings. The most extensive body of data available for this purpose is found in the report by Dr. Ruth Harwood, who studied a number of Peruvian primary schools in May 1964 as part of her work as staff anthropologist with the Teachers College, Columbia University, team that was cooperating in a program of educational development with the Ministry of Education through an AID contract. Those sections that have been selected for inclusion here give a precise and vivid picture of the school setting, its daily routine, and classroom activity.

A PRIMARY SCHOOL FOR GIRLS IN LIMA [1]

Description

The school lies in a *barriada* section of Lima in the district known as San Martin de Porras, on the far side of the River Rimac. It consists of 13 classrooms enclosed by a wall and arranged around a courtyard, or patio, of somewhat cracked and uneven cement. The wall and classrooms are painted dull yellow and the roofs are of reddish tile and corrugated metal.

Most of the construction of the school was done by the parents' organization, the *Padres de Familia*. They held fiestas and other fundraising activities and, since many of the parents were construction workers by trade, they themselves built all the school rooms along the sides and rear of the patio, paved the patio, built the school wall, put on the roofs, and, in short, made all but the front three classrooms, which were originally donated by the Ministry of Education. Two of the rooms had been intended for a library and reading room, but these have long since been converted into classrooms. Three new and badly-needed classrooms are now being built by the Ministry of Education with the assistance of the *Padres de Familia*.

The principal's office lies between the wall and the front row of classrooms. A cement wall from the gate branches off to the office, with the other branch leading to the pavement of the schoolyard. Nevertheless, dust and sand cover parts of the cement walk and rise in small clouds around the feet of hurrying students. On the far side of the courtyard are one or two bathrooms, but the rest of the space is devoted to classrooms, all of which are overcrowded and somewhat poorly lighted. Although most of the rooms have a window or two, the

[1] Ruth Harwood, *A Primary School for Girls in Lima* (New York: Teachers College, Columbia University, 1965), pp. 1–25 (mimeographed).

classrooms to the far side of the yard are shaded by the wall itself and thus get little light.

The overall appearance of the school is somewhat crude and run down. It has the appearance of an old building that has been patched, repaired, and added to many times since its initial construction.

The buildings actually serve three different schools during the course of the day. In the morning, from 8 a.m. to 1 p.m., it contains the girl's school we are about to describe, *Escuela Primaria de Mujeres No. 4330*. In the afternoon, from 1:00 to 5:30, a boy's school occupies the premises, *Escuela Primarie de Varones No. 520*. In the early evening, for about 2½ hours, a school for adults is set up that holds evening classes for women, *Escuela Vespertina de Mujeres No. 187*. A completely different set of faculty and students attend each school.

Background

OF THE COMMUNITY. The district of San Martin de Porras is a *barriada* section on the outskirts of Lima. It was the first *barriada* to be formed and is therefore the oldest one, having been started about 15 to 20 years ago. Yet many of the buildings appear new and freshly painted, and rather well constructed. It seems that one of the former Presidents of Peru, Manuel Odria, built a housing project there 20 years ago in an attempt to rehabilitate the area. The people were encouraged to move into the new buildings and to pay for them over a period of 20 years. Hence some families now completely own their own homes. About 30 percent of the population live in these houses, whereas the rest live in *barriadas*.

The people of the community are either day laborers or have small businesses of their own. The day laborers are factory workers and construction workers mainly, as well as chauffeurs and *empleados*. The rest, who constitute the majority, own roadside stands, small shops, or other small businesses.

OF THE STUDENTS. The parents of the students of this area display a great deal of interest in educating their children. Nearly all want to send their children to school and keep them there, and the dropout rate between transition and fifth grade is only 2 percent. Their interest in educating their children is also demonstrated by the activeness of the parents' association, which has built most of the school and kept it in repair. The parents, in general, are willing to cooperate in any way they can to make the school a better one. They are poor, however, and most cannot afford textbooks or other eduactional aids for their children.

Some of the families originated in the highlands of Peru, but the majority came from coastal areas. In the highlands, the Department of Junin was the area from which most originated, especially the cities of Huancayo, Tarma, and Junin. A few, however, migrated from Cerro de Pasco. The coastal regions from which the majority of families originated were Ica and Ancash.

The students themselves tend to be underfed, undernourished, and consequently not able to work well in school. The teachers complain that the children are hungry when they come to school because of having had little or no breakfast. As a result they become tired by the middle of the morning and can no longer concentrate on their studies. Moreover, some are actually sick, and others are mentally retarded. It would be impossible to say how many belong in these latter categories, but enough so that the teachers all cited them as problems.

To the outside observer, the most noticeable characteristic of the students is a lack of energy and initiative. These qualities, however, are no doubt partly attributable to the cultural emphasis on obedience and submissiveness for children in Latin America, as well as to the strict discipline maintained in the classroom. Yet poor nutrition may also be a factor here. Even at recess time, one does not observe the racing and whooping that goes on in North American school yards. The general behavior of these children is noticeably subdued.

A Typical Day

BREAKFAST. In an attempt to solve the problem of undernourishment among the students, the Ministry of Public Health has instituted a program of donating a certain number of breakfasts and/or lunches to each school. Here at San Martin de Porras, 100 breakfasts are provided each day. With a school enrolment of 619 pupils, the 100 breakfasts are hardly sufficient, but at least a small percentage of the girls (for the most part those who get no breakfast at all at home) are provided with some nourishment each day.

Breakfast is served from 7:30 to 8:30 in one of the classrooms. Since all 100 girls cannot be served at once due to lack of space, they come in groups during the hour, have their breakfast, and leave. Breakfast consists of a hard roll and a tin cup of milk, which they take to the desks and eat. The roll is served cold, but the milk is warm.

A large metal milk can has been placed at the front of the room. Beside it is a table covered with tin cups. A basket of hard rolls also sits on the table. Two ladies of the community preside over the food, ladling out milk from the can into the cups as the children file past, and handing each child a roll. These ladies have previously boiled the water and mixed the powdered milk into it in the large can. Cocoa, sugar, and Quaker oats have also been added to the milk, for the children will not drink it plain. The girls bring a few centavos from home each day so that the extra ingredients may be added. The milk is stirred from time to time by the ladies as they ladle it out in an attempt to cool the mixture.

A teacher stands near the back of the room to see that the girls behave in an orderly fashion and do not leave any crumbs on the desks. The girls themselves are quiet and well behaved. No noise or whispering is audible. When they finish, they take their cups to the front of the room and place them in a large basket and file out. A new group of girls then enters and the process is repeated. During the hour, successive groups of girls enter and leave until all 100 have been served.

The director told me that it has been found necessary to issue a card to each child who is entitled to have breakfast; otherwise, other children tend to break in. The teacher at the rear of the room looks at each child's card during the meal. The director said that she finds it hard to turn children away, since so many more need breakfast than can be provided for. Therefore the card system has proved to be the best. The same 100 children are served every day. If they changed off and had a different group each week or month, none would really benefit in the long run, she said.

THE LINE-UP. While breakfast is being served in one of the classrooms the children outside are lining up for their morning ceremony and drill. The lines begin to form at about 7:45. The children are lined up by grade or by section (if a grade contains more than one section) with the youngest section of the transition class nearest the gate and the fifth grade on the opposite side of the yard. The teacher of each grade or section stands at the head of her own line. She inspects the line to see that each child is standing straight and has clean hands and face. Occasionally a child is sent to the washroom to wash. One teacher acts as director each week and stands in front of the others.

Finally, when all lines are formed and inspected and ready, the teacher in charge calls out "Attention" and all the children stand stiffly straight. She then begins the ceremony with prayers. The students repeat each line after the teacher, and all cross themselves during the benediction. This is followed by the singing of the national anthem and several other songs. The teacher in charge then calls out, "At ease." She now begins to make announcements, to admonish them as to the necessity of good behavior in class, and finally comments on the fact that a distinguished "doctora" from the United States is honoring them with a visit and how important it is to conduct themselves with the utmost propriety at all times during her stay.

She then orders them to "Attention" once more and all straighten up stiffly, ready to march. She then calls out "Face front," and then

"March!" The first line, the youngest transition section, marches around in front of the other lines to its classroom with its teacher walking beside it. Then the second section of transition goes, and then first grade, and so on until the fifth grade finally marches off to its classroom and the exercises are finished.

THIRD GRADE. As we enter the third grade, a class of 45 girls rises to greet us. The teacher introduces us to the class, saying that we (my interpreter and I) are from the Ministry of Education and that "Señorita Ruth" lives in the United States. She then makes a little speech about how fortunate they are to have such a good lady come to visit their humble neighborhood. She says it makes them very happy to have me at their school and they would like to give me a round of applause. The children clap. We are then led to a seat at the front of the room.

The room is one of the large front rooms that were built by the Ministry of Education. These rooms have two windows each and are lighter and better ventilated than are the rear rooms, most of which have no windows at all. The walls are painted a faded pink color and the ceiling is of white adobe. The floor is paved with tiles. The only ornament in the room is a statue of Jesus in a glass case reposing on a shelf over the blackboard. A vase of flowers has been placed in front of the statue. Two bare electric light bulbs hang down from the ceiling.

The children's desks are long, narrow, unpainted, and somewhat crudely made of wood. Each is built to hold two students, and each has a bench beneath with one narrow slat for a backrest. The teacher's desk in the front of the room is also of wood and is in a somewhat dilapidated condition. A crude table and two wooden chairs in one corner are where we are asked to sit to observe the class.

The girls wear uniforms consisting of navy blue pleated skirts and white or striped blouses. Over the uniform, some girls are wearing pinafores of a faded blue color. All of the children wear shoes and socks—none is barefooted.

The class had already begun before we entered the room. It is a class in health education and today's topic is the human body. On the board is written the date, and "Health Education. Theme: The Human Body." Below this are five questions:

1. What is the human body?
2. How is the human body divided?
3. What is the soul?
4. What is the soft part of the body called?
5. What is the hard part called?

The teacher gives a little lecture about the human body. She says that part of the body is liquid such as the blood, the saliva, and so forth; part of the body is made up of organs; and part of the body consists of bones. Then she speaks about what is contained in each region of the body: the trunk, for example, contains the breast, the ribs, the heart, lungs, liver, etc.

Then she asks the names of the more obvious parts of the body. What are the upper limbs called? What are the lower limbs called? Hands are raised in answer to each question, and she calls on various girls to reply. Most give the right answer, since the questions are rather simple. She writes the name of each limb or part of the body on the board as it is given.

Now the children are told to copy the five questions from the board into their notebooks. The room becomes very quiet.

After an interval of fifteen minutes or so, the teacher begins to ask the questions aloud, one by one:

"How is the human body divided?" Hands go up. Several wrong answers are given. Then she asks:

"What is the body?" Immediately she turns to the blackboard and begins to write the answers down under the title "Response." She seems somewhat embarrassed by the fact that the children have given several wrong answers, and so now begins to write the answer before calling on anyone to reply. Each child when called upon therefore now reads the answer from the board.

The children begin copying the list of answers into their notebooks. On one side of the notebook each child has written the five original questions under the heading of "Theme." On the opposite page, under the heading of "Response," each is now copying the answers, of which there are about ten. Some of the answers are as follows:

8. The parts of the head are two: the skull and the face.
9. The parts of the trunk are two: the part in front is called the breast, and the part behind is called the back.
10. Inside the trunk we have the following organs: heart, lungs, stomach, and intestines.

The room is very quiet while the children are occupied in copying the answers from the board in neat handwriting. As we walk around and look at the notebooks, we see an occasional copy of *Enciclopedia Bruno, Tercer Ano de Primaria.* This is the textbook, the teacher tells us. Only five or six children seem to have one and they are not being used in the lesson.

Finally the teacher asks them to close their notebooks and says they will now have a lesson in writing (*caligrafia*). At this point my interpreter and I stand up, and indicate that we are now going to visit another class. The children stand, the teacher thanks us for coming, and my interpreter makes a speech about how much we have enjoyed the class. All clap, and we depart.

FIFTH GRADE. We now go to the classroom of the first section of the fifth grade, known as "Fifth Year A." There are 48 girls in this class, all about the same age as those of the other section of fifth grade, which we visited before recess. That is, the ages range from twelve to fifteen, with the majority being twelve or thirteen years old. Yet despite the similarity in age and educational level, the atmosphere in this fifth grade section is noticeably different from that of the other. For one thing, the girls all appear taller, although this may have been a coincidence. For another, they seem much more *lively* and, as the lesson goes on, display a good deal more initiative.

The teacher is a pleasant, motherly sort of woman who, as she reveals later, has four children of her own. She is less strict with the girls than was the other fifth grade teacher and, as a result, an air of informality prevails. The girls do not seem in the least nervous or shy when she calls upon them in class, but instead speak out with confidence. The general atmosphere is that of a group of bright girls who are eager for a chance to perform in class. Somehow this teacher seems to have inspired confidence and a pride in learning on the part of the girls.

They are beginning a lesson in geography as we enter the classroom. The teacher draws a map of Peru on the blackboard, and then asks questions concerning it; the girls often come to the board and point out the answers on the map. Apparently this lesson is a review, and the girls seem to know the answers well.

Teacher: We are going to see how the Andes Mountain chain crosses Peru. It comes in two branches, one that comes from Chile, the other branch that comes from Bolivia. These branches come together . . . in what district? In a review you ought to know . . . in what district?

Students (in unison): In the province of Cuzco.

Teacher: Forming what junction?

Students (in unison): The junction of Vilcanota.

Teacher: Then the Andes mountain chain penetrates with how may branches?

Students (in unison): Two branches.

Teacher: With two branches making a route from south to north. From this junction of Vilcanota begin 3 branches: 1, 2, 3 branches [pointing to them on the map] that come together again at the junction of—

Students (in unison): Pasco.

Teacher: At the junction of Pasco. And from the junction of Pasco go again 3 branches: two following the western branch, that is the one that borders the Pacific Ocean, along the coast, and another begins forming the other mountain chain that forms the famous Callejon de—

Students (together): Huaylas.

Teacher: The famous Callejon de Huaylas that is in the province of Ancash. This is interesting because there are two types of mountain chains: The one next to the Sierra that is the highest, is white in color and completely covered with snow. Thus it is called the White Mountain Chain; and the one that is next to the coast which is a little larger is called:

Students (in unison): The Black Mountain Chain.

Teacher: Through the center is formed, as we have said, the Callejon de Huaylas. And what river is it that crosses the Callejon?

Students (together): The Santa River.

Teacher: That has some of the most beautiful scenery in Peru, the Callejon de Huaylas. The three mountain chains continue, and do you know in which direction?

Students (together): To the north.

Teacher: Towards the north, and come together at the junction . . .

Students: The junction of Loja.

Teacher: The junction of Loja. The Andes mountain chain, what route does it make?

Students: The Andes mountain chain runs from south to north.

Teacher: It runs from south to north. Lets see, Marianne [nodding to one of the students]. With how many branches does the Andes mountain chain cross Peru?

Marianne: With two branches, one that extends from Chile . . .

Teacher: Let's see, explain.

Marianne: One that extends from Chile, and one that comes from Bolivia. From the junction of Vilcanota go three branches.

Teacher: Let's see, Sylvia [nodding to another girl], how is the mountain chain formed? Loudly.

Sylvia: The Andes mountain chain is formed by one branch from Chile, and the other from Bolivia, and they come together at the junction of Vilcanota which is in Cuzco.

Teacher: Which is in—

Sylvia: Cuzco.

Teacher: From Cuzco.

Sylvia: Three branches go out which form the Pasco junction. From the Pasco junction go three branches.

Teacher: The one of the western mountain chain with the . . .

Sylvia: From the central part of the western chain extend the White and Black mountain chains.

Teacher: What thing forms the White and Black mountain chain? Let's see, Isabel [pointing]. Loudly. What does the White and Black mountain chain form?

Isabel: The White and Black mountain chain forms the Callejon de Huaylas.

Teacher: Now, what names do these mountain chains have? The mountain chain that is next to the ocean, what is it called?

Students (together): The Western mountain chain.

Teacher: The other that goes to the center is called Central, and that which is toward the east is called Eastern. What does the Andes chain in our territory make? What particular form? Three regions completely different from each other. We have this beauty in our land because the Andes mountain chain makes three regions different from each other. The one which borders the coast and which is bathed by the Pacific Ocean is called the Costa; the region which is traversed by the mountain chain of the Andes is called the Sierra; and the other region that is a plateau that is all green and crisscrossed by a great number of rivers is called the Selva. Then what does the Andes mountain chain form when it crosses Peru? [Points to a student]

Student: The Andes mountain chain on . . .

Teacher: When crossing Peru forms what . . . What thing? Three regions.

Student: Three regions. One washed by the Pacific Ocean is called the Costa, and another formed by the Andes mountain chain is called the Sierra, and that which is . . .

Teacher: Crisscrossed by rivers and is almost a plateau is called . . .

Student: Selva.

Teacher: Selva. Now these natural regions have different climates, different soil. Whenever one has high altitudes, mountains, plains, peaks and mesetas, and the other region does not, they have different climates and different soils and also different products, producers, and people with different occupations. Because people of the coast are not going to do the same things as those in the Sierra or those of the jungle. Thus, this is what the Cordillera of the Andes makes, the Costa, Sierra, and Selva. Well, the coastal region is the narrowest region which is right next to the Pacific Ocean. This region is characterized by the fact that it is bathed by the Pacific Ocean. Because of that we have a climate that can be called temperate without great rains or cold. We have an ideal climate, that of the coast. Very little rain, merely a drizzle. A fine rain which we know by the name of . . .

Students (together): drizzle.

Teacher: Drizzle—that is what we have here on the coast. On the other hand the mountain climate is completely different. In the mountains there are heavy rain storms. Hail falls. In the mountains the climate is also dry and very good. On the other hand in the jungle the climate is very warm; it is not like the coast nor like the Sierra. It has a great quantity of rivers and of rains and the hot sun warms the rivers. Then there is no evaporation. There are great rainfalls, and the climate is especially bad in the afternoons. Now they are going to build great roads in order to be able to get to the jungle to take advantage of all the products, and to take them to the coast for the benefit of our country, Peru.

She indicated that this was the end of the geography lesson and, in fact, the end of school for the day.

The sound of feet shuffling past the door had been audible for the last half hour. This was due to the fact that the lower grades go home earlier than the upper grades. In fact, after the transition class leaves at 12:00, the first grade is the next to go at 12:20, and from that time on succeeding grades leave at ten-minute intervals. It was now 1:00 p.m. and time for the two fifth grade sections to depart.

A PRIMARY SCHOOL FOR BOYS
IN CHINCHA, PERU [2]

Description

The school is situated in an outlying farming district of Chincha known as Grocio Prado. It was founded fifteen years ago by a man named Anselmo Abad de la Cruz and so is called, after him, the *Escuela Primaria de Varones Anselmo Abad de la Cruz No. 567.*

In appearance it is a large, airy, neatly painted school built in the shape of a U around a long, paved patio. At one end of the patio is a stage with a roof and a curtain, which can be drawn across the front. It is well constructed with large windows that let in plenty of light and air.

The whole school was built by the *Padres de Familia,* and they keep it in excellent repair. It has no doubt been recently repainted, for example, judging by its sparkling white walls and fresh green trimmings. The classrooms also have been revamped recently, and they too have a new look. So the overall appearance is that of a brand new school, and it is hard to believe that the first classrooms were built fifteen years ago.

Background

OF THE COMMUNITY. The community has been in existence for a long time, but has only been an official district of Chincha for eighteen

[2] Ruth Harwood, *A Primary School for Boys in Chincha, Peru* (New York: Teachers College, Columbia University, 1965), pp. 1–21 (mimeographed).

years. It is known as the district of Grocio Prado. Although a part of the city, it is a rural farming area and consists mainly of *minifundios*— small, independently-owned plots of land. On these small farms are grown grapes, cotton, and fruit for sale. The area is the chief supplier of such products for Lima, and trucks are sent from Lima to Grocio Prado twice a week to pick up garden produce for its markets. There is one wine factory in the community owned by a second generation Italian. I was told, however, that most families sell the grapes and make wine for home consumption only.

OF THE STUDENTS. The students of this community, therefore, come from homes where there is a strong interest in progress and in education. Many adults attend the night classes held at the school, for example. Since their parents are relatively well off, more of the students are supplied with textbooks, notebooks, paper, pens, and other school materials than have been observed elsewhere. Moreover, all of them seem to have khaki uniforms, which are in good condition. The younger students wear white coats, similar to lab coats, over their uniforms. In general, the students appear to be well-clothed and well-shod—none is barefooted.

Due to the progressive attitude of the majority of community members in Grocio Prado, as well as their relatively good economic conditions, many students from this school have gone on to study at the university and become doctors and lawyers, I was told. When this happens, they usually leave the community and go to live in the city. Yet everyone knows their families and the community is proud of them. Thus the tradition of upward mobility is strong and motivates the students to continue their studies whenever possible.

There are 377 students currently enrolled in the school. This includes two sections of transition and one section of each of the five grades. The classes are very large, with 75 pupils in the first grade and 68 in the third, for example. After the third grade there is a sharp drop in numbers. In fact I was told by the director that the dropout rate is 50 percent, and mostly takes place after the third grade. The reason for this is that the boys are then old enough to help on the farm. Since this is an area of individual landowners and the *mini-fundios* are relatively large, every able-bodied boy must give a hand on the farm.

A Typical Day

THE LINE-UP. At about 8:30 a whistle is blown by the teacher in charge of the morning drill. The boys who have arrived early and are playing in the yard now begin to get into lines with others of their own class. More boys come running in from outside the school yard and also join the lines. As in the Lima schools, the youngest classes are on the left side of the yard and the oldest on the right, with the intermediate classes in between. The teacher of each grade walks up and down to see that his children are standing in a straight line; then he begins to inspect to see that all have clean hands and faces. Occasionally a boy is sent to wash.

Finally, the teacher in charge calls out "Attention!," and all the boys stand stiffly erect. He then calls "At ease!," and all relax. He then has the boys sing the Peruvian National Anthem, after which he announces that two distinguished visitors from the Ministry of Education are with them and delivers a short tribute to us, admonishing the boys to be very well behaved during our visit.

One or two more announcements are then made and the military drill is begun. He calls out "Attention" once more, then "Face front," and finally "March!" One by one the lines move off to their classrooms, stepping smartly, two by two, the older boys using a kind of goose-step. I was told that a soldier had been hired by the *Padres de Familia* to come over once a week and give the students professional military drill. As a result, the boys march with great precision in a high-stepping soldierly fashion. The last class finally goose-steps off to its classroom and the school yard becomes quiet once more.

SECOND GRADE. The director comes to the class with us, but after the introductions he departs this time, since I had emphasized the fact that we would like to have the class go on as if we were not there.

They are in the middle of an arithmetic lesson in which they are learning the metric system. The teacher has long strips of white cardboard that are marked off in decimeters and centimeters. There is a long white pole marked off in decimeters and centimeters standing upright near her desk. A blue crosspiece can be moved up and down to measure the heights of the boys.

The room is large and airy with plenty of light from the rear windows. The desks are unpainted and somewhat scarred, but sturdy and well made. The benches, too, look used but solidly built.

The teacher is a normal school graduate of the first category. She is pleasant, but seems somewhat nervous at having visitors. Nevertheless, she goes on with her teaching without interruption, as the director has asked her to do.

Teacher: The decimeter that I have in my hand is divided into even smaller parts. You see what I have here, don't you? They are all the same, and each one of those parts is called? . . .
Students: Centimeter.

Teacher: Each one of those small parts is called a centimeter. Can any one of you tell me how many centimeters I need to form a decimeter?

Students: Ten.

Teacher: Ten centimeters to form a decimeter. Ten centimeters to form what?

Students: A decimeter.

Teacher: And to form a complete meter how many centimeters do I need?

Students: Ten.

Teacher: That's for a decimeter, and each decimeter has ten centimeters. To form a *meter* how many centimeters do I need? How many centimeters? A hundred centimeters. To form two decimeters how many centimeters do I need? Edward? How many centimeters do I need to form two decimeters?

Edward: Twenty.

Teacher: Twenty centimeters. To form half a meter, how many centimeters do I need? Seven hundred? How many centimeters do I need to form a half a meter?

Students: Fifty centimeters.

Teacher: Fifty centimeters. To form eight decimeters . . . you know that each one of these parts is called a decimeter . . . To form eight decimeters how many centimeters do I need? Eighty centimeters. If I take one of those very small parts called a centimeter, it is even divided into smaller parts, ten. Each one of these little small parts is called a millimeter. How many of these millimeters do I need to form a centimeter? Only a centimeter. Ten. To form a centimeter, you need ten what, Matilde?

Matilde: Millimeters.

Teacher: To form two centimeters, how many millimeters do I need?

Students: Twenty.

Teacher: Twenty. And to form five centimeters how many millimeters do I need? Raul?

Raul: Fifty.

Teacher: Fifty . . . millimeters. To form a decimeter how many millimeters do I need?

Students: Fifty.

Teacher: To form a *decimeter* how many millimeters do I need?

Students: Ten? A hundred.

Teacher: A hundred millimeters. To form two decimeters how many millimeters do I need?

Students: Two hundred.

Teacher: And to form a meter, how many millimeters do I need? One thousand. One child is going to take out his notebook and measure it. How long is his notebook? You will tell me how many decimeters it has, how many centimeters, and how many millimeters. In length . . . will you say it loudly so that your other companions can hear? Twenty-two what? [A student measures his notebook with cardboard strip in front of the class.]

Student: Twenty-two centimeters.

Teacher: How many decimeters are there in twenty-two centimeters? How many decimeters? Two decimeters plus two centimeters left over. How many millimeters does it have now? Two hundred twenty. To your place please. Now, measure your pencil, the length of your pencil. The length of your pencil. How many centimeters does it have? How many centimeters? How many *centimeters*? The pencil. Let's see, this other child. Take your pencil. See how many centimeters that pencil has. Fifteen centimeters. How many decimeters? How many decimeters are there in fifteen centimeters. Decimeters. How many decimeters in fifteen centimeters? Remember that the decimeter is larger than the centimeter. Marcelino? [Marcelino measures his pencil with cardboard strip.]

Marcelino: A decimeter and a half.

Teacher: Then the pencil measures fifteen centimeters, and has a decimeter and a half. How many milimeters does it have? How many millimeters does that pencil have? One hundred . . .

Student: Fifty.

Teacher: Fifty. To your place. Measure the length of one of your desks. Another friend is going to come and help, as this boy doesn't know. How many centimeters long is your desk? If you have a ruler you can all measure the length of your desks. How many? How many centimeters in the length of the desk? Nine and a half? No. Nine decimeters, seven centimeters. Now measure your ruler. Measure the length of your ruler. How many centimeters does it have in length? Thirty one. How many decimeters in thirty one centimeters? Three and one centimeter. How many millimeters are there in those three decimeters? Three hundred millimeters. Marcelino is going to measure the blackboard.

The class continues as she calls on first one boy to measure one object, then another to measure something else. She asks them to give the answer in centimeters, decimeters, and millimeters. The boys appear to be absorbed in these measurements and, in fact, to understand the principle very well. She does not try to convert the metric quantities to feet and inches, but stays within the system itself. The textbook being used is Victor Alvarez, *Mi Guia y Mi Tesoro* (Segundo Ano de Educacion Primaria, Editorial Salesiana, Lima).

While the class continues its measurements of various objects by means of the metric system, the whistle for recess is blown.

RECESS. Unlike the Lima schools reported on, this one has two-ten-minute recesses in the morning, and two in the afternoon. In other words, there is a ten-minute break every hour—at 10:00 and 11:00 a.m., and at 3:00 and 4:00 p.m. The director feels this is more beneficial than the one twenty-minute break each session that most schools give. The boys become so restless, he says, that it is better to give them a short recess every hour.

The boys line up in their classrooms at recess time and march out into the school yard. They are allowed to race, run, and play with no restraints for the duration of recess. At the end of ten minutes, the teacher in charge blows a whistle and the boys get in line to march back to their classrooms. The whole process takes about fifteen minutes.

CONCLUSION. In summary, it may be said that this school has faced the same problems as other Peruvian schools: namely, lack of space, overcrowded classrooms, lack of teachers, equipment, furnishings, and so on. Yet in a very remarkable way the association of *Padres de Familia* has pitched in and solved them. They have built the school, put in bathrooms and other refinements, raised money for desks, chairs, blackboards, and teaching materials, provided drums and helmets for a school band, procured military instruction for the boys, and collaborated with the teachers in every way possible to make a better school for their children. But there are a few things that even this enterprising group of parents cannot achieve—such as more land for enlarging the school, more teachers, a library, and a refectory for serving meals. One is left with the distinct impression, however, that somehow they will eventually manage to obtain these, too.

This school is an example of what a thriving community can accomplish on its own with practically no help from the Ministry of Education. It has been built, equipped, and watched over by the parents for fifteen years. Nearly everything that has been needed for the school has, through resourcefulness and initiative, been attained. A good deal of this is due to the relatively well-to-do economic circumstances of the community members, of course—they have been able to raise funds for improvements and supplies more easily than could poorer communities. Yet one cannot help being impressed also by the amount of determination and drive manifested by the association of *Padres de Familia*. They will stop at nothing to obtain whatever they feel the school should have. Education is highly valued here, even though many boys are forced to leave school to help on the farms. But of those boys who *can* stay on and graduate, a large proportion are sent to secondary school and many to professional schools after that. The community is upwardly mobile and many of its efforts in this direction are concentrated on the school.

OBSERVATIONS[3]

These excerpts give us some taste for the richness that lies in the detail of observation. Altogether Dr. Harwood visited five primary schools

[3] Ruth Harwood, *Five Primary Schools in Peru: A Preliminary Report* (New York: Teachers College, Columbia University, 1965), pp. 1–24 (mineographed).

in a range of settings—urban, rural, coastal, and mountain. Everywhere she encountered a basic pattern in pedagogical style and student
response, in parental participation, and in frustration and resentment
toward the centralized and remote Ministry of Education. These are
best expressed by presenting selected portions of her summary:

This section will be concerned primarily with similarities rather
than with differences, since these were the more striking wherever we
went. We found, for example, that each school tended to have the same
types of problems and to have adopted similar methods of dealing with
them; that teaching methods were very much alike wherever we went;
that attitudes toward education and toward the Ministry of Education
were similar everywhere, and so on. To have explored the regional differences between schools would have necessitated a thorough social and
cultural study, and this we did not have time to do. From what we observed in the schools alone, therefore, the similarities were far more
striking than the differences.

Padres de Familias

This group, the association of parents, were found to be the back-
bone of the school system everywhere we went. The *padres* themselves,
for example, had built the whole school in two of the communities we
visited, those of the Grocio Prado district of Chincha and of Vilcacoto
in Huancayo. They had raised the money by means of holding raffles,
sales, bazaars, and other fund-raising activites. In San Martin de
Porras, all but the three front rooms had been built by the *padres*, the
patio paved, the roof mended, and all other improvements and additions installed by them. Not only did they build schools everywhere,
but in Grocio Prado in particular the *padres* had made all the desks,
chairs, tables, the main gate, installed bathrooms, built a stage at one
end of the patio, and had several times painted the whole school.
Moreover, when they felt that someone was needed to instruct the
boys in military drill, one of the parents went to the police station in
Chincha and arranged to have a solider (a guard, that is) sent to the
school regularly to do this.

In all of the primary schools the parents provided notebooks,
pencils, crayons, and pencil-sharpeners for their children, and those
who could afford it bought textbooks too.

In the girls' school in Chincha, which is located in a rented house,
the *padres de familias* had raised 25,000 *soles* to buy land on which
to construct a school. But the price of land had gone up from 30 *soles*
per square meter to 120 during the years they had been raising the
money, so their funds were still not sufficient. They had asked the city

for land but had been turned down. These parents badly want a new school for their children and are doing all they can to raise money for the land and materials.

Moreover, the *padres* at this same school had built an extra room in the school yard for the transition class, they had bought all the furnishings for the school, such as tables, desks, chalk, and other materials, and each parent had supplied his daughter with a chair to take to school. At the end of every school year the children take their chairs home again.

In Vilcacoto, Huancayo, although the director complained that the *padres de familias* were very uncooperative, lacking in interest, and that they seldom showed up when she called a meeting, nevertheless they did build the whole school themselves and the community had given the land for it. Furthermore, they had made all of the desks except ten, which came from the Ministry of Education, they had made tables and chairs, and they had raised 800 *soles* to be used for paving the patio. The director said that many parents in this community had no interest in sending their children to school, but that those who *did* were willing to make any sacrifice to do so. It was this small but interested group of *padres* who had built and furnished the school. Yet even the most dedicated parents would take their children out of school during the harvest time to work in the fields.

In short, it appeared that the *padres de familias* in every community we visited were willing to do all in their power to provide an education for their children. This included building and furnishing the whole school, raising money for materials, and doing everything short of teaching the classes themselves. There was, of course, in every area a group of distinterested parents who did not send their children to school at all, but we were not able to determine its size or extent. The major reasons for lack of attendance, moreover, appeared to be primarily those of lack of space, lack of teachers, or too great a commuting distance from the school.

The Teaching Process

In all of the schools I visited, the teachers were teaching very large numbers of pupils. The sizes of the classes varied from 32 to 75 students, with the majority of classes containing more than 40. There were often two sections of some of the grades, each of which contained 40–50 pupils.

The method of teaching used everywhere seemed to be a question and answer approach, first orally by repeating many times the question and correct answer, then in writing by copying the questions and answers over and over down a page in the notebook. Usually a set of questions was written on the blackboard at the beginning of the hour. After a short lecture on the subject, the teacher asked these questions aloud one by one. After the first question the class would answer in unison, and she would have them repeat the answer several times. She would then ask the same question again and call upon individual children to answer. (Even after all that repetition, a few did not get it right.) Finally, when she was satisfied that nearly all could repeat the answer correctly, she went on to the next qeustion, and so on until all (usually four or five) questions had been answered over and over many times. Then she would ask them to take out their notebooks. They would copy the questions. Then, she would either ask individuals to come to the board and write answers to the different questions (this always took place if the class was in arithmetic, for example), or she would put the answers on the board herself and they would copy them. At any rate, the lessons were divided into two parts: oral recitation (repeating over and over in exact words the answers to questions) and written work (copying set phrases or sentences from the board many times).

Textbooks were practically never used, as far as I could determine. There were always one or two students who owned one, but, since the majority did not, the teacher made no assignments in them. Perhaps they were helpful for reference to those who owned them, but I did not see them being used in any class.

In general, the students tended to be passive and quiet. Whenever the class seemed restless, a teacher would order them all to stand up and then to sit down, and this might be repeated two or three time. In another case, when boys were tapping on their desks with pencils, the teacher made all put their arms behind their backs for a while. But for the most part the classes were quiet and only a low murmur could be heard with an occasional pupil calling out, "Señorita!" The lack of activity and noise is all the more surprising when one considers the large size of most classes and the fact that usually two or three students are crowded together at each desk.

In summary, the teaching process was observed to consist largely of memorization by means of oral repetition and copywork. Almost no visual aids were employed. The children were passive, obedient, and respectful to the teacher, but displayed little initiative or independence, and were not encouraged to do so.

Attitude Toward the Ministry of Education

Everywhere we went we found that the scapegoat for all frustrations resulting from inadequate facilities was the Ministry of Education. Sooner or later we would begin to sense the resentment that was felt toward the Ministry by both teachers and parents at every school. The Ministry was blamed for not doing anything for them, for not doing enough, or for actually hindering the parents in their attempts to do more for their schools. The feeling seemed to be that the Ministry had an obligation to help them, but that it was not doing so—instead, it was turning its back and ignoring their very existence.

At one school the parents told me that the *padres de familias* had built almost the whole school, paved the patio, and later put new roofs on several classrooms. The Ministry not only gave them no materials or help, but instead now criticizes their work and claims that the school is poorly built. The parents feel that this criticism is unfair because they did the best they could with no outside help or professional advice.

At another school, where the parents have built the whole school, made most of the desks and chairs, and put in such extras as a stage for the auditorium, the director told me that all the Ministry has done is to prevent the parents from doing some of the things they have wanted to do for the school. The teachers felt that the Ministry should start helping their school because the parents are getting tired of doing everything themselves.

The resentment toward the Ministry seems to stem in part from a feeling of neglect, a feeling that the Ministry neither knows nor cares a thing about their schools. A real appreciation of the interest *we* were taking in their school, however, was shown in the hearty welcome that was given to us in each community. We were wined and dined by everyone from the director on down. Teachers, parents, and students all seemed delighted that we were studying their school. The parents helped entertain us by bringing food and gifts, even though they were not invited to the dinner parties by the teachers. The students crowded around or looked in windows of the classrooms we visited. Some brought gifts of fruit or flowers. The general attitude seemed to be, "*Ojala* that someone from the Ministry is at last taking an interest in our school!"

The Effects of the Centralized System of Administration on the Schools

The effect of the system of educational administration that prevails in Peru is to place the school directors and parents in the position of continually begging for supplies—and, moreover, of usually being turned down. The standard procedure in Chincha seemed to be for the director to go (or send a parent) to the Inspector of Education with a request for certain materials for his school. At that office he would wait in line to see the Inspector. The Inspector would then have his secretary type out a letter of request to the Ministry, which he would sign, stamp with his official stamp, and seal. The letter was then taken by one of the *padres de familias* to Lima to the Ministry of Education. Here the parent would join one of the long lines in that building to present his official request. I was not able to ascertain just how long it usually took to reach the source of supply, but it was a lengthy task at best, and often a fruitless one.

In San Martin de Porras, Lima, the director of the boys' school told me that he himself takes the requisition for supplies to the Ministry and goes to the third floor to present it. He told me that the Ministry never issues materials to the schools voluntarily, but that each school has to put in a request for whatever it needs. Thus he spends a good deal of time at the Ministry building trying to obtain supplies. There is no other way to obtain them, he said, but to go in person.

Requests for teachers entail an even longer process and many more frustrations. In one area we visited, at the regional center for education, there were long lines of people waiting to see the director in order to ask for a teacher. We talked to one, apparently angry, group of women (parents) crowded around the door to his office. They said that they had been standing there for four hours, and had been coming every day for three days. It was nearly six o'clock and the lights in the building were being extinguished. As we departed, the last lights were turned off and these ladies were left standing in the dark. (Later we found out that the director had long since departed by another door.) We never found out how many more days and hours these women spent there, but all indications were that no teachers would be forthcoming for quite some time.

In short, the centralized system of education in Peru operates in such a way as to place both parents and school directors in a demeaning and frustrating position—they must go in person to the highest authorities and beg for favors. This system no doubt gives rise to much of the resentment felt by parents and teachers toward the Ministry.

TOWARD AN ETHNOGRAPHY OF THE SCHOOL

The reader should be impressed by the similarity in organization and pedagogy that is repeated in the several schools visited by Harwood. That such uniformity should appear in a range encompassing populations that were wholly Indian, mixed Indian-mextizo, stable small farmers, and industrial workers, and a metropolitan district inhabited by the respectable poor, is indicative of a basic cultural homogeneity.

I have been informed that private schools attended by children of the well-to-do are also comparable.

These excerpts provide a vivid, if brief, glimpse of students and teachers as actors in the school setting and of their relation to community and the nation. As such, they give substance to earlier generalities of the congruences between education and culture in Peru. Moreover, they also exemplify the kind of data an anthropologist accumulates to produce an ethnography of a school in which observation ranges from community setting to classroom behavior.

Data must be comprehensive in scope, precise in their detail, and must record the behavior and interaction of individuals in the setting of place and sequence of time. From such detail comes the basis for constructing categories of differences and formulating statements about process. These are the essentials for initial understanding and for subsequent planning of change. Moreover, they permit comparisons between educational systems at a level beyond the superficial and they foster contextual insights rather than those based on apriorisms.

Even these limited data permit analysis beyond what will be attempted here and the involved reader is invited to apply his skill. A first step is to designate the major groupings as categories. As example, these include students (distinguished on the basis of sex, age, and grade achievement), teachers, parents, and Ministry bureaucrats. Careful examination of the data will uncover representatives of a few other types that intrude themselves and with special consequences. There are other categories that should also be identified, such as those based upon cultural definitions of ethnic variation or social class.

Such categorizations give us the major social and cultural divisions and open the way for the specification of the structure of the school as a social organization and of its relationships with other agencies and institutions. The gross characteristics of structure may be presented descriptively in which we derive an ordering based upon status or function. For example, we can describe the internal divisions within the school, or the relationship between school and central Ministry, or of *Padres de Familias* with both. Representatives of civil and religious organizations are also injected from time to time for special purposes.

Interaction analysis provides us with another device in which relationships may be detailed. In this approach, we identify those who initiate and those who respond, and the order of action. This method can be applied for its own ends or for verification of the gross structural arrangements based upon other criteria.

These approaches can be used in conjunction with still another— event analysis. As a first step, a rough inventory can be made of all the types of happenings. The school day could be counted as an event, but obviously within such an encompassing unit there are many sub-events, such as the morning line-up, recess, etc. Each of these can be examined in relation to space—where they occur—to time—their relation to preceding and following sequences—to activity, personnel, relationships, and order of action. With this approach, the several dimensions of a social system begin to appear. Comparisons can then be made among types of events, their internal structural relations, and the other aspects already mentioned. Such an analysis leads to specifications of similarities and differences of a kind beyond those of cultural categorization.

Humans always carry out their activities within certain conditions that can be specified and that affect the activities. The extent to which the environmental setting affects the teaching process, school organization, or other aspects of institutional operation can be made explicit through comparison. For example, our data are inadequate to permit us to know how the lack of textbooks really affects teacher behavior and student performance, but if this was an important consideration it would not be too difficult to make empirical observations, if we were in Peru, to establish the fact. The repeated comment by teachers that the pupils were adversely affected by lack of sufficient breakfast exemplifies an observed relationship between conditions and performance. Before we fully accepted the validity of such statements, we would need much more detailed information than is currently available. In any event, analysis requires continuous attention to the conditions within which happenings occur.

Finally, our analysis should attempt to specify the values that explain the observed behavior. This is not always an easy task, since verbal affirmation and actual behavior are often in conflict with each other. But values can be extracted by inference from many sources. For example, the subject matter taught, the controls of behavior, the organization of groups, the use of time and space may all be treated as indicators of values.

Such analyses are essential to a full understanding of the organization and process of education and of the relation of the schools to other aspects of the society. There is a larger purpose to be served by this type of detailed operation, however. It is from such a base line of knowledge of structure and process that the preparation of new national goals in education can be projected. From this base it then becomes possible to prepare a plan for educational development that might not otherwise be possible. It is this type of research that all developing nations must engage in if they are going to utilize education as a major instrument in the reconstruction of their societies.

17. EDUCATION AND DEVELOPMENTAL CHANGE

The use of education for purposes of public policy may not be new, but it has evoked increased attention since the end of the Second World War. For example, over the past several years the United States Congress and some state legislatures have enacted legislation that encourages the provision of facilities and training of students for occupations that serve the national or state interest. Large numbers of students have received scholarships or other aids to learn the skills of medicine, nursing, teaching, engineering, and science. Thousands of others who already are in professional practice have been awarded grants to upgrade their competencies through additional study. More recently, attention has been directed toward the economically backward sections of the country and segments of the population. The Appalachia program, for example, is designed to broaden economic opportunities and thus to reduce or eliminate poverty, and a great deal of emphasis, and hope, is being placed upon the expected results from formal education.

When we look beyond the borders of our own country, we discover that many other nations have embarked upon accelerated programs of educational expansion and modernization. Other Western nations are responding to much the same pressures as those that stimulate our own efforts. The new, underdeveloped nations are in a great rush to catch up. Their leaders know that industrialization produces the wealth that can support public services and raise the standard of living, but they have also learned that without an ade-

"Education and Developmental Change," in Art Gallaher, Jr., Ed., *Perspectives in Developmental Change* (Lexington: University of Kentucky Press, 1968), pp. 71–100.

quately educated personnel, neither public nor private enterprise can prosper.

The facts of life in this regard are so simple that in retrospect it is difficult to understand how they could have been so badly misinterpreted. It is true, of course, that the economists only recently have begun to assign a capital value to education. It is also true that the extractive industries of lumbering, mining, or plantation agriculture required only common labor from an indigenous population. Capital and technical skill were imported, and the output was absorbed by industrial economies that were already developed. The situation changes, however, when a population develops national aspirations, and expanded internal markets arise from recently acquired higher standards of living. The deficiency in skills that require formal education becomes a major block to the development of new resources or the transformation of existing practices—particularly in agriculture. Out of this reality came the awakening that led to a new assessment of the role of education.

It is somewhat ironic that the rationale for this preeminence of education can be traced to the pronouncements of the economists, and not to those of the educators. The educators have never doubted the worth of their contribution, but their message was heeded little until the powerful force of manpower requirements for economic development and national security arose. Manpower specialists have become increasingly influential among those who make national policy and allocate funds. It is argued that a nation that already is rich and powerful can maintain that position only if it can muster a determinate proportion of skills for its many needs. The nations that wish to sit among the elect must do the same. Since trained manpower is a consequence of formal education, the logic inexorably leads to the conclusion that education occupies a top priority in the allocation of resources.

Educators have also found persuasive the arguments of human resource development as a condition of economic growth. The Ashby Commission's recommendation for educational development in Nigeria, submitted in 1960, relied almost exclusively upon the analysis of the skilled manpower needs in Nigeria made by Professor Frederick Harbison. The report's projections of educational facilities and personnel needs were justified by economic considerations. It is noteworthy that the report was titled "Investment in Education."

Although the economic value of an education has long been recognized, customarily we have not viewed the expenditures for it as an investment in the same sense that we would consider the purchase of machinery or the building of hydroelectric projects an investment. For certain purposes, however, an economic frame of reference helps to focus our thinking in terms of the problems of development. In this context educational costs may be counted as a public expenditure necessary to provide trained personnel to expand and improve public services and productive enterprises. Irrespective of the justifying rationale, whether it be purely pragmatic or highly idealistic, the fact remains that formal education is a crucial adjunct in the development process.

A recent book by Harbison and Myers, entitled *Education, Manpower, and Economic Growth*,[1] supports the gross relation between educational attainment and national productivity. The authors group 75 countries into four levels of human resource development—underdeveloped, partially developed, semiadvanced, and advanced. Within these major groupings they found a high degree of correlation between seven educational indicators and economic factors. The correlation was less pronounced within the groupings because of (they believed) other variables, such as natural resources, that influenced the results. Their evidence supports clearly the general conclusion that education pays off.

We can rejoice with educators in their new-found ally among economists. It is difficult to conceive of a more convincing argument for adequate financial support of education than one that promises increased wealth and economic growth as a consequence. But a rationale based on economic premises has not been, nor should it be, the compelling force behind educational objectives. Our national goals have been conceived on a much broader base than mere physical well-being. Need we mention our belief in providing opportunities for individual achievement and self-development or of educating for responsible participation in a political democracy, or of the cultivation of the intellectual and esthetic capacities? These are aspirations that education should and has served. They, too, should be counted as essential goals in any program for development.

We must be careful to distinguish, however, between educational functions in a society such as ours, which is in a continuing state of transformation, and educational functions in less developed societies, which only now are emerging from an agrarian or tribal past. Our problem is to keep our educational machinery abreast of other societal changes. Among developing nations when national ambitions and an upsurge in aspirations by the people unite on the common denominator of education as a solution to their problems, however, education may be called upon to produce results that are not possible to attain. As

[1] Frederick Harbison and Charles A. Myers, *Education, Manpower, and Economic Growth* (New York: McGraw-Hill, 1964).

John Wilson, an expert on African education, described it for that continent, "The fact is that in Africa, education is in such demand that no political leadership dare withhold it or slow down its proliferation by pausing to enquire into its quality." [2] The problem lies, then, not in preaching the value of education but in the danger that education will be counted as a panacea to correct all deficiencies.

Where formal education represents a new institutional experience, the people may not possess the ability to judge its quality and adequacy. In such instances the responsibility for judgment will almost certainly fall upon educators. But do they not have the same responsibility in our own society? The answer to this question can no longer be a categorial "yes." Even with such a limited linkage as that between national development and education, economic considerations now exert a powerful force. Furthermore, there are other national goals with equally strong and legitimate assertions for the right to be included. The multifaceted functions of education now require competencies beyond those that are unique to educators. They include, among other things, an understanding of the relationship between the educational process and the institutions and culture of a people. It is in this latter sphere that the social sciences can and must make their contribution.

From the description and interpretation of society and culture, the contribution of sociology and anthropology, comes our understanding of the organization and behavior of humans in social groupings. These disciplines provide the basic knowledge that specialists in education must possess if they are to understand the social function of education and are to fashion a curriculum that trains and educates future generations. Emile Durkheim, the eminent French sociologist and pedagogist, who in his later career occupied the chair of "science of education" at the Sorbonne, insisted that the goals of education are wholly social, and, as a function of society, education ensures the perpetuation of collective life. He stated, "Education is, then, only the means by which society prepares, within the children, the essential conditions of its very existence." [3] Hence, Durkheim reasoned, educators must turn to sociology to gain the knowledge and ideas they have a responsibility to transmit.

Since Durkheim's day we have broadened the area of inquiry and clarified some of the concepts he used, but his prescription of the dependence of pedagogy upon sociology still holds. Formal education

    [2] John Wilson, *Education and Changing West African Culture* (New York: Teachers College Press, 1963).
    [3] Emile Durkheim, *Education and Sociology,* trans. Sherwood D. Fox (Glencoe: The Free Press, 1956).

remains primarily concerned with the process of transmission of knowledge, morals, and skills. It determines the manner and shape of presentation of subject matter, but only rarely does it create subject matter. It exploits multiple sources for the materials it utilizes. But educators are properly concerned with everything that is relevant to the process of teaching and learning. What, then, are the more general as well as the specific contributions the respective social sciences have to offer?

There are three such areas that I believe have direct application. As social scientists we are interested in the organizational forms through which human beings group themselves. These include the community and the subsidiary institutional arrangements, one of which is education. Second, we wish to understand those cultural patterns, the ways of behaving and their associated cultural values, that provide the breath of humanity to social groups. One such pattern includes the educational process and its stated or implied philosophy. Lastly, we wish to understand the processes that govern the repetitive regularities of social behavior as well as those that can explicate the transformation of a society. One such process is embodied in the concepts of the transmission of culture and the socialization of the child.

These, then, are three general areas of direct relevance—the organizational form within which educational activity occurs; the patterned activity expressed in techniques, procedures, and values of teaching and learning; and the processes that are utilized to bring about change or that ensure stability.

One of the errors that those who work in cross-cultural situations are likely to make has been based on the bland assumption that underneath the obvious differences, which are often viewed as only superficial, the people of diverse cultures are basically alike. This view may also be interpreted as meaning that they are not really different from me. Those who hold such a view, and what for them is a generous projection of humanness to others, often experience a rude shock when their most artful attempts to bring new wisdom or alter traditional ways of behaving to others of different cultures find their efforts either have little effect or produce unintended consequences.

Anthropologists, who have successfully predicted the frequent frustration and failure of those who attempt to work outside a known cultural framework, have advocated that the development technician learn the ways of the people among whom he works. But anthropologists, in their efforts to help others to work cross-culturally, have also gained some new perspectives. They have learned that conscious awareness of the behavior, values, and assumptions of one's own culture may be of equal or even greater importance for successful performance in culturally divergent situations than is precise knowledge of the other culture itself. (Among those who have attempted to interpret American culture are Edward T. Hall, who worked for five years in the Point Four Training Program of the State Department between 1950 and 1955, and Conrad Arensberg, whose essay "American Cultural Values" [4] has been widely quoted.)

If there is any one aspect of culture in which sensitivity to traditional behavior would seem to be desirable, it is in the area of innovation or reform of educational organization and practices. The record shows, however, that just the opposite has been true. During the period when much of the world was under colonial administration, the educational facilities provided by the governing nation were almost always faithful, if inferior, copies of the school system in the mother country. In fact, as Wilson reports for Africa, "There was, indeed, a naïve belief that Africa had no education, and there was no understanding of the fact that education is itself part of the social organization of any society, whether or not that society has anything which might be recognized as a school." [5] In India, where an indigenous formal system of schooling served a limited portion of the population, the British ignored the indigenous practices and established their own imported system.

In the United States the Indian Service replicated the traditional American school and operated it under an avowed policy of Americanizing and detribalizing the Indian. Boys and girls in the boarding schools were taught presumably useful vocations, most of which had no relation to reservation life and often very little applicability in an industrializing America. Even the valiant efforts of John Collier when he was Commissioner of Indian Affairs had only little effect. He did succeed in removing the worst features of the reform school atmosphere that these schools previously had, but the task of breaking the stranglehold of traditional practices proved difficult. The recent study by Murray and Rosalie Wax [6] of the Pine Ridge Reservation School reports the need of educational reorientation to meet both cultural and curriculum problems.

Attempts at educational reform have also had an interesting history among dependent people. Only rarely have these projects sought to examine the needs of a colonial people, a notable exception being the Phelps-Stokes study of African education. Usually they were the

[4] Conrad M. Arensberg, "American Cultural Values," in Conrad M. Arensberg and Arthur N. Niehoff, Introducing Social Change (Chicago: Aldine Publishing Co., 1964), Chapter VI.

[5] Wilson, Changing West African Culture, p. 17.

[6] Murray Wax and Rosalie Wax, "Formal Education in an American Indian Community," Social Problems, XI(1) (1964).

result of the extension of reforms that had been generated in the governing country, reforms that were designed to modernize its own educational system and not for forwarding the development of a dependent territory.

Whatever the original intent, philosophy, or source of the educational systems of the underdeveloped countries in Asia, Africa, and Latin America, the point to be remembered now is that with political autonomy, whether recently won or stretching back over a century and a half, these countries have the power to choose which educational practices and viewpoints they believe are the most advantageous for their own growth and development. On second thought, however, we are forced to narrow the breadth of the discretion they hold. Their new, or old, rulers are already bound by traditions that stretch into the past. In the former French and British colonies in Africa all aspects of schooling clearly reveal their respective Gallic and Anglo-Saxon origins, and at the moment the tendency to perpetuate and intensify these traditions is much stronger than any impulse that might cast them out. The educational systems of South America reach back to Spain and Portugal. A recent overlay reflects influence from the French Enlightenment, and later minimal innovations from the United States.

If the progressive political leaders of the developing nations wish to bring their countries into the orbit of industrial civilization, they must recast and add to traditional education. This is not a fact about which they need to be informed, however. The decision to modernize an educational system is a relatively easy one. The difficult problem is to know what to do and how. This can be a portentous decision, however, because reform of education cannot be accomplished without changes in other segments of the society. Once the course is set, there can be no reconstitution of the tribal, plantation, peasant, or rigid-class societies that are swept aside as a consequence. But to set in motion the processes that transform a society is far more difficult— even with violent revolution—than might be supposed.

These difficulties, as they apply to educational modernization, can be better understood by looking at a sample of those nations where traditional practices in education continue to flourish. The purpose is to indicate some of the social and cultural characteristics that must be reckoned with in any attempt to transform the existing situation. The diversities among the examples should also provide the basis for comparative analysis and demonstrate that each culture requires its own distinctive formula for change.

Korea, Brazil, and Peru are the three countries from which the illustrative material will be drawn. Although the focus in each will be somewhat different, the basic similarities are considerable and in this respect resemble other developing nations. Korea demonstrates the consistency within the values honoring the great achievements of a classical tradition. Brazil illuminates the tight interconnections among values, behavior, institutions, and education. The Peruvian case gives some insight into the utilization of social science principles in bringing change in educational practice.

The practices and values that shape the mode of life of a people are found within their culture. Ordinarily a culture exhibits a high degree of consistency among its separate aspects, and we do not expect to find any serious contradictions or disharmonies between areas of activity and their correlative institutions, except under conditions of rapid change. This generalization should serve to alert the educator who has been asked to recommend innovations to seek first for the congruencies between the organization, practice, and philosophy of education and comparable aspects in other institutions. Such knowledge helps to delimit the scope and direction which educational advice might take, as is shown in the report by Don Adams [7] of his experience in Korea, which I shall summarize.

The traditional culture of Korea honors authority as represented by the aged, by those in positions of power, and as it is contained in the wisdom transmitted from the past. "The Good Life has been defined completely in terms of past living; where history has largely been viewed as cyclical, with the future regarded as a mere repetition of some portion of the past; and where innovations in terms of things bigger and better may be disrespectful to one's ancestors." [8] The relationship to nature is one that asks of mankind a harmonious adjustment, resignation, even self-discipline. The barriers and forces of the physical world do not provide the challenge or evoke the will to mastery that they have for Western man. In a cultural environment that reverences the past it is not surprising that the traditional educational system emphasized the academic and the esthetic. The student "studied to imitate rather than to exceed, to conform rather than to create. Education that was prized was divorced entirely from the social, economic, and scientific problems of the present." [9]

Other cultural features reflecting the older Chinese and more recent Japanese influences are found in persisting traditions concerning

[7] Donald Adams, "The Monkey and the Fish," in Gove Hambridge, Ed., *Dynamics of Development: An International Reader* (New York: Praeger, 1964), pp. 361–368.

[8] *Ibid.*, p. 362.

[9] *Ibid.*, p. 363.

language, script, texts, and preferred courses of study, but enough has been reported to indicate some of the cultural barriers that have inhibited the reconstruction of education on a Western model. Educational procedures that attempt to develop self-reliance and cooperation challenge the authority rooted in family and social distinctions. A curriculum that educates for the future violates commitment to the past. Veneration for the scholar denigrates learning that directs one toward pragmatic goals, so vocational or technical training holds little esteem. Innovation itself is disrespectful. Yet Korea is being thrust toward the modern world at a slow, uneven, and painful pace. In such a situation the contribution of education is no less significant, but as Adams describes the role of the educational adviser in this "sensitive and difficult" setting, it is a minor but vital one that might lessen the traumatic effects of change. This is indeed far removed from grandiose plans of rapid educational transformation, but it may well be the only course of action that is feasible.

Perhaps the most important of all the insights that those who seek development through education must acquire is that the educative process can be understood only as we understand its social and cultural setting. The significance of this principle was shown briefly in connection with the values that shape the perspective of life among Koreans. But we can deepen our understanding if we attempt to see a society whole. With this objective in mind I will outline some relevant aspects of the institutions and culture of Brazil in their relationship to the structure, practices, and values in formal education. This description should also dramatize that the values and goals that the United States attaches to education are not held universally.

Brazil is a nation in transition from a traditional plantation pattern, which effloresced in the seventeenth and eighteenth centuries, and a system of subsistence agriculture, whose roots extend to pre-Columbian cultures of the aborigines. Approximately 50 percent of its one hundred million inhabitants are rural residents. Much of the urban population is concentrated in towns and cities along the coastal fringe and two of these, Rio de Janeiro and São Paulo, together have about twenty million inhabitants. Urbanism as a way of life is as old in Brazilian culture as are the great sugar plantations or cattle *fazendas,* but the new commercialism and newer industrialism have injected a vitality, but hardly an orderliness, into some sections of the country. The northeast, for example, has barely been touched by the modern world and represents a backwater of stagnation and poverty. In contrast, the industrial urban complex in the city and state of São Paulo approximates, in many respects, that of the most advanced nations. In spite of these diversities, Brazil presents a high degree of national unity attributable largely to the uniformity of its social institutions and way of life.[10]

The history of Brazil from its earliest settlement to the present reflects the desire to accumulate wealth and power, which has encouraged ruthless exploitation. This exploitation included the natural resources of forests, soil, and minerals; of aborigines, slaves, and laborers; and of the institutions of government and religion. Occasional voices of protest have been raised and efforts made to mitigate the extreme abuses as, for example, the attempt of the Jesuits to protect the Indians in the early colonial period. In a later day, leaders imbued with the spirit of the Enlightenment sought broad reforms in the institutional life, and with the growth of cities and industrialism much progressive legislation was enacted. Mostly, however, these efforts stand as monuments to the good intentions of a few and were never incorporated as integral parts of the social fabric. The attempts at educational reform have suffered much the same fate as those made in other segments of national life, an aspect we shall examine more fully a little later.

No single factor can explain the predatory and conservative nature of Brazilian life, but in the nexus of institutional and cultural behavior we can observe some of its manifestations by examining the structure of the family, the strong sense of individualism, the relative absence of a community or public consciousness, and the internal cultural divisions, which we can label social class.

The history of Brazil and the functioning of its institutions cannot be understood apart from the structure of the traditional family. In the classic analysis, *The Masters and the Slaves*, Gilberto Freyre [11] documents the pivotal position of the family in the colonial and subsequent periods. The analyses in the writings of Wagley, Hutchinson, Willems, and Nogueira support the same conclusion for contemporary Brazil, even though they note some recent modifications. But family in Brazil in no sense approximates what we mean when we refer to family in the United States. There it includes an extended and interlocking network of kin, often subdivided into smaller units of closely related nuclear families. From this large kinship group, the *parentela,* came those who dominated the political, religious, and economic life of the country. In their other institutional roles they acted not only as

---

[10] Charles Wagley, *An Introduction to Brazil* (New York: Columbia University Press, 1963), Chapter I.

[11] Gilberto Freyre, *The Masters and the Slaves: A Study in the Development of Brazilian Civilization* (New York: Knopf, 1964).

representatives of their own kin but of those joined with them through an extension of the family in the system of godparents, the *compadrio,* and of those for whom they served as patrons, the employees and *agregados* of the lower classes. Thus, the family and its extensions cut through and included members of all social levels. In fact, as recently as thirty years ago some of the patriarchal family heads in the country's interior maintained private armies for their protection and aggrandizement.

The sense of the evidence should convince us of the significance of the connections that attachment to a family provided. It should also help us to understand how the development of Brazil cannot escape from the mold that family imposes. Its influence cannot be underestimated, as Wagley has stated: "The persistence of familism has acted as a block to the formation of national political parties, the creation of an impersonal bureaucratic system of government, and the development of economic enterprises that would enlist wide public participation." [12] We might add that the failure of educational reform and modernization can also be traced to the same source.

The preeminence of family helps to explain the absence of a public consciousness of community involvement as we in the United States know it. Here where the primary obligation is to kin or others who are personally dependent upon an individual, the business of government or community assumes a lesser importance. The arena of government often is viewed as the locale in which special interests jockey for favorable position through political maneuvering. This view is partially applicable to Brazil, but in this instance the special interests are those of the family and the social class it represents. Hence individuals seek special favors or government appointments for members of their families, and nepotism is an accepted value. The schools are not exempt from such practices, and in some instances a change in the party in power in a municipality will result in the dismissal of one group of teachers and the appointment of another.

There is another tradition, however, that Brazil inherited from its Portuguese background and that continues to have a strong influence in the culture. Government was originally viewed as an extension of the power of the king and later of the ruling clique, which in traditional Brazil meant the oligarchy of family. The power of government was utilized to benefit those who controlled it, not to bring benefits to a people. Through government the ruling class exploited others, but it also exploited the structure of government itself. There is no dispensa-

[12] Wagley, *Introduction to Brazil,* pp. 203–204.

tion that sets a ministry of education or any specific school apart from the general principle. Nepotism, corruption, incompetence, and inefficiency are as likely to be found within education as in any other activity. We can claim no more or no less for any other country.

There is a further aspect of Brazilian culture and personality about which we should know if we are to understand the educational process—namely, individualism. The sense in which this manifests itself is rather different than among United States citizens, so some additional explanation is desirable. Among Brazilians, the distinction between "public" and "private" spheres is far sharper than it is among Americans. The private world encompasses the intimates of family and friends, and here one is bound by an elaborate code of behavior and mutual obligations. The public world, in contrast, is one in which the individual may mingle freely, and he is not bound by the normal constraining obligations. This may help to explain why public mixing of class or race is of such little consequence, as epitomized in the social leveling at times of carnival. It also helps to explain the double code of ethics, which prescribes one set of behavior for the stranger and another for one's intimates.

Individualism, however, is more than this. Each individual, whether from the high or low class, posesses an autonomy that he is expected to defend. If encroachment occurs and is not protested, then one suffers shame. Extreme provocation may lead to violence. What we might interpret as helpful supervision becomes in Brazil a reflection on one's capabilities and inhibits freedom to act. Also for this reason the enforcement of law and the application of legal rules is a personal, erratic, but, to the Brazilian, completely understandable uncertainty. The public official does not view himself as a servant of the people, as that would be a demeaning posture. Relationships with others are not governed by bureaucratic procedure, but, preferably, they are handled on a personal basis. Even those with high social position cannot count upon equal or disinterested treatment by a clerk. Each encounter is treated as a game in which each contestant attempts to preserve his individuality and self-respect. As a consequence, public institutions and their functionaries occupy a different position than in the United States. The public school, as an extension of government, is not a community institution, and the school teacher, as a public employee, is not accountable to her public. Leeds stated the case quite aptly:

Brazilian schools, in general, are virtually autonomous with respect to the communities in which they are situated. Teachers are their own law, as respects the locality, regardless of whether they are part of the state or county (municipio) school systems, or if they run private schools. What authority there is over the schools stems from political units administratively superior to the locality, and in any case, does not apply to the privately run schools. There are virtually no community organizations, formal or informal, like the citizens' associations for better schools such as one finds here and there in the United States. There are no significant parent contacts with the schools, much less organized parent-teacher organizations. Further, no systematic effort, indeed virtually no effort at all, is made by the schools to influence, proselytize, or propagandize the community to accept desired values or forms of actions as is so widely the case in American education. Thus, as a rule, with respect to community involvement, Brazilian and American schools are at opposite poles.[13]

These two dimensions, the separateness of the school from the community and the tie between individualism and autonomy among teachers, as aspects of widespread cultural and organizational characteristics, demonstrate once again that the assumptions and procedures of educational development must be elicted from within the culture. We can see how unworkable our own notions of supervision and administration would be in this situation. The basic principle applies with equal validity to innovations in our own educational system. Even so, we blithely make changes with little appreciation of their social consequences.

In considering the social and cultural conditions that affect the practice of education in Brazil we must give attention to the cultural variations that we label social class. Once again, however, our perspective is not fully transferable. In Brazil the strong sense of individual initiative and self-improvement is lacking. In no sense does this deny the fortitude and energy of those who sought to gain wealth through exploitation, such as the *bandeirantes* of São Paulo or those who carved out great estates for cattle, sugar cane, coffee, or cocoa production. But the pattern of latifundium included no middle class, which in our society gave individual striving its distinctive flavor. In the towns and capital cities the basic social divisions were not much different from those of the countryside, and only recently with the introduction of industrialism have significant changes in the class structure appeared. Those few whose social status placed them between an elite and the bottom existed as institutional functionaries or engaged in minor commercial pursuits. Traditionally, Brazil has been a two-class society, and some measure of its magnitude and limited change can be seen in Table 1.

Admittedly, these figures conceal the differential distribution that

[13] Anthony Leeds, *Cultural Factors in Education: Some Problems of Applied Anthropology* (Washington, D.C.: Pan American Union, 1961), pp. 12–13.

TABLE 1. PERCENTAGE OF TOTAL POPULATION, BY CLASS.

Class	1870	1920	1955
Upper and upper middle	3.3	3.5	6.0
Middle	4.8	9.5	16.0
Lower	91.9	87.0	78.0

Source: Adapted from J. Roberto Moreira, *Educação e Desenvolvimento No Brasil* (Rio de Janeiro, 1961).

characterizes the regions of traditional agrarian or modern urban industrialism. They do confirm, however, not only the relative numerical inferiority of the middle class, but also its gradual expansion.

This background of the relationship between the social and cultural aspects of Brazilian life makes it easier to understand the educational system. It should be noted that instead of first attempting to describe its characteristics or to define and explain its problems, I have given primary attention to the environment within which it operates. I decided on this strategy not only because I believe educational process should be viewed as a derivative, but also because those who attempt to use education as the vehicle for development must understand that a direct assault on educational problems, by attempts at reform, can frequently lead nowhere, as has been the case for most such efforts in Brazil.

For the purposes of analysis we can examine school attendance as one aspect of the problem. Only a few statements will show its magnitude. Of the population between the ages of seven and eleven, about 30 percent are not attending school. More than half of those who do enroll abandon their studies in the course of the first year. Less than one fifth of those who begin school finish a four-year primary series. It is fairly obvious that Brazil cannot become a modern nation with this type of educational record. It is also obvious that much more is needed than just money. There has to be restructuring of the school system, and this is not possible unless there is a restructuring of the society. A closer look will reveal what is meant by these statements.

The intimate linkage between an elite, organized in large interconnecting families, and the other institutional arrangements of Brazil already has been described. It should not be surprising that the school system is controlled by and serves the interest of this group first. In this context, then, the purpose of formal education is not to educate (at least not to educate the mass of the population), but to perpetuate the existing social system. The statistics I have presented demonstrate the effectiveness with which this is accomplished, a fact recognized by several analysts and stated bluntly by Leeds, who said, "Brazilian education is meant to conserve privilege for the privileged, and to create a manipulatable lower class for exploitation by the privileged classes." [14] Only in the large cities where a class structure with some resemblance to that of the United States has developed can we see any break with the predominant pattern. Even here the main features of the discriminatory system remain—evident in the allocation of resources, in the types of schools, in the differing standards for determining the salaries of teachers, and, in fact, in every respect. Those who think that a more equitable distribution (an impossibility under present circumstances) would make any difference are in for a rude shock. The very heart of education found in its philosophy, curriculum, and practice would continue to perpetuate the status quo.

The explicit social and pedagogical purpose of the schools is to reject all of those who cannot demonstrate through examinations a narrowly conceived intellectual capacity, that of rote memorization. The evidence of its success is found in the annual withdrawal of more than half of those who enter the first grade and the low number of students who complete a four-year primary series. The mechanism through which this objective is achieved is explained by the Brazilian sociologist-educator Dr. Roberto Moreira, who stated that what is considered important in learning "is the acquisition of the ability to reply to questions, whose answers permit one to check if certain facts were, or were not memorized." [15] In further elaboration on this point, he wrote:

We see, moreover, it is the teacher who determines tasks, exercises, memorizations, without any concern with the possibility of concrete application of these acquisitions. The knowledge memorized, the information obtained, the exercise, are accomplished in themselves and for themselves, independently either of the inclinations and interests of the child, or of a social practice in which they might have meaning or concrete application. It is significant that in all of this the school is not properly concerned either with the child, nor with the community or society. Its concern is with the compliance to a schedule and a program according to formal processes within a preestablished and invariable routine.[16]

We might extend the analysis to include secondary and higher education, but in doing so we would add nothing substantial to the conclusion reached thus far. We should mention, however, that the new

14 *Ibid.,* p. 32.
15 J. Roberto Moreira, *Educação e Desenvolvimento No Brazil* (Rio de Janeiro, 1961), p. 234.
16 *Ibid.,* p. 249.

industrialism has provided an environment within which a slow but healthy growth of technical education is found. But in its purposes and institutional linkages this development is entirely apart from the traditional education system. The fact is of great significance to those who advocate educational reform for Brazil. I once proposed that the situation called for "a new system of primary education for the 70 to 80 percent of Brazilian children for whom the present system does not work." [17] I argued that such a policy was not nearly so radical as is the present attempt to impose values and cultural aspirations of an elite upon the lower class through formal schooling. Nor am I surprised that, for whatever wisdom my words of advice may have contained, they had no effect whatever.

The relationship between education as an instrument for development and social engineering that must accompany change is a crucial problem. The specific relationship between professional education and applied social science also is important. Unfortunately, I do not believe that we have moved much beyond the preliminary stage of the polite fencing with each other that precedes the beginning of serious planning and action. I intended for the material on Brazil to demonstrate the intimate connections among family, institution, social class, cultural perspective, and the education system. I also intended to show that educational planning and reform would have to take all of these factors into account. The next step, it seems to me, is to look at a situation in which the concepts of social science have been incorporated into a program for development, an example of which is found in Peru.

Thus far our attention has been focused upon some of the cultural and organizational barriers that educators face in attempting to reconstruct an educational system to advance national development. The serious problem is not deciding what a program should be. If the goal is to use education for economic development, it is relatively easy to determine the number and distribution of technical personnel needed to carry a country to a more advanced level of industrial production. It may be somewhat more difficult to find the money to build and equip facilities and to train or import personnel to staff technical schools. An even more serious problem likely will be encountered in assembling a qualified student body from a population in which all manual labor is held in low repute and traditional formal education has been seen as the road to white-collar prestige and affluence. The fate of other programs such as those attempting to eliminate illiteracy or to reform primary education may be affected adversely by the direct encounter

[17] Solon T. Kimball, "Primary Education in Brazil," *Comparative Education Review*, IV(1) (1960), 49–54. (See Chapter 15 above.)

with other powerful cultural conditions. We should switch now, however, from the perspective of the nation to that of the locality.

Community development, as one example of a program intended to bring beneficial change to those who followed a traditional subsistence and agricultural way of life, sought to produce changes on a broad front and from within the group. We are fortunate in possessing a fairly substantial documentation of the relative successes and failures of this approach in the report on Chonin in Brazil by Oberg and Rios.[18] I think it is reasonable to say, however, that the basic principles undergirding the practices of community development remain as sound today as ever, although there have been occasional shifts in tactics or emphasis. (As one example, there has been increased use of relative novices in technical aids such as those found in the Peace Corps or other such groups.)

Of the several aspects of a community development project, what is of immediate interest to us is the contribution of education. We can narrow our field of concern even further by excluding adult education, as exemplified by extension workers who seek to improve practices associated with health or agriculture. Our focus is the school as an agency seeking to bring change. As example, I will describe a project called CRECER, now under way in Peru. It illustrates the direct contribution social science can make to community development through education, and it provides a model of operation that I believe has worldwide applicability, including the United States. A brief summary statement of the characteristics of Peru will give some sense of the setting within which this project operates.

Peru resembles many other countries of the world in its slow but gradually accelerating movement toward a modern, urban, and technological society. As is so frequently the case, the forces favoring change are inhibited by deficiencies in the cultural and technological matrix, by the inertia of traditional social arrangements, and by the opposition of vested interests. The political and economic life has been dominated by a combination of a ruling, hereditary oligarchy, sometimes referred to as the Forty Families, and internationally financed enterprises that control the extraction of minerals and are heavily invested in banking, transportation, and commercial agriculture.

More than a tenth of Peru's eleven million inhabitants are concentrated in its capital city, Lima, which has experienced a phenomenal growth in the past two decades. Only slightly over half of the eleven million speak Spanish as their native language, and the remainder

[18] Kalervo Oberg and Arthur Rios, "A Community Improvement Project in Brazil," in Benjamin D. Paul, Ed., *Health, Culture, and Community* (New York: Russell Sage Foundation, 1955).

speak a variety of Indian tongues with Aymara and Quechua pre-
dominating. About 55 percent of the adult population is counted as
literate. The population is unevenly distributed in the three major
climatic zones of desert, sierra, and tropical forest, but the mountainous
masses that separate the coast from the tropical areas create difficulties
in communication and, until recently, have contributed to isolation and
separatism.

To this quick casting of the balance sheet of assets and debits
should be added the progressive intention of the present government, a
powerful factor. But the machinery of government, built to serve and
to perpetuate a traditional, static social system, also must be transformed if the goals of the nation's leadership are to be realized. The
modernization and expansion of the educational system is one such
goal. The present centralized control in the Ministry of Education
theoretically should facilitate change, but such an assumption fails
to recognize the glacial movement of bureaucratic machinery. Often
it is easier to get an entirely new program under way than it is to make
a minor modification in some ongoing operation. This may not be an
adequate explanation for the inception of the project I am about to
describe, but, in my view, this program represents a radical innovation
and demonstrates the successful linkage of the methods of community
study and education for the purposes of community development.

Preliminary planning for this program, which carries the short
title of CRECER (Campaña para la Reforma Eficaz de las Comunidades Escolares de la Republica), began auspiciously in late 1963
under the aegis of Dr. Adrico Via Ortega of the Ministry of Education.
Dr. William C. Sayres, an applied anthropologist with the Teachers
College, Columbia University, advisory team to the Ministry of Education, served as the Alliance for Progress counterpart and technical
adviser. The cooperative endeavors of these two have provided the
inspiration and the direction.

CRECER was conceived as an experimental attempt to enlist the
active participation of school teachers in educational and community
betterment. But action programs were to be preceded by a systematic
study of existing conditions and needs, including consultation with
those who became the field participants. In both of these phases, the
gathering and analysis of data and the determination of programs for
development, the assistance of the professional social scientist was
crucial. All of the devices that are customary in training field workers
were utilized. To ensure comparability in the information to be col-
lected, planners prepared a manual of instruction, outlining guides to
the collection of information about history, geography, demography,
economic activities, cultural characteristics, and social groupings. The

manual also described methods of recording observations and interviews and grouping comparable data in a filing system. It also prescribed ethics that govern the protection of informants.

When the program got under way in the early months of 1964, about one hundred teachers had been enrolled. Most of these lived in small communities in all sections of the nation. Participation was on a purely voluntary basis, and no one received additional salary. The initiation of the project had its problems, and because of distance, limited personnel, and other reasons, it had to be flexibly structured.

In February 1965, the participating teachers were invited to a two-week reporting and evaluation conference in Lima. Although no money was available for traveling expenses, nearly one-half the teachers attended. Furthermore, their enthusiasm was so great that they decided to continue their discussions for an additional week. Dr. Sayres wrote an interpretive assessment in a letter to me describing the conference:

The CRECER workshop turned out better than we had expected. I cannot say enough for these teachers. They had two important things going for them: (1) motivation (they go about their community studies with more interest and enthusiasm and dedication than any group of graduate anthropology students I have known; the project gives them a tremendous professional boost, especially those in the outlying rural communities who for the first time feel they can do something significant and be a part of something nationwide and even international), and (2) opportunity (they are there year after year, with a defined and accepted community role). If they are unsophisticated in techniques of community study (they are nevertheless progressing and on the whole are doing a creditable job), they are at the same time considerably more sophisticated than the average anthropologist in the workings of the educational system which is to be linked to community development. We feel that through this project, and without fuss or feathers or red tape, these teachers are quietly going about the business of clarifying the dimensions of Peruvian community life, aiding in human resource development (the teachers are after all in daily contact with the growing generations and have an explicit responsibility in such development), and harnessing the school to the task of socioeconomic development geared to cultural realities.

What seems increasingly clear is that among these teachers—and presumably among many others—there has been a predisposition to participate in a project of this kind. It is as if they had just been waiting for such a vehicle. In this sense CRECER is itself a piece of culture serving an array of professional and personal needs among Peruvian teachers. It gives more meaning, direction, and status to what they do. There is also some evidence that at least in certain communities the act of being studied gives a kind of cultural satisfaction. There is a paradigm with such facets as: "The teacher is the most educated person here. He is interested in us. He wants to learn about us. If we are worthy of such attention, perhaps we do not matter as little as we had been led to believe." And of course there is a changing image of the teacher as one who no longer contents himself with academic navel gazing, but who is actively concerned with community development.

CRECER as an experiment is still in a developmental stage, and it is much too soon to attempt a definitive assessment. Additions and modifications have already been proposed. An intensive plan of development is now under way in what may become a demonstration community. A supplementary manual recently has been completed, and plans have been made to establish four regional centers to improve the communication between the leadership and the teachers. But the results achieved thus far do permit some observations in addition to those offered by Dr. Sayres.[19]

We are all aware that the changes experts desire to achieve through their plans are not realized except as those within a community modify their practices, their values, and their groupings. We ought to be aware, also, that neither fiat nor force works. What is often effective, however, is changing the conditions within which individuals or groups live. In this instance the activity, and as a result the role, of the teacher have been modified by the provision of a constructive opportunity to increase the intensity and effectiveness of his connection with the community within which he lives and works. If successful, the change in his function inevitably affects the quality of his work and the nature of his relationship to others. There has thus been achieved a simultaneous change in the cultural and social aspects of an individual and of his relationships with others. From such minute changes appear the gross changes that in their sum we call development.

The procedures and the consequences of CRECER also help to confirm another of the principles that experience has shown to be valid. There will be no valid change—valid in the sense of internalized ways of acting and believing—except as a program allows those for whom it has been planned to learn on their own how to act out the new ways. Such a statement does not negate the vital role of those who make

19 CRECER did not survive. Much can be learned about the nature of change, however, from its demise. By mid 1969 the two men who gave it birth and leadership had gone. The Ministry of Education let the program wither away through inattention, as it does all new programs that threaten the established order. In the pattern of Latin American "personalismo," each man adulates his own monument. The participating teachers, now leaderless and abandoned, fell apart. A similar fate befell the nucleo schools for the Indians of the Sierra when the United States withdrew its support. An analysis of success and failure in educational intervention in Peru can be found in the article by Rolland G. Paulston in the Council on Anthropology and Education Newsletter (May 1971).

policy and plan programs, as they are also essential. But their aims can be effective only to the extent that they arrange the conditions within which accomplishment may be realized, not to the extent that they perfect modes of supervision or direction.

There are other lessons that we might derive from CRECER, but our main purpose has been served—that of demonstrating one contribution that social science can make to the uses of education and development.

Although we have neither examined all of the interconnections between education and development, nor explored all of the implications of a working relationship between educators and applied social scientists, enough has been said to illuminate the nature of the problem. There is little need to argue the value of potentiality of education in bringing change, as there seems to be common agreement upon its value. The immediate problem is to develop a working relationship between social scientists and educators to plan what needs to be done and the strategy for its accomplishment. Herein lies the simple and the overwhelming difficulty. Where traditional cultures, such as those of Korea and Brazil, inhibit innovation, the need for collaboration is clear. We should have learned at least that the educational practices from one culture cannot be transferred to another with the expectation of gaining the same results.

This analysis also is relevant to the educational enterprise in the United States. For example, are those who are responsible for programs that affect the residents of Appalachia aware of and using some of the social science principles that now are accepted? It is relatively easy to generate special attention for problem areas, but ought we not also to be concerned about our new metropolitan areas? In New York City, for example, we find a system of school organization and administration that is archaic, a curriculum that is outmoded, and instructional practices that emphasize a custodial rather than a learning function. The goal of using education for developmental change is no less important for our own country than it is for other areas of the world.

There is every reason why educators and social scientists should join together to help create an educational enterprise that serves the goals of humanity everywhere. The ease with which such an ideal may be formulated is quite other than the hard task of its realization. It is far more likely that, with a few notable exceptions, cooperation between educators and social scientists will remain minimal for a long time. Among educators the vested interest is far too great for them to relinquish willingly any portion of their domain to outsiders. Furthermore, the limited horizon that leads them to define their goals as primarily improving the quality of instruction in the classroom and the training of teachers does not really accept that the educational enterprise has any significant relationship to the society in which it operates. The narrow commitment that such a definition of function produces additionally restricts educational endeavor. Under such conditions we should not expect that educators will, or can, take the initiative in calling upon social scientists to help solve their problems. In fact, as these problems are now defined, it is not certain that social science would have much to offer anyway.

If cooperation from educators is not likely, what help may we expect from social scientists? Unfortunately, the situation in that quarter seems little if at all better than that among educators. Only recently has there been any significant interest in defining the social dimensions of the educational enterprise, excluding the few notable exceptions, and serious study of the processes of cultural transmission are now just beginning. In short, what social science has to offer in the way of specifically applicable research findings is greatly limited, even though most of what is available is not being used. In addition, only a few social scientists have any sophistication in educational organization and practices or any commitment to professional education.

The situation is far from hopeless, however, and for the strongest of reasons—namely, the values of our type of society cannot tolerate an ineffective educational system. Our society requires a system of formal education in which the social consequences of education are clearly understood and social goals become incorporated into school organization and curriculum. The current group of professional educators do not possess the requisite knowledge or skill to bring this about. If this analysis is correct, then the developmental task that confronts American educators is immense. The next question to decide, then, is what is to be done about it.

It is not the purpose of this paper to formulate a program to meet the need, but it does seem appropriate to make a few suggestions. These are offered under the assumption that the primary task is to build stable linkages between educators and social scientists and that this goal may be accomplished through finding areas of common concern and of institutionalizing joint efforts in seeking answers to these problems. There should be no difficulty in finding enough projects of mutual concern, but the difficulty may be that of creating a suitable institutional framework. Two closely related activities offer the greatest hope. The first is research, and the second is shared responsibility in an ongoing development project. These activities could be pursued separately or combined. If successful, they should result in achieving the primary goal, which is the stable working relationship between the disciplines of social science and professional education.

18. EDUCATION IN COMMUNITY DEVELOPMENT

Community development as an idea and a method has captured the imagination and interest of the segment of the professional and governmental world that is concerned with improvement and change among underdeveloped peoples. In its more common usage the term refers to the attempts to improve the physical, social, and economic well-being of primarily agrarian peoples. Agencies of the United States through its Point Four program, of the United Nations, and of the cooperating countries have supplied most of the money and personnel for these ventures.

Technical assistance programs have made it possible for technicians from such areas as health, education, and agriculture to survey conditions, recommend or institute remedial changes, or train and educate members of local communities in skills needed to achieve certain types of objectives. Sometimes a rural sociologist or cultural anthropologist has been available to advise ways and means of introducing new cultural practices or to point out some of the problems involved in relating these programs to native cultures. Only a small portion of this total effort, however, may be properly labeled as community development. Much of it consists of technical assistance that includes large-scale developments beyond the capabilities of villagers, or more modest ventures such as malaria control or skills in utilizing fertilizers. This type of assistance has been an administrative function in cooperation with the central government. Technical assistance has been incorporated as a policy of government in many countries, but only in India has there been achieved a full-scale indigenous community

"The Role of Education in Community Development," *Teachers College Record,* Vol. 57, No. 6 (March 1956), pp. 386–391.

development program, although a good beginning has been made in some of the countries of the Moslem world, in Southeast Asia, and in a few places elsewhere.

I should like to raise a question whether the methods and techniques of community development can be applied with approximately equal success to the problems of contemporary industrial cities.

This is not an easy problem with which to deal. One difficulty is the absence of empirical experience based upon this type of approach within an industrial city. In addition, the contrast between agrarian and industrial community life is so great that doubt may be expressed as to their comparability. Furthermore, it is questionable whether we possess understandings of the dynamics of urban life that remotely approximate those understandings that have been achieved from the many studies made of peasant communities. Such studies have aided immeasurably in showing the nature and significance of socio-cultural aspects of community life. The magnitude of the task of comprehending the diversities of urban life and organization when compared with the simplicities of village life may leave us discouraged. Nevertheless, if the community development process releases energies that lead to new achievements as well as possibilities for future growth, cannot similar procedures do the same for industrial communities?

Fortunately, it is not our task to attempt a solution for the problems of the industrial metropolis. Instead, we have limited ourselves to problems involved in the transference of a specific type of approach. We can discern an existing pattern among those who are now struggling with the physical and social problems that afflict our big cities. The numerous commissions and agencies, public and private, that work with problems of disease, poverty, unemployment, sanitation, congestion, crime, housing, transportation, education, recreation, and cultural activities contribute greatly to ameliorating the lot of the unfortunate and provide services of varying quality for the remainder. Whatever the results, neither the organization nor the philosophy of these government and private agencies meets the criteria of community development. To delineate these criteria, let us turn to a statement from a report issued by the Foreign Operations Administration.[1]

Community Development is a technique for stimulating organized self-help undertakings through the democratic process. It aims to mobilize the principal resource of most underdeveloped areas—their manpower and their

---

[1] Foreign Operations Administration "FOA Policy, Concept, Methods and Organization with Respect to Community Development," Washington, D.C., September 4, 1954 (mimeographed).

interest in improving their own lot—once they have become aware that improvement is possible. It is not a technical assistance project in and of itself, but rather is one method of carrying out technical assistance programs. It is not community development unless it aids in securing a coordinated, rather than a segmented, approach to the interrelated problems of a community.

This definition provides us with two key aspects that set community development apart from the kind of routine or special activities that characterize the formalized administrative functions of an industrial city. These are, first, "organized self-help undertakings" that, second, seek "a coordinated, rather than a segmented, approach to the interrelated problems of a community."

For a program to meet the requirements of community development it must be people-centered. It is people who determine the needs, provide the leadership, guide and participate in the action, and in their own way incorporate changes into a way of life. They hold both a right and an obligation for control of the communal destiny.

In this sense may we not then include as community development the natural history of all human communities? Since we are seeking to discover if there are similarities between community development method and community activities of men in the ancient or recent past, let us consider two contrasting approaches. The vast engineering projects of the Roman Empire in North Africa and the Middle East brought new life, for a time at least, to the settled peoples of these regions. These efforts resemble large-scale technical assistance projects of today but do not fit our definition. In contrast to these centrally planned and administered improvements we have the activities of early settlers of town and countryside in the newly opened western lands of the United States. Should we say these pioneers, in their communal efforts to build roads, schools, and churches, and to establish industry and commerce, were also within the tradition of community development?

The tradition of community improvement continues to run strong in contemporary American life. Some of the efforts have become institutionalized on national, state, or local levels. And although it is not our purpose to provide an inventory of such activities, brief reference to some of them will show the magnitude of the effort. Among the groups interested in one or more aspects of community life are the Chambers of Commerce, industrial development committees, city planning commissions, councils of social agencies, luncheon clubs, schools, churches, citizen councils, and a variety of governmental agencies. Prominent in this latter category is the agricultural extension service as well as the extension and adult education programs of many colleges and universities. Two foundations, the Sloan and the Kellogg, have been particularly active in developing techniques for stimulating community-centered programs.

Are we justified in concluding that the range of activities through which citizens of American communities meet their civic, political, educational, economic, and religious needs, considered as an inclusive whole, represents the counterpart of village community development within an urban industrial society? On the individual level the fundamental needs are the same. The differences in cultural tradition and social and technological complexity are very great indeed, and it may well be that the solution of such problems as traffic congestion is beyond the competence of a people-centered program. (At least the social devices we now use to find solutions for such problems seem vastly remote from the populace.)

We cannot really grapple with the problem of transference of the community development method to the urban scene unless there is some agreement that the present institutional arrangements do not and cannot meet adequately the standards of human living that we desire and that we can achieve. There have always been a few who have protested vigorously against the laissez-faire growth of our cities and who have advanced concrete proposals for reform. A leader among these has been Lewis Mumford. But unfortunately his prescriptions have been largely ignored. A. A. Berle, Jr., has summarized the serious plight in which New York City finds itself. He sketches with broad strokes and appropriate detail an outline of the chaos that afflicts this city and places primary responsibility for the difficulties upon antiquated or conflicting governmental structures. His solution envisages types of political structure that meet the interlocking needs of a metropolitan area inhabited by sixteen million people, yet preserve "the historical collectivity of the city for the things it can do" and at the same time "liberate and protect the village for the things only a village can do." In writing of this latter aspect, his words and those of community development advocates are much alike.

When the plight of our cities is faced up to at last, a fundamental attack on the whole problem of government in densely populated areas seems inescapable. Before this attack can take place, some basic ideas must be clear. There are human values that can only be preserved by thinking in terms of small areas: the neighborly associations, homes and their qualities, contact between parents and schools. Even a New Yorker thinks not of the city or of his borough but of Gramercy Park or Brooklyn Heights, of West End Avenue or Kew Gardens, of his nearby school, his precinct police station, his familiar grocery. These are qualities of the village. For the rest, the city is a vast blur operated by political machines, a mayor—and other elected officials whose very names he hardly knows.[2]

The creation of new governmental devices does not in itself solve the problems of human living. They may be desirable and necessary rearrangements to meet the new conditions of human grouping but they do not and cannot provide the kind of results that community development has brought to village life. It is entirely possible that New York and other great cities may be able to solve by legislation the administrative snarls that prevent urban governments from providing the kinds of services for their inhabitants that our time permits. Legislation alone, however, will not hold in check the morass of formlessness that bureaucratic centralization forces upon a people; in fact it may even hasten the ultimate emptiness of urban life.

Although we have postponed consideration of the role of education in community development in order to make clear how this approach includes aspects usually absent from technical assistance, urban administration, or improvement projects, and to state our problem in relation to the method, we are now prepared to narrow our focus to educational process and the school. Our first step is to ask if the metropolitan school system provides a favorable environment within which a community development program might be started.

It would be surprising indeed if the problems facing urban education varied extensively from those that face other public agencies. There are the perennial deficiencies of money, personnel, facilities, and public support. As an example, in New York City more tax monies are used each year for the care of indigents than are available for public education. Additional funds, however, will not solve other types of equally crucial problems. The task of administering an educational program of great magnitude has inevitably led to bureaucratization, with its resultant rigidities. Teachers and administrators find themselves with the alternative of accepting current conditions or facing endless frustrations in attempts to bring change.

The loss of the tie between teachers and local community and the concomitant diminution of the importance of the school as a significant local institution are characteristic of the urban school. Assignment of teachers to a particular school is made only incidentally on the basis of residence or of knowledge of a given locality. If they happen to live within the area served by the school it is a fortuitous circumstance that helps some in their participation in local community affairs.

The decline of the school as a center of community life and the

[2] A. A. Berle, Jr., "New York, The Runaway City," *The Reporter* (September 8, 1955), p. 17.

absence of feeling that the school belongs to the people of the area also contribute to the unfavorable situation. Without local control there can be little responsibility. Furthermore, it is doubtful that central bureaucracy would welcome any measure of local participation. It is even more doubtful that the administrators would known how to stimulate such activity or to cooperate with it if it were established.

Fortunately there are exceptions to this generally bleak picture. There are instances of excellent schools with local participation that would exemplify the best in school-community relations and of the fulfillment of the function of the school as a significant community institution. Such schools are testimonials to a dedicated school staff and community support, and perhaps can serve as models for the kind of educational program that may be attained.

In general, however, there is little evidence that either the current philosophy or the organization of urban school systems lends itself to the promotion of community development. We must not necessarily accept the present situation as one without hope; and the schools, with all their deficiencies, may offer the most fruitful area for change. Institutional education, however, is only one facet of the total educational process, and we should also remember that community development is a coordinated, not a segmented, approach.

Community development method teaches us some lessons that we should heed and that should be understood by those who constitute the great and growing body of planners and administrators, if they are to meet the ills of urban industrial society. The principles are very simple, but apparently they must be learned the hard way. Experience has shown that conditions cannot be corrected by law, decree, or experts alone, although all of these are useful in their place. The local group must shape the program in terms of its definition of needs. The goal must be one that those who are participants can understand, and the means to accomplish the objectives must lie within their capabilities. At times help from the outside is needed and requested, but its application is under local direction. Sometimes it is necessary to create new social devices, but these, to be effective, must be consonant with the cultural pattern of cooperative achievement, with opportunity for citizen leadership to be expressed and strengthened.

This is one of the aspects of community development to which Tannous, who has had long experience in this field, gives major emphasis. He writes that "the stimulation and development of adequate leadership constitute the most dynamic and productive approach to community development." [3] And he then points out that there has been

---

[3] Afif I. Tannous, "Assumptions and Implications of Community Development in Underdeveloped Countries," *Human Organization*, Vol. 13, No. 3 (1954), p. 3.

"a tragic neglect or abuse of this resource of leadership." What he describes is, unfortunately, an oft-repeated story because of the inability or unwillingness of those who control services for communities to utilize the dynamic forces within the local group.

There is no intention to exclude the expert in the process of change, but it is primarily as a technician and an outsider that he works within the community. India has met its problem through establishing training centers at which selected villagers receive training from an expert staff. These multiple-purpose workers then return to the areas from which they came, and are responsible for a number of villages. Through this device the skills of the highly trained professional worker are carried to a much larger population and more effectively incorporated into ways of living. Taylor [4] proposes that the training of "grass roots" workers is necessary for successful community development programs.

Are the barriers of administrative prerogative and professional status so great in our urban culture that we cannot or dare not try to overcome them? If not, then the community development process cannot be transferred, because at its heart is the principle that people must achieve for themselves. This the people cannot do if the structures of control and action remain remote from them or if the cult of expertness places responsibility for decision in the hands of the highly trained alone. Since the factors of administration and professionalism are so deeply intertwined in community organization, any change in their definition or operation will be most difficult. It is not impossible, however. The reclamation of civic responsibility is an ardous task hampered by inertia and by ineptitude in social skills. The reformation of professional attitudes has hardly gotten under way, but there are encouraging signs of receptivity for new approaches. Once we achieve some unanimity on the nature of the problem and need for action, then we can forge the new working relationships through which solutions can be found.

In its final analysis community development may thus be seen as almost entirely an educational problem, using this term in its broadest sense. Its application in the underdeveloped areas has always had to overcome the blindness or rejection of administrators and experts on the one hand and of peoples bound to traditional ways on the other. Each group has had to learn how to communicate with the other, but the main burden of responsibility rests with those who are attempting to bring change.

[4] Carl C. Taylor, "Community Development Programs and Methods," Washington, D.C., June 1954 (mimeographed).

PART IV *The Educational Challenge*

19. ANTHROPOLOGY AS POLICY SCIENCE

The social turbulence that in 1914 broke through the deceptive calm of a supposedly ordered world has expanded in breadth and magnitude until all peoples are caught up in its consequences. Its dramatic episodes are chronicled as wars, economic booms or busts, the demise of colonialism and the rise of the new nation-states of the Third World, a proliferated technology epitomized in the moon-shots, and domestic turmoil. Included in the latter are a redistribution of rights and privileges and a change in the relationships between the affluent and the deprived, the shape and function of our institutions, and the customs that regulate the relationships between men and women and between old and young.

We would probably agree, however, that except for the senseless destruction of war and the thoughtless corruption of our environment, most peoples of the world are probably better off materially than before. Yet the jealousies and fears among nations, the inequities and injustices of use and access to knowledge and resources, and the exclusion from participation in the processes of social and economic decision breed further turmoil. Meanwhile, new technology and institutional reformation contribute their charge to the flow of change, sometimes ameliorating, sometimes exacerbating the situation.

The cumulative consequences of these changes have indeed been great. Some have viewed our age as a revolutionary one and the violence that has accompanied the contest for the control of political power in some areas of the world gives support to such labeling. But these brief, spectacular explosions should more properly be viewed as manifestations rather than as causes of what Williams [1] has called

[1] Raymond Williams, *The Long Revolution* (New York: Columbia University Press, 1961).

"The Long Revolution," and what I perceive as the erratic but powerful tides of change that are eroding the remnant tribal and agrarian
styles of civilization, whether concentrated in the Third World or
residual in urban industrial societies, simultaneously nurturing the
emergence of a new way for mankind. The language of simile gives us
the imagery but it does not spell out the variables, the systems, or the
processes. These are the responsibilities of the disciplines of thought
and inquiry and the philosophy and methodology of science. These are
indeed the powerful intellectual tools with which ultimately, "Man
Takes Control," as Charles Erasmus [2] has phrased it.

The awareness that the responsibility for the ordering of the
world rests squarely on mankind is in itself an event of great por-
tentousness. No longer can we avoid the requirements of our future by
seeking comfort in the benign guidance of a divinely conceived plan
nor in blaming vague forces beyond our control for our own inepti-
tudes. In the wake of our assertion we have shouldered the burden of
our destiny.

The challenge of the moment and of the future is urgent. If we
are to survive, to validate our claims to hegemony through the intelligence to live in harmony with the universe, there are two requirements that must be met. We must have knowledge and we must
learn how to use it constructively and from use gain further knowledge. The scope is far greater than that of relating to the physical environment through technology; it also encompasses all dimensions of
natural and social phenomena and of their interconnections. In the
natural sphere, the applications include the management of our natural
resources, the production of foodstuffs, and the physiology of life. In
the social sphere, we particularly need to understand the relations
between institutions in community and society, and man's practices
and beliefs. Their modification and control require social engineering.
Once we have decided upon the limits of our problem, we must then
consider the instrumentalities we need to achieve our purposes. As
exemplification, in the remainder of this chapter I shall focus on the
uses of anthropology in formal education.

THE EDUCATIONAL ENTERPRISE

In the period since the end of the Second World War, the universities
of the Western world, particularly those of North America, have experienced a radical restructuring in response to new demands and accelerated growth. Higher education has now joined the corporate

[2] Charles J. Erasmus, *Man Takes Control: Cultural Development and American Aid* (Indianapolis: Bobbs Merrill, 1961).

systems of government and business to create the powerful institutional triad of our society. This strategic position has been won because of two reasons. The great research universities, probably not more than thirty in number, generated the new knowledge that had technological relevance for social policy and governmental objectives, and with the professional colleges they trained highly skilled scientific and professional personnel. In fact, Lord Snow estimates that "since 1945 American universities have carried out about 80 percent of all the science and scholarship in the western world, and a very high proportion of the science and scholarship in the whole planet. That is the effort of a single generation." [3]

Although industry and government expend huge sums for research, only a fraction of this is used to generate new knowledge. Much of the effort is directed toward product development, testing, and acceptance, and an uncertain portion is either trivial or frivolous. Apparently, groups dedicated to production for profit or exercise of political power do not provide an optimum ambience for creativity. Their innovative qualities appear better suited to developing new technology, production and distribution of products, and administering programs. Their capabilities as repositories and transmitters of knowledge, functions that are central to educational institutions, are limited and marginal to their other activities.

Thus, in the modern multi-faceted university with its combined functions of generator, repository, and transmitter of knowledge, we possess the instrumentality through which the principles that explain the dynamic wholeness of the universe become known to us and man establishes that harmony between himself and nature. Only recently have we been jolted into an awareness of the serious consequences we face if we fail to solve our problems. We now recognize the intimate linkage between an excessive population, a misuse and over-use of our resources, the deterioration of our cities, and the inability or failure of our institutions to rise to the challenge.

During the same decades that higher education achieved a new eminence of societal significance, the lower schools, the secondary and primary levels, were subjected to a multiplicity of investigations and a barrage of adverse criticisms. The magnitude, variety, and intensity of the probings and accusations are in startling contrast to the widely-held esteem of higher education, until student protest tarnished some of the glitter, and invite speculation as to the difference. There can be no doubt that the magnitude of the controversy attests the crucial function we attach to schooling in our society.

[3] C. P. Snow, quoted in *Gainesville Sun*, July 12, 1971.

In retrospect, the early protagonists were mild-mannered, even constructive in their criticisms when compared with the later fury of attack. For example, Arthur E. Bestor, Jr., in *Educational Wastelands* [4] charged that the empire building motives of the educationists subordinated the primary intellectual purposes of the schools. When John Gardner [5] called for "excellence" in education in a book of the same title in 1961, he was an advocate of the cultivation of the intellect as an educational goal, a message that had much greater impact in academe than elsewhere. The prescriptions that issued from James Bryant Conant's several studies of schools and of teacher training were designed to shore up the system, not to transform it. [6] The rapier-like thrusts by Jacques Barzun on the educational cloak of cant and hypocrisy may have titillated or irritated, depending upon one's sympathies, but they did not strike deeply. [7] Finally, the comprehensive survey by Martin Mayer, simply titled *The Schools*, revealed the cohesiveless melange but did not castigate or prescribe. [8]

Beginning in 1964, with the appearance of John Holt's *How Children Fail*, [9] the crescendo and the vehemence of the attacks on the schools began to mount. Other books, some of them based on the precise methods of social science research and others drawn from first-hand experience, followed in rapid succession. Representative of the latter group is Paul Goodman's *Compulsory Mis-Education*, [10] Herbert Kohl's *36 Children*, [11] James Herndon's *The Way It Spozed to Be*, [12] and George Dennison's *The Lives of Children*. [13] Examples of studies based on systematic studies include *Realities of the Urban Classroom*, [14] by G. Alexander Moore; *Walk the White Line: A Profile of Urban Education*, [15] by Elizabeth Eddy; *Life in Classrooms*, [16] by Philip W.

[4] Arthur Bestor, *Educational Wastelands* (Urbana: University of Illinois Press, 1953).

[5] John W. Gardner, *Excellence* (New York: Harper and Brothers, 1961).

[6] James Bryant Conant, *The Education of American Teachers* (New York: McGraw-Hill, 1963); and James Bryant Conant, *Shaping Educational Policy* (New York: McGraw-Hill, 1964).

[7] Jacques Barzun, *House of Intellect* (New York: Harper and Brothers, 1959).

[8] Martin Mayer, *The Schools* (New York: Harper and Brothers, 1961).

[9] John Holt, *How Children Fail* (New York: Pitman Publishing Corp., 1964).

[10] Paul Goodman, *Compulsory Mis-Education* (New York: Horizon Press, 1965).

[11] Herbert Kohl, *36 Children* (New York: New American Library, 1967).

[12] James Herndon, *The Way It Spozed to Be* (New York: Simon and Schuster, 1968).

[13] George Dennison, *The Lives of Children* (New York: Random House, 1969).

[14] G. Alexander Moore, *Realities of the Urban Classroom* (Garden City: Doubleday Anchor, 1967).

[15] Elizabeth M. Eddy, *Walk the White Line: A Profile of Urban Education* (New York: Frederick A. Praeger, Inc., 1968).

[16] Philip W. Jackson, *Life in Classrooms* (New York: Holt, Rinehart & Winston, 1968).

Jackson; and *Teaching and Learning in City Schools*,[17] by Eleanor Burke Leacock. Although the majority of these authors concentrate in the experiences of minority children and their teachers in the inner-city schools, sufficient evidence is drawn from middle-class situations to establish that educational malfunctioning is widespread. The tide of outpourings continue as does the vehemence of condemnation. Ivan Illich [18] is ready to abolish the classroom system entirely and well we might if the recent conclusion of sociologist Christopher Jencks,[19] that the contribution of the school to the intellectual development of the child is relatively unimportant, is true. The Carnegie Corporation of New York, in an attempt to achieve an unbiased evaluation of the situation, commissioned Charles E. Silberman of Fortune Magazine to conduct a thorough investigation. Between 1966 and 1969 and with $300,000 in support, he did just that. *Crisis in the Classroom* [20] was the title of his comprehensive survey. He concluded that only a radical reordering of the schools could eliminate the grim and sterile environment that now exists.

From the cacaphony of accusing voices can be isolated the range of specific charges of the critics. They are as varied as are the perspectives of those who make them. They charge that the schools foster racial and social class biases; sexism; anti-intellectualism; monolithic uniformity; radical equalitarianism; religiosity; and paganism. Moreover, teachers are incompetent, insensitive, middle-class oriented disciplinarians; examinations and tests favor white middle-class biases; the administrative structure is a bureaucratic entanglement imposing mediocrity; school boards are conservative representatives of the establishment; and teacher training institutions, state boards of education, and educational professional associations are mutually joined in a self-perpetuating oligarchy designed to protect their territorial and professional self-interests.

The vociferous and persistent have kept the pot of controversy boiling and have effected some minor changes, for better or for worse, depending upon your view. A decision of the United States Supreme Court has upheld the protest of those who deemed religious prayers a violation of the constitutional separation of church and state. Some schools have dropped the Christmas and Easter pageantry following protests from Jewish parents. School libraries have removed Tom Sawyer and Huckleberry Finn from their shelves in response to Black

[17] Eleanor Burke Leacock, *Teaching and Learning in City Schools* (New York: Basic Books, 1969).

[18] Ivan D. Illich, *Deschooling Society* (New York: Harper and Row, 1971).

[19] Christopher Jencks, *Inequality: A Reassessment of the Effect of Family and Schooling in America* (New York: Basic Books, 1972).

[20] Charles E. Silberman, *Crisis in the Classroom: The Remaking of American Education* (New York: Random House, 1970).

complaints. Children in some schools no longer hear their teachers read traditional fairy stories since spokeswomen for Female Liberation have condemned them as sexist. The John Birch Society has scrutinized textbooks hoping to discover and root out offending socialist views on such matters as public housing or unions. And Fundamentalists who stake their past and future on the literal interpretation of the Word have harried those who taught Darwinian views.

Indeed, some attacks seek to strike at the very vitals of the ideology that justifies schooling as an essential instrument of our society. One indignant revisionist, Colin Greer,[21] believes that the legend of the urban public schools as the ladder providing upward mobility for the poor and the ethnic is a falsehood. He believes that the effect, if not the intent, of schooling has been to perpetuate the ethnic and racial minorities and the poor in their lowly status. In fact, this critic is tempted to condemn the situation as a conspiracy of the middle-class WASP (White Anglo-Saxon Protestant). (The school systems of the major urban cities of the Northeast have been in the hands of ethnics for at least two generations.)

The wide-ranging nature of the items one includes on a roster of complaint and action do not readily lend themselves to any simple categorization such as conservative versus liberal. Instead, we must view these diversities as evidence of a complex and segmented society and one that is in ferment. Perhaps we would be well advised to assess this turmoil as further evidence in support of the contention advanced by James McClellan [22] that the Public School Movement is dead. If indeed there is no longer agreement on the value of a particular pattern of schooling—a distinctively American creation as McClellan views it—then we should suspect that society and education are in a phase of noncongruence.

As new adjustments are sought, tensions appear in such areas as race, sex, religion, patriotism, or in beliefs about curriculum and pedagogy, or in the relationships among students, teachers, administrators, and parents. Practices or developments that are seen as threatening by any of these groups, or by other special interest groups, almost certainly will lead to protests, as those who have taken part in demonstrations against desegregation of schools have shown. In these contests of control, the courts have become the ultimate arbiters of disputes and through legal decisions imposed an arbitrary solution on

---

[21] Colin Greer, *The Great School Legend: A Revisionist Interpretation of American Education* (New York: Basic Book, 1972).

[22] James E. McClellan, *Toward an Effective Critique of American Education* (Philadelphia: J. B. Lippincott, 1968).

all. The courts also provide protection for such variant behavior as that found among the Amish and Jehovah's Witnesses.

How do teachers—those who carry the instructional burden—view the situation? If we turn to the writings in the professional journals, we must conclude that with a little tinkering and some new gimmicks all would be well—at least in the classroom. This suffocating blandness ignores the sound and the fury that issue from the critics. But there is a new surging militancy among teachers that cannot be ignored. The American Federation of Teachers recruits furiously while the traditional National and State Education Associations transform themselves into collective bargaining agencies. Teachers now strike and picket like any other hunkey. They want better pay, fringe benefits, precisely defined duties, police protection from unruly students, and all the other goodies of the working man. Their cry of protest has been for better treatment, not for the reform of the schools.

But there is a gentler and more idealistic view of teachers. We are led to believe that what teachers desire above all else is the chance to teach. That is the career for which they have prepared and that is their commitment. Obstacles breed frustrations. Dumb kids, unruly kids, intractable kids either will not or cannot learn and interfere with teaching or at least order in the classroom. Parents are also a source of trouble, directly when they intrude in the teaching process and indirectly through the misbehavior of their children. Administrators and supervisory staff can also become irritants. They issue orders, require reports, and are either inefficient or deficient in securing textbooks, supplies, and the necessary materials. The majority might well contend that no such crisis exists. But, if so, place the blame where it belongs, on students, parents, and community. These are the sources and the causes of the disturbances.

The view from the classroom, however, does not permit comprehension of the problem as a whole, although teachers have been forced to cope with some of its manifestations. Educators tend to see the problem as the need to update curriculum and methods of instruction, but it is clear that improvement here has not diminished the difficulties nor the cries of the critics. For example, curricular development for secondary schools in such areas as physics, geography, and biology has been sponsored by the National Science Foundation. The high hopes Jerrold Zacharias generated through reformation in the teaching of physics have not been realized in other areas, but it may still be too soon for an assessment of their effects. Other innovations, such as team teaching, ungraded classrooms, and modular scheduling, may all be steps in the right direction of school practice, but these efforts do not solve the basic task of bringing school and community into productive collaboration, ensuring participation by learners in the educative process. The present system inhibits such an achievement and blindness prevents acknowledgment that solution of the social dimensions is crucial.

SCHOOLING AND THE INDIVIDUAL

Americans have been taught to believe that their country is a land of opportunity. We commemorate the lives of those who through adversity but with single-minded tenacity have won through to great deeds and national acclaim. In fact, the locality that cannot report with pride the accomplishments of some "local boy who made good" must indeed be a rarity. The myths accompanying this pantheon of national and local heroes, of past and present, constitute a model for others to emulate and in their successes thereby they validate the myth.

In the language of social science we label achievement aspiration as the "mobility model." It is associated with an open-class society in which achievement is rewarded by increased prestige, material goods, and advances in status—necessary and worthy goals in a land of opportunity. Intelligence, talent, hard work, honesty, good judgment, with some assistance from "lady luck," were the qualities deemed necessary for those who aspired to raise themselves. Others found the witches' brew of corrupting public officials, exploiting labor, plundering the public, financial shenanigans, or outright theft as more tempting to their taste, although the basic formula still applied. But high achievement, whether won fairly or by chicanery, was indeed rare. Subsistence farmers and industrial laborers were frozen in an occupational mold that offered little opportunity for advancement. Even the aspiring middle classes mistook the gradually broadening affluence for all and the increased status that maturity bestows as proof of the validity of mobility striving. With a perspective limited by the narrow orbit of his acquaintances, it was almost inevitable that the individual concluded that success or failure was a matter of individual determination. Furthermore, the intimate connection between schooling and social standing was clearly apparent to the observant—the educated held the trump cards in the game of life.

Through mutual reinforcement, the combination of the American dream as a land of opportunity, an open class society with its mobility model, and formal schooling as the source of instrumental qualities for success, became deeply interconnected in American culture. But as the society became more complex through industrialization, schools became disconnected from both family and community, as Thomas and

Wahrhaftig [23] have described for the folk Anglo-Saxons and Cherokees of eastern Oklahoma and recently dramatized by accounts of contemporary schools in the inner city. Schools in both of these contrasting situations now respond and are accountable to external forces of a bureaucratized pseudo-professionalism. Ironically an ersatz version of John Dewey's philosophy developed into a supporting ideology as prospective teachers were exhorted to teach not subject matter but the "whole child" in the "democratic" classroom and school. Whatever the preachments of the teachers' colleges may have been, they seem not to have been derived from the realities of the classroom. But what is now obvious to us is that the schools never did serve as the instrumentality of mobility for great segments of our population. What then is the function of the school?

If we accept the principle that the educative process ensures the transmission from one generation to the next of the cultural heritage, then education should be viewed as a conservative influence. But also reflect that the heritage may be one that stipulates that the world is in a state of rapid change and each individual's place in it is largely the consequence of his own efforts. Is it not then logical that any strategem, any device or means that assists in the development of the individual, is at the same time congruent with the goals of the society? As we trace out the logical implications of this position as it applies to the school, does it not also follow that each child should be viewed as a distinct personality with his own needs and potentials, different from other children or students, and requiring variant approaches to stimulate the flowering of his potentials? No stronger rationale than this one is needed to justify the whole range of practices now advocated by professional educators when they propose to intensify the relationship between teacher and student by limited class size (a practice that reaches its ultimate with the assignment of only one teacher to one child), adjusting the curriculum to each child's level (although grouping students by similarities is frowned upon or condemned), individualized instruction (which if achieved through electronic devices under the control of students sitting in cubicles and using earphones can eliminate the teacher entirely), and individual student control (which can be translated as no set rules for discipline cases). These pedagogical guidelines place added burdens upon both teacher and student. If the latter fails to progress satisfactorily, you cannot fault the teacher since the curriculum and practice have been tailored to student needs,

[23] Robert K. Thomas and Albert L. Wahrhaftig, "Indians, Hillbillies, and the 'Education Problem'," in Murray L. Wax, Stanley Diamond, and Fred D. Gearing (Eds.), *Anthropological Perspectives on Education* (New York: Basic Books, 1971), pp. 230–251.

but if the student doesn't respond at all then there is the strong suspicion that it is the teacher who is incompetent. Why the finger of
responsibility for failure so seldom points toward supervisors, experts,
or administrators is a fact worthy of more thought.

Practices associated with evaluation are generally consistent with
an emphasis upon individual accomplishment figured as a point on a
scale or by age or grade level. Throughout his school career, each
student is subject to a succession of tests that reveal his progression
and fix his relative ranking as a percentile. Arranging results along a
continuum from high to low and issuing grades according to their
percentage distribution is called grading on the curve, a practice that
ensures that some will always outrank others and vice versa. Viewed in
the context of individualization and social mobility, these practices
represent the ultimate in individual isolation and rewards based on a
numerical statement of achievement. The scores are not only fateful
indicators of success or failure in the system of schooling, but they are
marks that can have a powerful impact on the career pattern as an
adult.

But we should consider this emphasis upon ranking from another
perspective, namely, that the intense preoccupation with individualization excludes if it does not deny, and even condemns, any measurement of achievement based upon group cooperation. Instead the
dyadic, superior-inferior teacher-pupil relationship is the only acceptable official one. Achievement of educational goals is inhibited
by the stresses that such a system generates. Burnett shows that if the
students accepted the work model that the teacher imposes, the work-
in-isolation pattern, not only would student achievement be lessened
but teachers would have a much heavier teaching burden. Instead,
students turn to each other for mutual help in solving the tasks that
the school presents.[24] Truly isolated children, those who are not
part of the student system, must either turn to the teacher for help,
possess the inner capabilities to solve teacher posed problems, or else
they are lost. So deep is the attachment to the classroom organized
curriculum as the heart of schooling that few educators would either
believe or accept evidence that showed that most of the significant
learning acquired in school is generated quite apart from the official
program.

Schooling and its consequences cannot be separated from other
aspects of the society. What connections might we trace, for example,
between the imposed order of the classroom and the relatively unre-

[24] Jacquetta Hill Burnett, "Workflow versus Classroom Models of Academic
Work," *Michigan Journal of Secondary Education*, Vol. 9, No. 2 (Winter 1968),
14–23.

strained clusterings of adolescents? Their dramatic representation has been expressed in the several youth movements, the drug culture, student protest, communes, the generation gap, and rock festivals, all of which might be subsumed by the concept counter-culture. The components of this movement are indeed complex. It includes the narcissistic exploration of the self, the hedonistic savoring of sensual delights, anti-intellectualism, the mockery of sham and hypocrisy, the assault upon authority, and the extolling of the present. It is indeed ironic that these manifestations of youthful revolt against the values and institutions of an older generation might also be interpreted as evidence of the success of parents in inculcating independence training, which is a core value of the middle class. The flagrant assault upon other values, however, was hardly a welcomed resultant.

Although these youthful upheavals have been interpreted in many ways, it is quite unlikely that they will ever be judged as wholesome as are mother and apple pie, but they must be counted as fully within the American tradition. There seems to be a connective thread that joins the assertion of the right of each individual to "do his own thing" with those who croon "don't fence me in," the lonely struggle of conscience in "High Noon" or the policy of isolated learning in schooling. That the reality is quite other than this fanciful illusion of rarified individualism does not alter the rhetoric. Nor should we be surprised at the emergence of different and apparently contradictory emphases, for a complex culture such as ours is rich in diverse themes that furnish alternative rationales for the rhythmic swings of its cultural manifestation.

THE VIEW FROM ANTHROPOLOGY

The concern of anthropology with the behavior of individuals in groups makes it a particularly appropriate discipline for the study of the processes and practices associated with education. The community into which one is born harbors the cultural model of the social adult into which each individual is shaped. The socializing experiences instill the identities of sex, age, family, and all other distinctions that participation signifies. Through a gradually widening horizon of diverse participation, the infant moves into early childhood and beyond, and in the sequence acquires patterns of articulate speech, of associated body movement and stance, of time and situation, and of communication modes linked with cognitive responses and affective states. Later he learns that signs stand separately from the articulations that in literate societies have been elaborated in a written language, the learning of which becomes a specialized function of organization and practice. In the contrasts that separate one society and its culture from another, there are exhibited the specifics of a social setting, of a life style, and even of a distinct learning process. From comparisons between them, of Navajo with Hopi, of Japanese with American, of Bantu with Arab, comes the opportunity to derive those generalities that encompass all varieties of social life and that also appear to be universal attributes of humanity.

Such a synoptic review reminds us once again of the broad sweep of anthropology. The phylogenetic focus has been upon man's place in the animal kingdom and his biologic antecedents and characteristics. The cultural focus has been upon the human in his individual and group behavior and in his adaptation of the environment to his purposes. Through the study of symbolism in language and mythology, of custom in habituated practices, of the structure of groups in the achievement of cooperative goals, and in the utilization of the environment through technology, anthropologists have cast a wide net of inquiry.

In the decades since the 1920's and 1930's, when the functional focus of Malinowski and Radcliffe-Brown opened new vistas, there has been a succession of theoretical and methodological innovations that have both expanded and deepened our understanding of man and his society. These include the work of Chapple and Arensberg in interactional analysis, of community-study by Warner and others, of network analysis by Barnes and other British social anthropologists, of event analysis by Kimball and Pearsall, of kinesics by Birdwhistell, of proxemics by E. T. Hall, of cognition by Goodenough and Romney, of sociolinguistics by Hymes, of comparative socialization by Caudill, of revitalization by Wallace, and a new burst of interest in van Gennep's rites of passage theory led by Turner.

These new theories and procedures, when considered as a whole, represent a formidable arsenal of intellectual weapons for dispelling our ignorance about the nature of man. Presumably knowledge can be considered as an end in itself, but in a dynamic society like ours we can hardly justify its mere accumulation or the pleasure experienced in its acquisition. And there are some anthropologists who believe that their perspective and findings constitute a powerful resource that can and should be utilized for the advancement of the welfare of man.

In the spring of 1941, a group of like-minded anthropologists gathered at Harvard University and brought into existence the Society for Applied Anthropology. In its original conception and over the years, one of the goals of this organization has been to develop a body of principles that explain the nature and process of change. From its inception, it has also insisted upon its disciplinary and professional cosmopolitanism by encouraging the participation from the entire range of behavioral sciences and a broad spectrum of the professions. That this stance has been reasonably successful is attested by the range of articles published in its journal, *Human Organization,* and in the program of its annual meetings. A sampling of the subjects covered includes the fields of health, education, industry, community development, social work, administration, and government. The geographic and cultural range has been world-wide.

In the succeeding decades a great deal has been learned about the dynamics of social systems. Through the case study method, attention was focused upon the order of action between categories of personnel, the sequence of happenings, the associated activities, and the impact of varied conditions upon the behavior of individuals in a group. From the analyses of such events, it has usually been possible to offer explanations that account for resistance or acceptance of change and the success or failure of directed innovation. Furthermore, it has become possible to formulate rules of procedure that, if observed by those attempting to initiate change, prove felicitous in practice. Finally, a few general principles that have cross-cultural validity and multi-institutional applicability to explain the process of change have been formulated.

As illustration of these capabilities, we can state in quite precise behavioral language why apparent changes that arise from coercive pressure are in truth illusory; why involvement is a necessary condition of learning; why a custodial environment inhibits or destroys initiatory capacities; or why highly structured supervisory systems produce individual pathologies and low productivity. With these and other understandings it is not difficult to account for at least some of the causes that lead to industrial strife, political uprisings, the negative response of recipient countries to foreign aid programs, the disorder in our cities, or the failure of our schools to educate. From this backlog of understanding it is possible to suggest courses of action that could ameliorate many of our social ailments and begin to move our society in a more positive and constructive direction. Unhappily, the managers of our institutions have little knowledge about the capability of anthropology to contribute to the solution of problems of human organization and to effect change. Only rarely, if at all, is anthropological counsel sought on the crucial or even minor problems of our society and its institutions. The prevailing image that identifies anthropology with backward and remote peoples, an image that admittedly corresponds with the focus of interest of many anthropologists, has undoubtedly been a potent contributor to this neglect.

The effort to make the capabilities of anthropology more widely known and utilized must be intensified. It is not sufficient merely to assert the nature of the operating contributions. In education, as in other fields, anthropologists must join with the practitioners in the formulation of the goals and in the strategies of their achievement. Such a broadened mantle of responsibility projects anthropology into the arena of public scrutiny and debate and inevitably leads to the development of a new dimension as a policy science.

The concept of policy science has gradually emerged in recent years as one consequence of the growing maturity of the social sciences. Its most noted advocate, Harold Lasswell, offers this succinct statement of its scope. "The policy sciences study the process of deciding or choosing and evaluate the relevance of available knowledge for the solution of particular problems." [25] He further elaborates that it differs from earlier or competing bases for policy decision in that the rationale or source of decision derives from scientific evidence in contrast to theological, metaphysical, or other explanatory systems. Utilizing this formulation as our definition, let us now explore the policy science implications of anthropology for education.

BEHAVIORAL DIMENSIONS OF POLICY AND PRACTICE

Initially, we should recognize that there are contrasts if not contradictions between the conventional thought and logic of the culture of any given society and that contained in the anthropological perspective. Specifically, there are differences in the explanations about the origin and development of man and the processes of change. There is a deep intellectual antithesis between the prevalent Western world view, which organizes experience within the framework of the dialectics of polarity, and one that views the world as one of interrelated ongoing systems. As example, the conflict between the individual and the society, as posited by Rousseau and revived in the contemporary challenge to the Establishment by the assertion of the primacy of individual rights, reflects a polar ordering of abstractions. In contrast, systemic analysis views such a dichotomy as spurious, a position that is supported by anthropological learning theory, which contends that you cannot separate the consequence of experience as learning from the social setting in which it occurs. In other words, the individual becomes human within a social context and is part of the whole.

When, for example, educationists advocate adapting the curriculum to the needs of the individual, the objection is not to the existence of individual differences nor to the value of identifying them,

[25] Harold D. Lasswell, "Policy Sciences," *International Encyclopedia of the Social Sciences,* Vol. 12 (New York: Macmillan, 1968), p. 181.

but rather to the assumption that the difference can be reckoned as a sum of a listing of traits—achievement scores, reading level, I.Q., etc. In contrast, individual difference should be seen as the consequence of the variety of cultural and social learning contexts in the natural history of the individual. No test score can inform us in the least detail of learning patterns upon which curricular programs should be created. When statistical measures are applied to scores, the result is a lineal scalar statement of range and frequency distribution. If enough samples are available, comparisons can be made between populations— age, sex, nationality, race, etc.—a game educators like to play when they wish either to impress or to deplore. I reiterate that the systemic approach of the anthropologists, in contrast to the particularistic one of educators, directs attention toward the social and cultural contexts of learning as the significant variables, rather than toward statistical intervals.

This approach contrasts with the logistically hopeless goal of individualized instruction, based on trait listing of qualities, with one in which pedagogy and curriculum actually are a function of individual difference as determined by the cultural background and social participation out of which students come. Alan Howard's study of the public schools of Hawaii reveals some of the coping procedures Hawaiian-American children use to avoid conforming with a curriculum that stresses individualized competitive performances.[26] Studies by Wax and Wax of the Pine Ridge Sioux,[27] by Dumont of the Cherokee,[28] and by King of the Mission school at Mopass [29] confirm the failure of the traditional model of instruction as an effective learning device in cross-cultural situations but also show the school to be a deculturating influence that fosters alienation from the community. The evidence from these and other situations leads us to conclude that schools fail to achieve their instructional goals. Their deficiencies are rooted in the structure of an organization that imposes conformity, although their rhetoric extolls the individual; in pseudo-professionalism that has disconnected them from community; in a model of instruction that seeks validation through statistical formulas; in a philosophy of learning that emphasizes particularistic acquisition and rejects varia-

[26] Alan Howard, *Learning to Be Rotuman* (New York: Teachers College Press, 1970).

[27] Murray Wax, Rosalie Wax, and Robert V. Dumont, Jr., "Formal Education in an American Indian Community," *Social Problems*, Vol. 11, No. 4 (Supplement 1964).

[28] Robert V. Dumont, Jr., "Cherokee Children and the Teacher," *Social Education*, Vol. 33, No. 1 (January 1969), 70–72.

[29] A. Richard King, *The School at Mopass: A Problem of Identity* (New York: Holt, Rinehart and Winston, 1967).

bility in learning style; and in a curriculum and method of presentation that are fractionated and isolating rather than whole and systemic.

If it were possible to organize an educational system that utilized anthropological principles, it would require no less than a radical reworking of present policy and practice. The dimensions of such change have already been indicated in several of the preceding chapters. In Chapter 9, the relation between school organization and learning was the subject of concern. It was pointed out that the big urban school systems, and some of their simulated versions in smaller cities, organizationally resemble other municipal bureaus and departments. They are hierarchically organized bureaucracies designed to accumulate and store records, to maintain property control and exercise fiscal responsibility, to supervise personnel, and oftentimes to provide some kind of service to the public. In any large organization, there is always the need for caretakers and record keepers, but these should be peripheral activities unless it is the warehousing business. Schools are not warehouses, but that would appear to be the way in which some of them are operated.

If the educational objective of our schools can be achieved through the teacher-learner relationship, then the support structure of the school should be built around this focus. Of necessity then the overburden of a status ranked hierarchy of administrators and experts would need to be reevaluated in terms of its function. Instead of a line-of-command type of structure, suppose we organize students into learning groups that send forth requests to facilitators, who are then rated on their ability to meet requests. Such a reversal of existing initiatory practice is not as ludicrous as it may seem, although recognizably impossible of attainment in present circumstances.

But the restructuring cannot be limited merely to the formal structure of school organization, it must extend to all the activities and relationships of the school setting. Consider, for example, the current practices that attend the teaching of reading, writing, and arithmetic, and compare this with the pattern of learning the child used in acquiring the ability to speak and count previous to his sequestration in a formal learning situation. All children become articulate in the natural settings of family and peers with congruency between verbal usage and situation. How utterly contrary is much of the classroom practice, in which we induce or coerce the young to read, write, and figure. The tests educators use to measure achievement in these areas reveal all too starkly the magnitude of their failure, a failure readily attributed to the child's underprivileged environment, inadequate intellect, character deficiency, or lack of motivation. And what are the solutions that are proposed to remedy this sorry state of affairs? In effect, remedial programs extend even further the outreach of the bureaucratic structure down into the tender years of childhood and into the privacy of the home. Any acceptance that the artificial and dehumanized structure of schooling may in itself be contributory to the malaise seems to be lacking. The half-knowledge on which policy and program are now promulgated is simply inadequate.

The biological-cultural linkage of language acquisition with becoming human is clear. The cosmic sweep of anthropology views the phylogenetic sequence of homo sapiens as a tortuous ascent into humanity, during a momentous duration of perhaps a million years or more, when the consequences of articulate speech melded with the genetic system to shape the brain. In a rough sort of way, individual ontogeny parallels the evolution of the species. The striking contrast with other forms of life is found in the importance of the "super-organic," as Kroeber once called it, the culture of the group, which provides the initial nurturance and gradually prepares the developing individual to achieve maturity and perpetuate the species. Speech as the articulate form of an abstract language is one of the acquisitions. Neither language nor speech is an abstraction to unsophisticated users, but they become so to us because we have created linguists, who reveal their inner structure and dynamics. Writing and its comprehension by reading should be viewed as a further elaboration of language and the process of their acquisition in the natural setting of human beings carrying on their essential activities.

How under heaven then can we justify, by logic or by scientific evidence, the separation of the learning of communication skills from the natural setting in which they are used? Those who have listened to the stilted school-book speech of students who acquired literacy in culturally alien mission or colonial schools can appreciate the out-of-context imprint. The consequences of specific cultural influences have been explored by Margaret Mead through cross-cultural analysis. She establishes how subtle are the variations that have affected the incorporation of literate skills into a culture.[30]

Social structure is usually ignored as a significant dimension of the educative process. By structure we refer to the nature of the relationships, in addition to activity and situation, that obtain between individuals in a group. For example, once the appropriate skills have been mastered by a military drill team, by a chorus line, or by automobile assembly line workers, little if any additional learning occurs with subsequent performances of the group. The purpose of such

[30] Margaret Mead, "Early Childhood Experience and Later Education in Complex Cultures," in Wax, Diamond, and Gearing, *Anthropological Perspectives on Education*, pp. 67–90.

gatherings is to reenact past learning through repetitive performance, not to acquire new learning. All custodial situations lead to remarkably parallel consequences through routinization of the relationships between keepers and kept and the limitations of activities to the habitual. Obviously, the learning that does occur in such situations requires a relatively low level of cognitive effort, somewhat on the scale of that demanded by Skinner of his pigeons or by Pavlov of his dogs.

But what can anthropology tell us about the kind of group structure that provides the optimum conditions for learning? The answer to this question resides in the empirical evidence, from which we also derive explanatory principles, and directs us to a type of human grouping that is both ancient and universal and that in modern parlance we call the task force. The task force may be thought of as a group that has been assembled for the accomplishment of a common objective and whose members are differentiated on the basis of skill and ranking, responding to an accepted leadership, usually following a set course of action but retaining flexibility to adjust to changes in personnel or unanticipated conditions. The expedition assembled by Admiral Peary in 1908 to discover the North Pole or the Sioux Indian war party of the early nineteenth century both meet our specifications. Task forces may require technical skills as diverse as those necessary to build the atomic bomb in the Manhattan Project or the space rockets at Huntsville, or they may be as few, but still essential, as those utilized by the Shoshone in an antelope surround. War parties, trading expeditions, oceanographic exploration, harvesting rings are types of activities that fit the category. But most institutional activity does not, since all that is required is the repetitive performance of routine skills. The record keeping function of a government bureau, the assembly line of an automobile manufacturer, the animal processing of a packing plant, the custodial activities of prisons and hospitals are examples in which the establishment of routine procedures reduces the need for flexibility to near zero and in which innovation, requiring new learning, is minimal, if it exists at all.

The task force requires sustained, intimate interaction among its members; it operates in situations in which some of the conditions are unknown and considerable adaptability may be required; it actively innovates in the pursuit of its goal; and it rewards functional contribution rather than ascribed status. It is concerned with problems of a non-routine, and often non-recurring, type; it is flexible in organization with the capability of exercising a considerable degree of autonomy; its members are task oriented and highly motivated; and as an organizational form it can be utilized in a wide range of situations. New skills and knowledge are acquired coincident with exploration and meeting of new contingencies.

The effectiveness of the task force grouping as a device for promoting learning depends upon the nature of the problem and the organization of effort to provide answers. New knowledge was the major objective in the search for control of nuclear power at the Los Alamos laboratories as it is in the experimental and field activities of research scientists. Lest these more grandoise instances leave the impression of limited use, the task force organization can be a potential for any group or collaboration of freely associating individuals to accomplish either mundane and short-lived tasks or those that are long-term and difficult. They could range from annual grave-yard cleanups to complex governmental investigations.

The task force contrasts markedly with the routinized activities that are embedded in the customary practices of a household or the more complex institutional organization of a factory or school. The specific differences become quite clear when we examine, for example, the behavior of a classroom. In the elementary grades, there is the daily routine, which is initiated with a patriotic or religious observance, or both, and which proceeds in orderly sequence through each of several subject topics, with intervals for recess and lunch, also sequenced and timed, until the dismissal ritual of bell and phrase sends the children trooping homeward. Variation in pattern for secondary schools is insignificant. For both, the instructional pattern is one in which teachers assign, students prepare, and then teachers either talk or students recite. Special programs and activities embellish the hard core of school routine locked into the timed intervals of lesson plans within an ordered system of bureaucratic supervision and required reports.

The basic structure of the classroom is a simple one. The repetitive interaction is rank ordered between teacher and student. Rarely is there any activity that requires more than the teacher-student dyad for its completion. Perfect student response echoes teacher input faithfully, as the verbatim record of the Peruvian classroom presented in Chapter 16 showed. We must draw attention to the congruence between the rigidity of the school structure and the constrictions upon learning, in contrast to the flexibility of the task-force structure and its related contingency capabilities. Undoubtedly in task-force organization we possess a powerful device for organizing learning.

We turn now to connect the preceding analysis with the problem we posed earlier, namely, the uses of anthropology as a policy science for education, and specifically to consider whether the task-force approach should be viewed as complementary or as an alternative to the classroom model. No definitive answer may be expected, but the ramifications of the exploration will illuminate some of the courses of action available for the courageous. What Jesse Stuart accomplished with a small cluster of Kentucky mountain high school adolescents who together broke from the constraining walls of traditional instruction and classroom to search and grow together proved that, for that time and place, the grouping we label a task force worked.[31] Such a fortuitous combination of charisma and conditions, however, probably occurs too rarely to be repeated often. So we must turn to more familiar ground for exemplifying examples.

In most high schools, and to a lesser extent in the lower grades, there has evolved in American education a student oriented program of extracurricular activities. It is an aspect of schooling about whose educational consequences we have relatively little knowledge. But it is sufficiently widespread and of seeming significance to the students that they delegate each year to a select group of their peers the responsibility for documenting and reporting their activities in a yearbook. Even a cursory comparison of the contents of several of these, drawn from different sections of the country, reveals a great uniformity in the formal structure of student life. It also tells us a great deal about the relative importance of different activities and the degree of student involvement and participation. Male dominated competitive team sports hold the spotlight of attention. But their pretty female adjuncts, the cheer leaders, pep squad, and baton twirlers, also catch the roving eye. Other segments of student life that are recorded include student government; curriculum-related clubs in languages, vocational education, sciences and arts, the talent areas of writing, drama, music, dance, and speech; the areas of special interest, such as chess, stamp collecting, electronics, and the like; honor societies and service clubs; and the major social events. These groupings reflect a broad range of interests, some of them reflecting the diversity of the school program whereas others duplicate the adult divisions of the society from which their members are recruited. The astute observation by Jacquetta Burnett that the student system of the high school should be counted as the adolescent training ground for adult participation in the community has significant implications.[32]

If the measure of the importance of a program are the money, personnel, and other resources allocated to it, then we must conclude that educators view extracurricular activities, with the exception of

---

[31] Jesse Stuart, *The Thread that Runs So True* (New York: Scribner's, 1949).
[32] Jacquetta Hill Burnett, "Ceremony, Rites and Economy in the Student System of an American High School," *Human Organization,* Vol. 28, No. 1 (Spring 1969), 1–11.

competitive team sports, as of secondary importance. The pattern of rewards for those faculty who elect or are assigned to work with student groups varies, but the arrangement is basically an ad hoc one. And faculty complaints that such duties constitute an overload are not unknown. There are also other problems. The irregular timing of such events either interferes with normal class hours or requires adjustments for after-hours use of building and facilities, which can inconvenience custodial personnel and create problems of security. When property or money is involved, there are questions of accountability. Running a school would be much simpler if everything could be as fully routinized as is classroom instruction, and that is difficult enough, as most administrators would testify.

Extracurricular activities differ in several respects from the regular school program. For one thing, they are only indirectly connected with the stated objectives and management of formal education. Neither expansion nor curtailment would likely lead to any noticeable public response, unless athletics were adversely involved. Measures of evaluation are of an entirely different order from those used for academic subjects and, although some schools maintain records of participation, these do not form part of the individual's official school transcript. Participation is almost wholly voluntary and selective, with varying levels of student direction and autonomy. Problems of social control and discipline are solved primarily from within the group rather than being imposed from some external source. In these several characteristics there is a strong resemblance to the organization and objectives of a task force, and a marked contrast with that of the classroom. In such activities, once their educational worth is accepted, we possess a powerful supplemental or alternative approach to the present structure of education.

Another focus from which we can examine the extracurricular activities is that of their social functions. A great deal of the unsupervised play activity of the young in all societies is given over to games that simulate adult situations and roles. We are familiar with children playing "house," "dress-up," cops and robbers, doctor and nurse, "school," and games requiring miniature mechanical counterparts of our technology. Anthropologists reckon this repetitive, self-directed learning as an important preparation for the later assumption of adult roles. In contemporary Western nations, where the entrance into adulthood has been delayed well past puberty by mass education, it is not surprising that there has also been a corresponding upward extension of proto-adult "play," which replicates the more complex world into which they must enter. Nor is it surprising that some of these activities have become school-related. From this perspective, the variety of skills—intellectual, social, athletic, artistic, forensic, and vocational—that are sharpened through practice in student activities constitute a significant segment of the learning that is needed for participation in the adult world. The failure of the individual to learn these skills during the period of adolescence puts him at a disadvantage in later life.

It should be clear by now that educational policies based on principles from anthropology would differ substantially from those now current. It is not my purpose here to attempt to develop a set of such policies. That would be a project of considerable magnitude. But enough exemplifying data have been presented to indicate the direction and substance of such an effort. They would be based on our knowledge about learning and socialization; on the relation between learning and social setting; on the relation between institutions and community; and on a world view that seeks principles to explain change.

CONCLUDING OBSERVATION

It has not been the objective of this chapter to offer a prescription for rescuing the schools from the ailments they suffer. I claim no such capability. But its objective may be viewed as both modest and profound. The intent has been, first, to inform about the magnitude of the attacks to which the schools are subject; second, to provide some context for understanding the stresses that contribute to the situation; and last, to explain how principles based upon behavioral science developed in anthropology offer an approach for the assessment of the problem and development of a program for reconstituting the educational process to serve better the needs of individuals as participants in our society.

As yet, the formulation must be considered largely exploratory, not alone because of the absence of precedent in the relation between anthropology and education, but because the policy science aspect of anthropology is itself in an emergent state. The base upon which it is being built, however, is a solid one. Over the past several decades, applied anthropologists have been expanding and verifying their knowledge of the processes that explain change. They have observed the results of planned innovations and the unintended consequences that accrue from the mindless modifications of the conditions in which human groups work. They have observed the disparity between the rational goals set by policy makers, their reduction to plans and procedures, and the response of those subject to the resulting programs. And, as has been mentioned earlier, some of the most significant new theoretical contributions to understanding human behavior have been and are coming, either directly or indirectly, from concern with applied problems.

There is an additional dimension of anthropology that bears upon its contribution as a policy science. I refer to the concern for humans. This is a concern that unites both science and morality and has led some of our "hard" science colleagues to be confused about the nature of some of our data. They have judged them subjective, that is, not quite subject to respectable proof, a misunderstanding that can readily be dispelled when they come to accept that even the reality they observe is a variable. Depending on the perspective, a tree can be a botanical specimen, a specified number of cords of firewood, an esthetic value, an ecological variable, or a status symbol.

The humanistic tradition of anthropology is not derived from the romantic utopianism of the individual, just as its scientific tradition is not based in materialistic rigidities. Rather, its concern is with the nature of man and the comparative study of the customs that guide his behavior and the groups through which he solves his problems. In the study of the diversity in man's universe also arises an understanding of his potential. To utilize this knowledge for the amelioration of the human condition and hence for the realization of man's potential requires only the short step that an applied science of mankind promises.